THE GAME OF LOVE

THE GAME OF LOVE

TROUBADOUR WORDPLAY

LAURA KENDRICK

University of California Press
Berkeley · Los Angeles · London

University of California Press
Berkeley and Los Angeles, California

University of California Press, Ltd.
London, England

Library of Congress Cataloging-in-Publication Data

Kendrick, Laura.
The game of love.

Bibliography: p.
Includes index.
1. Provençal poetry—History and criticism.
2. Troubadours. 3. Play on words. 4. Provençal language—Style. 5. Love poetry, Provençal—History and criticism. I. Title
PC3304.K46 1988 849′.1′009 87–12981
ISBN 0–520–06055–5 (alk. paper)

Printed in the United States of America
1 2 3 4 5 6 7 8 9

In Memory of
W. T. H. Jackson

Contents

Illustrations

Following page 146

Acknowledgments

I would like to thank all those who have in any way helped to make this book possible. You know who you are. Of those who have given me the most immediate assistance, I thank the staff of the Bibliothèque Nationale in Paris, who bore the greatest burden of my research, and Madame Geneviève Brunel of the Institut de Recherche et d'Histoire des Textes. Several readers, Roger Dragonetti, Charles Muscatine, Sheila Delany, Robert Jordan, who hardly knew me at the time, were surprised to find parts of the manuscript in their mailboxes, and I am very grateful to them for their encouragement early in the writing process. Fine editors and readers for the University of California Press, Doris Kretschmer, Stephen G. Nichols, Jr., R. Howard Bloch, an anonymous Press reader, Rose Vekony, and Jane-Ellen Long, have made putting the manuscript into its final form a pleasure and an education.

I am also grateful to several institutions for their support of my work: the Rutgers Research Council, which provided travel grants and a publication subvention; the National Endowment for the Humanities, for a Junior Faculty Summer Fellowship; the American Council of Learned Societies, for a six-month postdoctoral fellowship that I diverted, in part, to research on this book. The photographic departments of the Bibliothèque Nationale, the Vatican Library, and the Pierpont Morgan Library have provided photographs from manuscripts in their collections and kindly given me permission to reproduce them in the following pages.

Provençal Songbooks Cited

A	Rome, Biblioteca Vaticana, lat. 5232
B	Paris, Bibliothèque Nationale, fr. 1592
C	Paris, Bibliothèque Nationale, fr. 856
D	Modena, Biblioteca Estense 45 [α, R, 4, 4]
E	Paris, Bibliothèque Nationale, fr. 1749
G	Milan, Biblioteca Ambrosiana, R, 71, sup.
H	Rome, Biblioteca Vaticana, lat. 3207
I	Paris, Bibliothèque Nationale, fr. 854
J	Florence, Biblioteca Nazionale, Conv. Sopp. F, 4, 776
K	Paris, Bibliothèque Nationale, fr. 12473
M	Paris, Bibliothèque Nationale, fr. 12474
N	New York, Pierpont Morgan Library, 819
N^2	Berlin, Staatsbibliothek, Phillips, 1910
P	Florence, Biblioteca Laurenziana, Plut. XLI, 42
Q	Florence, Biblioteca Riccardiana, 2909
R	Paris, Bibliothèque Nationale, fr. 22543
S	Oxford, Bodleian Library, Douce 269
Sg	Barcelona, Biblioteca de Cataluña, 146
V	Venice, Biblioteca Marciana, app. cod. XI
a^1	Modena, Biblioteca Estense, Càmpori, γ, N, 8, 4; 11, 12, 13

Frequently Cited Editions

Numbers following citations from these troubadours and Provençal works in the text refer to the following modern editions. In the notes these editions may be abbreviated to the last names of their editors or the short titles of *Leys* and *Flors*.

Bernart de Ventadorn	Carl Appel, *Bernart von Ventadorn* (Halle, 1915)
Bernart Marti	Ernest Hoepffner, *Les Poésies de Bernart Marti* (Paris, 1929)
Flors	Adolphe Gatien-Arnoult, ed., *Las Flors del gay saber*, 3 vols. (Toulouse, 1841–1843)
Giraut de Bornelh	Adolf Kolsen, *Sämtliche Lieder des Trobadors Giraut de Bornelh*, 2 vols. (Halle, 1907)
Guillaume IX	Nicolò Pasero, *Guglielmo IX d'Aquitania: Poesie* (Modena, 1973)
Jaufre Rudel	Rupert Pickens, *The Songs of Jaufré Rudel* (Toronto, 1978)
Leys	Guilhem Molinier, *Las Leys d'amors*, ed. Joseph Anglade, 4 vols. (Toulouse, 1919, 1920)
Marcabru	J. M. L. Dejeanne, *Poésies complètes du troubadour Marcabru* (Toulouse, 1909)
Peire d'Alvernhe	Alberto del Monte, *Peire d'Alvernha: Liriche* (Turin, 1955)
vidas	Jean Boutière and A. H. Schutz, *Biographies des troubadours*, 2d ed. (Paris, 1973)

I

Contests and Contexts

Las palabras sirven a la intencion
É non la intencion a las palabras.

Words serve intention
rather than intention's serving words.

—Archpriest of Hita,
Libro de buen amor

To prove that "words serve intention"—that understanding or interpretation controls words—and not the reverse, Juan Ruiz, alias Archpriest of Hita, author of the *Libro de buen amor*, uses the exemplum of the debate by means of the sign language of gesture between a learned Greek scholar and a Roman roughneck. The purpose of this debate is to determine whether or not the Romans are sophisticated enough to receive laws from the Greeks. Feeling themselves at a disadvantage, the Romans choose a pugnacious ruffian to represent them, dress him up in rich robes, and tell him to use whatever gestures he is inspired to use against the Greek opponent. The Greek scholar begins the debate by sticking out his index finger, to which the Roman roughneck responds by sticking out his thumb, index, and middle fingers. To this the Greek opens his palm, and the Roman clenches his fist, whereupon the Greek announces that the Romans deserve to be given laws.

When questioned afterwards by their respective sides, the Greek doctor and the Roman ruffian give opposing interpretations of the same text of manual signs:

> They asked the Greek what he had said to the Roman by his gestures, and what he had answered him. He said: "I said that there is one God; the Roman said He was One in Three Persons, and made a sign to that effect.
>
> Next I said that all was by the will of God; he answered that God held everything in his power, and he spoke truly. When I saw that they understood and believed in the Trinity, I understood that they deserved assurance of [receiving] laws."
>
> They asked the hoodlum what his notion was; he replied: "He said that

> with his finger he would smash my eye; I was mighty unhappy about this and I got mighty angry, and I answered him with rage, with anger, and with fury,
>
> that, right in front of everybody, I would smash his eyes with my two fingers and his teeth with my thumb; right after that he told me to watch him because he would give me a big slap on my ears [that would leave them] ringing.
>
> I answered him that I would give him such a punch that in all his life he would never get even for it. As soon as he saw that he had the quarrel in bad shape, he quit making threats in a spot where they thought nothing of him."[1]

Both parties to this debate read the other's signs precisely as they want to, as their own backgrounds and intentions lead them to: the learned Greek scholar—rather like a Christian theologian—seeks in all signs proof of the existence of the one true God; the Roman roughneck's intention is more competitive, and he is attuned to action in the present. The scholar's goal in reading signs is to discover unity; the common man reads the same signs in terms of divergence and the struggle of opposing forces.

The Archpriest of Hita uses this exemplum to put the responsibility for the message of his *Book of Good Love* squarely on the shoulders of the individual interpreter:

> This is why the proverb of the shrewd old woman says: "No word is bad if you don't take it badly." You will see that my word is well said if it is well understood: understand my book well and you will have a lovely lady.
>
> (Willis, p. 26)

The signs in themselves are ambiguous: the good reader will find a good message in them; the bad reader, a bad one. Centuries earlier, Augustine used a similar argument in his *De doctrina Christiana*. The good reading of the Scriptures is the one that overcomes difference and ambiguity to discover the unifying message of charity.

The search for true meaning, according to Augustine, is like a "voyage home," back to one's point of origin, back to a stable center.[2] In *Etymologies and Genealogies*, R. Howard Bloch has pointed out how medieval Christian thinkers tried to use etymology to reverse linguistic change and return to a still center of pure meaning:

> Just as, according to the Eusebian model, men evolve through time away from God, words devolve—through use, catastrophe, translation, and poetry (especially pagan verse)—away from Adam's primal act of naming.

> From an original univocal signification stems the multiplicity of tongues; and from the unity of the original couple stems the multiplicity of the races of men. Both history and grammar are bound by a common sense of loss and dispersion, by a common nostalgic longing for beginnings, and by a set of ontologically similar strategies of return.[3]

But not everyone in late antiquity or in the Middle Ages considered change to be a bad thing or the goal of interpretation to be a return to a paradise of monism. The "pagan," acentric worldview Augustine fought presumed a voyage in the opposite direction.

Lucretius in *De rerum natura*, Varro in *De lingua latina*, Ovid in his *Metamorphoses*—all move forward and sweep outward in their exploration of the forms and meanings of words and things. They are more interested in generation than in origins and try to follow divergences of meaning, valorizing the fertile multiplicity of forms, the productivity of difference. Lucretius derives something as precious as freedom of the will from the slight deflection of the elemental particles of matter in their fall through endless space;[4] such deflections, he reasons, cause the elemental particles to collide with one another and thus to assume the ever-changing, ever-moving configurations of all natural forms. Lucretius even uses linguistic examples to explain this:

> For the particles are the same in sky, sea, rivers,
> Earth, sun, all crops, all trees, all living things,
> But in different patterns and moving in different ways.
> It is not so different as you might think with verses,
> For so many letters are common to so many words,
> Yet the words and verses differ from one another
> And that is true of meaning as well as sound.
> And this is only a change in the order of elements;
> The variations for particles are more numerous
> And so make all the variations of nature.[5]

Lucretius enjoys contemplating these changing patterns of elements, the way identical particles, arranged differently, make wood or fire—or the words for wood or fire (*lignis* or *ignis*), with different meanings.

Varro, too, is fascinated by the infinite variation that can be produced from a finite group of elements. Whereas Lucretius is more interested in letters, the smallest parts of written language, Varro pays more attention in his *De lingua latina* to the "smallest indivisible part of spoken speech," the syllable or root word (which he calls simply the "word" [*verbum*, X.77]) in its infinite variation due to natural and voluntary declination (*declinatio naturalis* or inflectional morphology, and *declinatio voluntaria* or arbitrary derivation).[6] Although Varro claims to be tracing origins, his etymological speculations produce consanguineous groupings of words, all sharing certain elements or root syllables, rather than clear lineages leading back to Ur-ancestral words. His interpretations are not reductive but expansive, giving evidence of the richness of signifying possibilities in Latin. In short, Varro seems to be more interested in how words are shaped, and especially in ways poets have shaped them, than in discovering ultimate origins. At one point he compares the obscure poetic word to a miniature ivory carving by a great master. Over the course of time, poets, as well as other people, reshape words by subtracting or adding single letters, transposing or changing them, lengthening or shortening syllables, adding or subtracting them (V.6). Just as men use black haircloth as a background to show up the delicacy of the carving (by making the negative space, that which has been carved away, visible), so Varro justifies his practice in etymological explanations of adding a letter or taking one away from an obscure poetic word in order to show how the poet has reshaped the word, "that what underlies this expression may be more easily perceived" (VII.1).

In his extraordinary *Metaformations*, Frederick Ahl has recently tried to show how Ovid put into practice in his *Metamorphoses* Varronian (and Lucretian and Platonic) thinking about language, which emphasizes the variation of the basic elements of words and foregrounds the "matter" of language, rather than pretending it is transparent or of no consequence (because the locus of meaning is elsewhere), as Christian theologians later tended to do. Ahl generalizes:

> for Ovid, as for Plato, the letters within words are the substrate, the shifting reality which establishes, undermines, redefines meaning at the verbal level. The sentence is a movable configuration of *letters* and *syllables*, rather than of words, . . . of sounds at play.

This attitude toward language and poetic composition is particularly appropriate to Ovid's subject of metamorphosis:

> Ovid's poetical world is complex. People may lurk within animals or plants. . . . the elements, the ingredients, of all matter are shuffled to create new forms. Within one reality lurk the ingredients of another. . . . As the material elements shift, transforming men into animals or plants, so the elements of words are shuffled to reproduce changes in language itself.[7]

Such views of language did not die inevitably with the fall of Rome, nor were Christian theologians completely successful in eradicating them.

Although Isidore of Seville's *Etymologies* were also known as *Origins*, the implicit message of this encyclopedic pedagogical text for the Middle Ages is in many respects similar to Varro's. While claiming to focus on origins and, by discovering these, to bring us closer to truth, Isidore effectively demonstrates the extreme richness of signification, the variety, and the arbitrary nature of the Latin lexicon.[8] It is as easy to use his etymologies to expand and enrich as to concentrate and unify the meaning of words. The same might be said of the later medieval compilations by Rhabanus Maurus and others. All of their etymologies can be read not only as strategies of return to a still center of truth, as Bloch has pointed out, but also forward, taking pleasure in difference, in the variety of possible combinations of the same or slightly divergent letters or syllables, in the interplay or contest of verbal configurations that constitutes a dynamic linguistic order.

In *The City of God* Augustine argues against Varro that the pagan theology of difference—with people worshipping and fearing a multitude of lesser gods and trying always to encourage a healthy balance of power among a variety of divine forces, even to the point of inventing new, diversionary or counterbalancing ones—is not appropriate to a great empire, which can only be attributed to and supported by the one true God:

> Next let us ask, . . . out of so great a crowd of gods which the Romans worship, whom in especial, or what gods they believe to have extended and preserved that empire. Now, surely of this work, which is so excellent and so very full of the highest dignity, they dare not ascribe any part to the goddess Cloacina, or to Volupia, who has her appellation from voluptuousness; or to Libentina, who has her name from lust; or to Vaticanus, who presides over the screaming of infants; or to Cunina, who rules over their cradles. But how is it possible to recount in one part of this book all the names of gods or goddesses, which they could scarcely comprise in great volumes, distributing among these divinities their peculiar offices about single things? . . . Who would not have thought that goddess Segetia sufficient to take care of the standing corn until it had passed from the first green blades to the dry ears? Yet she was not enough for men, who loved a multitude of gods. . . . Therefore they set Proserpina over the germinating seeds; over the joints and knots of the stems, the god Nodotus; over the sheaths enfolding the ears, the goddess Volutina. . . . they dare by no means say that the Roman empire has been established, increased, and preserved by their deities, who had all their

> own functions assigned to them in such a way, that no general oversight was entrusted to any one of them. When, therefore, could Segetia take care of the empire, who was not allowed to take care of the corn and the trees? When could Cunina take thought about war, whose oversight was not allowed to go beyond the cradles of the babies? When could Nodotus give help in battle, who had nothing to do even with the sheath of the ear, but only with the knots of the joints?[9]

To read the text of nature in the way the pagan Romans did, accepting and even encouraging difference rather than trying to reduce it to unity, is, in Augustine's view, subversive of empire, of authority, of God.

Augustine's point is telling. It illuminates struggles over the meaning of signs and texts not only in his time but in our own. At the height of nineteenth-century European imperialism, when so many medieval texts were "definitively established," editors tried to eliminate ambiguity and return to "original" intentions. Their diagrams of the genealogy of texts, of textual "deviation," are to be read upward, back to the original ancestral text, the supreme authority. Furthermore, in the United States after the world wars, we saw much effort spent on applying Augustinian interpretation to all sorts of "definitive" medieval religious and secular texts in an attempt to unify their meanings as well as their forms. With respect to troubadour lyrics, our tendency was to idealize and reduce their meanings into a secular equivalent of *caritas*; we did this by focusing on the sameness of the lyrics, trying to read them all as if, albeit deviant in some ways that we tended to overlook as flaws, all troubadour lyrics were versions of an Ur-troubadour text that set the rules or conventions enabling the sublimation of erotic desire into verbal—poetic, artistic—aspiration for recognition by an unattainable lady. Behind the search for the "origin" of this refining, standardizing idea of "courtly love," which is largely the product of unifying interpretations of troubadour lyrics, lies a reductive, controlling intention.

Provençal scholars have by no means been the only readers with reductive aims. For example, the literature department where I teach requires all faculty to teach and all English majors to take a "core" course in which hundreds of students on several campuses of a large *uni*versity (etym. "turned toward one") are regularly forced to write on the same poem using the same set of leading questions reproduced in perfect sameness from the department's truly regal copying machine. Through the course of discussions among themselves, the students' writing gradually converges to a single interpretation; the papers approach uniformity, which gives the central committee that made up the leading questions and chose the poem a sense of great accomplishment, that is, of being in control.

Struggles over the meaning of texts are struggles for power—sublimated, involving figurative rather than real blows, played out in the liminal space of the margins, but, nonetheless, often crucial contests. This is clear nowadays when the heads of the two greatest imperial powers meet in a symbolically liminal space to argue over the interpretation of the text of a previous arms control treaty and, in the aftermath of these negotiations, when journalists and political analysts argue over the meaning of the "text" of the negotiating contest, trying to discover covert meanings and to decide which side came out ahead.

The politics of textual interpretation are also writ large in the thirteenth-century Inquisition in southern France, that "unifying" effort which resulted in the eradication of heretics (those whose interpretations differed from the Church's, thus threatening its authority) and in the installation of the French king as supreme secular ruler over the various conflicting local authorities that had previously controlled the region. An important and quite explicit thirteenth-century poetic resistance was made to the Church's and the French monarchy's efforts at "unification"—their textual politics during the Inquisition—but this is the subject of another study. In this book I will treat related but even earlier struggles over the meaning of the text, played out in the twelfth century by the first troubadours whose works have survived in writing, Guillaume IX (duke of Aquitaine), Marcabru, Jaufre Rudel, Bernart de Ventadorn, Raimbaut d'Orange, Giraut de Bornelh, and that most shadowy of "schools" of secular poet-interpreters, the *scola neblo*. In the remaining pages of this introductory chapter, I will outline the major lines of my argument concerning the early troubadours' textual practices and their cultural contexts, saving more extensive discussion for later chapters.

Troubadour verse demonstrates the lingering acentric worldview or *mentalité* of the people of southern and western France in the twelfth century. This old mental model of order mirrors what a largely agricultural society observed of the forces in nature: that "stability" is the ephemeral result of a temporary balance of conflicting forces—one might even call it a felicitous "indeterminacy"—before one force or another wins out, only to cede later to a stronger force. This acentric model of order as an ever-shifting configuration of competing forces is not only agonistic but also cyclical, because the same or very similar patterns and configurations can be expected to emerge repeatedly. Such a worldview valorizes multiplicity and complexity and divergence; it values change because only change—constant movement, constant renewal—insures the dynamic on which the centerless system depends.

Until about the mid-eleventh century, this acentric model of order also reflected fairly accurately the dominant social, political, and popular theological systems of the south and west of France. Among the most powerful extended families or clans of these regions, marriage alliances were more often temporary than permanent; brothers and even sisters shared inheritances on a co-proprietary basis;[10] politics was local and loyalties could shift quickly; religious beliefs were divergent, and a host of local saints and relics competed at garnering public devotion.[11] This dynamic social order of shifting alliances allowed—even required—individual and group enterprise to keep it moving. But no one group could expect to be a winner forever. Time favored change. Authority in such a system was based on action in the present and, to a lesser extent, on human memory of earlier deeds and words. The memory of living men was, however, a shifting force in itself, fallible and selective in its responses, just as likely to aid change as to hinder it (as written words more effectively do).[12]

Upon this sensitive, acentric order of change, the Church tried to impose a centered, hierarchized, stabilized order; the most powerful regional rulers, especially the French and English kings, who stood to gain the most, cooperated with the Church's centralizing efforts. No less was required than a reordering of everyday human relations, and this could not be done without the promotion of a new worldview, new representations of order that, on the one hand, filled the empty center of the "pagan" secular model, and, on the other, attacked and denigrated the acentric order as "chaos." The tympana of Romanesque portals, as at Autun, show the balance of powers—of good and evil, saved souls and damned—but the balancing is no longer gratuitous: the hand of God or of an archangel holds the scales. The concentric rings of voussoirs of such portals generate a multitude of natural vegetal, animal, and humanoid forms, as at Vézelay, but this multiplicity is ordered around and converges at unity, in a single, authoritative image of Christ in majesty. In his *Romanesque Signs*, Stephen G. Nichols, Jr., provides a valuable history of this centering process in the configurations of visual and verbal narratives of the eleventh and twelfth centuries.[13]

The hierarchical order of churches and the figurative representations of order on and in them—from the great cathedrals to the tiny parish churches, the magnificent edifices of the mother monastery to the lesser ones of its peripheral affiliates—was being written in stone as permanently as possible in the eleventh and twelfth centuries. By emphasizing the superior intercessory powers of Christ and Mary, churchmen attempted to channel and unify religious devotion; they tried to subordinate a multitude of competing local saints (each with fragmentary powers, much like the pagan deities) to the Virgin Mary, who topped the hierarchy of saints and figuratively represented the Church. Not only were the tympana of Romanesque portals clearly hierarchized and centered on Christ or Christ and Mary in majesty, but, once inside a great cathedral such as Chartres in the late twelfth century (earlier at St. Denis), the laity might read a similar message in stained glass in a great tree of Jesse. This figuration of Christ's human lineage on his mother's side is, nevertheless, phallocentric, for it places Jesse at the base of a series of kings that culminates in Mary and Christ—the "only begotten Son"—atop the branch that springs from the root (groin) of Jesse.[14] In this image generation returns man to God, thereby closing the circle. Above the tree of Jesse at Chartres shines the late medieval epitome of centered order: the great rose window of the west facade.

It is not necessary to go on naming examples of the ways the Church and the most powerful lords were trying to consolidate their power in the eleventh and twelfth centuries. In the long run, they were largely successful, not only in introducing a centered idea of order but at making real changes in the socioeconomic and political structures in the south and west of France (they had earlier accomplished such changes in the north). The clan was broken and the noble family was defined more narrowly by the permanent unit of man and wife and a hierarchy of children headed by the eldest son. Just as primogeniture replaced coproprietorship within the family, a hierarchy of binding feudal loyalties culminating at the top in the king rationalized and centered politicoeconomic relationships. Because of the eventual success of this centered, ideal "feudal" model of order and due to the bias in its favor of the majority of surviving written records, especially those "written" in stone, we tend to underestimate how difficult the model was to put across and how much resistance to it there was in the south and west of France in the eleventh and twelfth centuries.

Writing, in the broad sense of representation that is fixed in visual images, was the most effective means medieval religious and secular rulers used to impose a centered, hierarchical model of order and thus to consolidate their own power. At issue was the retention of control, over land, the wealth it produced, and men. In a society in which authority was based on action and in living memories of actions, including the action of the spoken word, it was very hard for a lord who had conquered or been given or otherwise acquired distant lands which he could not personally visit quite regularly to retain control over them for very long; these lands rapidly became the free possessions of those who were entrusted with their supervision, who actually did and were seen and remembered to rule the land and people living on it. The lord's supervisors became owners in their own right; the center did not hold because the "representation" was taken for the reality.

Oral cultures in which order is understood as a dynamic configuration of competing forces implicitly reject the basic principle of representation: that there can be authority in absence. This is perhaps clearest on the level of popular theology in the eleventh and twelfth centuries, the apogee of the cult of the Christian saints. Although the compilers and writers of medieval saints' lives and miracle collections often try to shape popular piety in more monotheistic directions (forcing us to read them against the grain of their writers' intentions),[15] their accounts make it obvious that local saints were commonly invoked, not as intercessors or representatives of God, but as powerful healers or protectors in their own right. Just as the old Roman gods were named after the natural processes over which they were supposed to have power, so one or more syllables of some medieval saints' vernacular names suggest body parts or diseases over which they were believed to have power (both to cure and to hurt). Thus, an invocation to "Saint Folcuin" or "Sainte Cunegonde" for relief of the pains of childbirth sounds rather like an imperative plea concerning the female sexual parts (*san con*).[16] The *sanh* or *san* (Provençal for "saint") has the power to *sanar* (from Latin *sano -are*); there is health in saints just as the word *health* inheres in the word *saint*—or, to use a Varronian analogy, there is fire in wood just as the letters *ignis* inhere in *lignis*.

The people's belief in the efficacy of saints to cure disease or otherwise intervene to preserve health does not involve representation. The saint or elements of the saint—active in death as in life—are still physically present in his tomb or reliquary. These saintly elements are believed to have the power to pass easily through the boundaries of other objects and persons, to impregnate them and, in so doing, to rearrange their elements in accordance with those of the saint, which heals the sick person. Such ideas may be natural to agricultural peoples who observe the conflict of forces in nature and the constant metamorphosis of forms made of the same matter. Although they did not formulate their observations into coherent theories involving the movement of elemental particles in space, medieval people got their notions, as Lucretius did, from observing generation and decline in nature. From the medieval belief in the power of saintly elements to pass through the apparent boundaries of objects, it follows that cure is possible, not only when saintly fragments are brought into direct contact with diseased persons, but also when intermediary objects that have been touched and changed by saintly particles are brought into contact with the diseased parts. In this category of intermediary objects are tombs and reliquaries containing saintly remains and objects the living saint touched, such as clothes. The hyperactivity of saintly elements enabled them to pass even beyond these intermediary objects to what might be called (but with no hierarchizing intention) twice-removed relics, those imbued with curative power through contact with an intermediary object that is or has been in contact with the saint or his remains. Although analysts generally call these twice-removed relics "representative relics," they were not representations in the medieval imagination, for medieval people believed them to contain real elements or fragments of the saint transmitted through contact. Such relics did not serve the purpose of *representing* the saint's power in his absence; rather, something of the saint was believed to be *really* present in these relics.

Likewise, the ex-voto objects left by pilgrims at the shrines of saints in the high Middle Ages were not, from the point of view of those who shaped them, representations. Perhaps because of the practical difficulty of maintaining actual physical contact with the saint's relics for very long and because of prohibitions against this in some cases, people often fashioned imitations of themselves or their diseased parts in wax: ex-voto objects. During the handling of these, the wax, an easily impregnable matter, was probably thought to become imbued with the living person. Hence also the custom of passing the string that would serve as the wick of the ex-voto candle around the person's body or the diseased part.[17] The motivation for fashioning these ex-voto objects was not to *represent* the miracle for the saint or for posterity; rather, the waxen object was a way of *really* linking the giver to the saint—of putting the sick person's elements in longer contact with the health-giving elements of the saint, on or near which the ex-voto object was deposited.

In the popular mind, reality usurped representation. This was true well into the fourteenth century with respect to the cult of the saints. Most late medieval miracles reportedly took place at a distance from the actual remains or relics of the saints—but in places where there were images or statues of the saints to be invoked and touched. Such images of the saints in effect served as relics;[18] people believed they were imbued with the saintly particles capable of working miracles on contact.

Just as the forms of relics were constantly changing as saintly power was imparted to new objects, so also new saints were continually being created or discovered and elevated to power by monastic and ecclesiastical communities. The lines of saintly force in any one region were constantly shifting with the competition between religious groups. The supplicant's role, which had never been passive, was even more active in this competitive situation. It was the supplicant who initiated the contact with the saintly relics; thus he was free to choose one saint over another competing one and even to try to play one saint off against another. The supplicant, however, could not expect to get something from the saint for nothing. The relationship between saint and supplicant was understood to be an "exchange" of elements and gifts. The people, like Lucretius, well knew that in nature nothing comes from nothing. Force could act only through presence, through matter. Representations of power did not work; they were either impotent or else they were taken for realities. The reason for the dearth of surviving early medieval "representations" of this acentric idea of order as an ever-shifting configuration of competing forces is that its adherents did not produce many, being oriented toward reality rather than toward representation. Even surviving objects from this period that we consider to be representations were not always so intended or so used by laymen.

The earliest written vernacular charters from the south and west of France, many of them contemporary with the earliest known troubadours, are very interesting in their reflection of the problems churchmen, religious lay groups such as the Templars, and secular rulers faced in the eleventh and twelfth centuries in trying to assert authority in absence through representatives. Besides the peculiar phonological (rather than morphological) groupings of letters in the earliest eleventh-century charters, what strikes the modern reader of them is their formulaic phrases indicating that they are not meant to be authoritative. Rather, these early charters tend to define themselves as written memory aids, in Latin *breve rememorationis* or *memorabile* or *memoriale*, in the vernacular simply *breu* or *breu memorial.*[19] In an effort to stabilize and orient human memory of gifts and obligations, churchmen wrote down and preserved the names of witnesses to particular transactions, the details of which they took increasing care to specify. Laymen began to follow suit.

Most ecclesiastical documents of this period are written in Latin, but some are macaronic, mixing vernacular phrases with the Latin. The combination seems to be deliberate, to make sure the layman understands what he is swearing, as, for example, in an oath of fidelity sworn by the son of the Viscountess of Narbonne in 1078 to the archbishop of that city. The first vernacular words in the tissue of the Latin descriptive formulas are *non decebrei*, "I will not deceive"; the next, "nor will I steal from him"; and the pattern continues with other significant verbs of action rendered in the vernacular.[20] Having been forced to swear such oaths of fidelity to churchmen, promising to behave as their faithful representatives (which did not necessarily prevent *engan* or deception), and having, even more important, witnessed the recording of their words in writing and perhaps also the verbatim replaying of these, secular lords began to see the value of writing as a technology and to try to use it themselves to prevent possessions from slipping so rapidly from their grasp. By means of writing, the Church was gradually taking pieces of donated and purchased land out of play—out of the old dynamic configuration. In order to counter this, some secular lords imitated ecclesiastics and began to use the new technology themselves. But this meant accepting representation, and, implicitly, a centered model of order. Only those secular lords who stood to gain by representation accepted it. Many stood to lose and actively opposed the authority of the written word.

This opposition may be glimpsed through the diction and forms of the early vernacular charters, the *breu* that announce themselves as mere servants of living memory. Indeed, it was not difficult to forge a written document.[21] Why should laymen who could not themselves write believe some marks on a piece of animal hide? Was it not wiser to believe the testimony of an assortment of living witnesses or their survivors? Such skepticism led the promoters of charters to invent authenticating devices, especially for laymen, who did not, as a rule, own personal seals. Sometimes, for example, the inscription was copied twice or more and divided between the copies along a line of letters of the alphabet so that the authentic documents' letters would match up when their cut edges were juxtaposed; this, at least, helped to convince people that the documents were not being switched on them.[22]

Gradually over the course of the eleventh and twelfth centuries, vernacular writing gained authority as the charter itself became the prime witness, and the closing list of men who had seen and heard the recorded transaction took second place, becoming guarantors of the authenticity of the written document more than of the original action. The inscription was no longer a mere aid to fallible but authoritative living memories, but a permanent embodiment of perfect recall. Much as a modern phonograph record enables us to reproduce a symphony, so the written charter enabled the reproduction of the original words of the swearer, giving priority to the words of the dead over those of the living: "Let it be known that I, [name] . . ."—so go the first-person opening formulas of later-twelfth-century charters. It was not possible to collapse and deny written representation in the way that popular piety conflated anthropomorphic representation with reality, the statue of a saint with the saint. The representation of writing was much more abstract; a charter was clearly not a man nor even a fragment of a man. To grant the authority of such written charters, to accept as authentic their representation of the verbal action of someone physically absent, is to center power in the past, in ancestors, in absent people. Writing was the technology with which churchmen, kings, and certain secular lords managed to revise earlier, acentric ideas of order. Closing formulas, first of ecclesiastical charters, eventually of those drawn up by secular lords, named regnal years of kings, emperors, bishops, not only to situate the particular transaction in time but also to authorize its written representation by reference to the centers of secular and ecclesiastical power that ruled representation.

R. Howard Bloch has observed that a "collective writing lesson" was going on in the eleventh and twelfth centuries, a lesson in which oral culture influenced literate culture as well as the reverse. He notes that the "dissemination [of writing] produced almost limitless possibilities for the dispersion of power alongside of its concentration"; there were "those ready to capitalize upon the institutional forms of power that writing permits—administrative, legal, economic—and those for whom it represents (consciously or not) the possibility of their subversion."[23] In this contest between oral and literate cultures, writing is, as Bloch insists, not the *cause* of conflict so much as the "vehicle" and "the terrain upon which it occurs."[24]

The audiovisual texts of early troubadour verses, which were both inscribed and performed aloud, were liminoid spaces within which these cultural conflicts were played out. The issue to be decided in the game of interpreting the troubadour text (and in interpretation I include composition or reinterpretation and recomposing of earlier texts) was whose model of interpretation was most powerful, that is, what extratextual model of order would be used to explain the meaning of written signs: oral culture's acentric idea of order as a series of temporary standoffs or indeterminacies in an ever-shifting configuration of competing, physically present forces, or literate (chiefly ecclesiastical) culture's idea of order as a stable hierarchy of forces centered on and controlled by one physically absent ruler. These two different ideas of order, like the differing intentions of the Greek scholar and the Roman ruffian of the Archpriest of Hita's exemplum, produced opposite interpretations of the same signs.

Troubadour verse began with a provocative intention: to challenge the authority of writing, the instrument through which the Church, along with the French and Anglo-Norman kings, was trying to impose its centered, hierarchizing moral and social order. The first known troubadour, Guillaume IX, Duke of Aquitaine, was the only troubadour who attacked ecclesiastical authority very directly and dramatically. When the Bishop of Angoulême excommunicated Guillaume for repudiating his wife and refusing to break off his liaison with the Viscountess of Châtellerault, Guillaume threatened the bishop with his sword in the cathedral and exiled him from Angoulême.[25] This sort of forceful opposition did not prove very effective. When the exiled bishop died, he was treated as a saint. Much more subversive of religious order was the laughter Guillaume provoked by means of his burlesques. At the height of the ascetic fervor of sudden conversions and monastic retreats (which also involved the donation of much land and the building of many monastic houses), William of Malmesbury reports that Guillaume founded a mock monastery of prostitutes, complete with abbess and liturgical song.[26] He set this up at Niort, a real place that also means "no place" according to a playful etymology (*ni-ort*).

Contemporary religious chroniclers criticize Guillaume for his immorality and for making audiences guffaw at his facetious verbal play "surpassing even that of the jongleurs."[27] *Foudatz*, facetiousness, making what he wanted to out of words—these were ways of resisting the legal power of the Church and the Anglo-Norman and French monarchies. Bertran de Born put this succinctly in "Ieu chan, que·l reys m'en a preguat": "Lo sen venserem ab foudat / nos Lemozi . . ." ("We will conquer sense with foolishness, / we Limousins").[28] Troubadour "foolishness" deauthorized and destabilized the written vernacular text by finding or inventing multiple, conflicting senses, by accepting and valorizing indeterminacy, variation, and difference, and by insisting on the primary importance of context(s) in determining meaning, with the chief of these being the will or desire of the interpreter, his intention. The troubadours shaped words artfully into new and different forms; they played with words as if they were material things that men might master and control, albeit only temporarily, until another interpreter got his hands on them to take them apart and put them together again in his own ways. "Foolishness"—which troubadours such as Guillaume IX exaggerated in a deliberately provocative way—is the Church's denigrating label for the acentric mentality of the secular, oral culture it opposed, for the radically relativizing interpretive behavior of those who did not share the Church's idealistic, monistic aims, but who preferred the ever-changing configuration of forces combining, fragmenting, and recombining into different patterns.

In the late eleventh and the twelfth centuries, groups of troubadours such as Guillaume's "companions" or the *scola neblo* ("school of Sir Eble" or "foolishly obfuscating school") parodied the religious school situation of textual interpretation. For such a secular audience, a vernacular lyric text might be performed, not by the authoritative voice of the cantor or schoolmaster, but by the completely unauthoritative one of the jongleur or mime who sang and gestured the verse or by a messenger who read and displayed it in the irregular graphology of a letter, a "brief," or a roll. After the verse's presentation began the game of its interpretation, which might be handled seriously or facetiously. The thirteenth-century didactic troubadour Daude de Pradas laments the death of a patron ruler who assured that lyrics were, at least in his court, "per razon complida," achieved appropriately or "completed" by the *razo*, the reasoned explication.[29] Sometimes this wrapping up comprised a whole series of interpretations, each more ingenious than the last, as each interpreter competed in demonstrating his prowess at *entendre* and *dire*, at understanding and explaining the verse. The game of interpretation did not always proceed soberly and reasonably. By using and abusing the techniques for interpreting Latin poetry and Scripture taught in religious schools—exegetical techniques of etymologizing and figurative interpretation as well as grammatical analysis of the inscribed letters—the facetious troubadours dissected their own vernacular texts in order to discover (*trobar*) as many meanings as possible in the verbal matter, by various combinations of its letters and sounds into words and phrases and by various constructions of the literal and figurative meanings of these. During the course of these interpretive games, the troubadours fabricated a literary language; they treated words as matter and used artisanal metaphors—planing, polishing, soldering, refining, weaving and interlacing, coloring—to describe their labor on the forms, sounds, and senses of the vernacular.

One of the most influential manipulators of words (especially of endings in order to make clever rhymes) was the early- to mid-twelfth-century troubadour Marcabru, who compared his own compositions to masonry, as though he were writing in stone:

E segon trobar naturau
Port la peir' e l'esc' e'l fozill,
Mas menut trobador bergau
  Entrebesquill,
Mi tornon mon chant en badau
  En fant gratill.[30]

And according to natural [or vernacular] composition, / I bring the stone and the mortar and the file, / but destructive minor troubadours / mix it up, / turning my song into a mockery, / doing just as they please with it.

Marcabru, who has many traits of a Christian ascetic, claims that his aim in composing is permanence; he insists on the stone-like integrity of words (although he may file off their edges—or endings—a bit). However, he finds that his intentions have been subverted by lesser troubadour-interpreters who mix his poems up according to their own foolish intentions.

In another lyric, "Per savi·l tenc ses doptanssa" (no. 37, p. 178), Marcabru attacks "infantile-minded troubadours" for ignoring the "truth" and turning interpretation and/or composition into a schoolish "discipline" that "breaks up the words by guesswork":

> Trobador, ab sen d'enfanssa,
> Movon als pros atahina,
> E tornon en disciplina
> So que veritatz autreia,
> E fant los motz, per esmanssa,
> Entrebeschatz de fraichura.

> Troubadours, with their infantile sense, / cause the worthy difficulty, / and turn into a discipline / that which truth grants, / and they make the words, by guesswork, / riddled with breaks.

What "truth grants" may be the singular, virtuous sense of Marcabru's texts, the sense that Marcabru himself intends in praising "fin amors" or *caritas* and in composing in the service of Christian doctrine.[31]

In "L'iverns vai e·l temps s'aizina" (no. 31, p. 149), Marcabru rejects the "troba neblo" because it maintains "sentenssa follatina" (foolish Latin, or foolish-tongued explication) against "razo" (right reason):

> Ja non farai mai plevina
> Ieu per la troba n'Eblo,
> Que sentenssa follatina
> Manten encontra razo;
>   Ai!
> Qu'ieu dis e dic e dirai
> Quez amors et amars brai,
>   Hoc,
> E qui blasm' Amor buzina.

> I will never engage myself on the side / of Lord Eble's kind [or, the obfuscating kind] of composition, / which maintains foolish-tongued meaning [or, interpretation] / against right reason; / Oh! / For I have said and say and will say / that love is silent and false love [love of art] sings loudly, / yes, / and whoever blames love slings cow dung.

With his castigation of other troubadours for misusing learning and misinterpreting his texts, Marcabru seems to have polarized the situation and created a debate among troubadours, adding zest to the game of interpretation. Marcabru himself used etymologizing techniques to demonstrate by the meaning of separate syllables the true nature of the troubadours' love, not a pure, whole *amors*, but a "bitter" *amars* springing from *am-ars* (love of art, recollecting Ovid's "*ars am*-atoria") and from burning sexual desire (*am-ars*, playing on the Latin verb *ardeo*, used by the Christian fathers to describe lust). Marcabru contrasted *amors* with *amars* thus:

> Bon' Amors porta meizina
> Per garir son compaigno,
> Amars lo sieu disciplina
> E·l met en perdicio.
> (no. 31, p. 146)

Good love brings medicine / to cure its companion; / bitter love disciplines its [companion] / and sends him to perdition.

Caritas heals and leads to salvation; false (artful, sexual) love involves discipline and leads to hell.

Whereas Marcabru castigates the troubadours for breaking up and mixing up his words and changing his meaning, Guillaume IX, Jaufre Rudel, Raimbaut d'Orange, and several other troubadours, especially the noble ones (the *rics*), deliberately opened their verse to interpretation, challenging the listener/reader to find as many meanings in it as possible. Their art is elitist or "closed" (*trobar clus*) only to the extent that we refuse to participate in the game of elaborating the meanings of the verbal matter; it is closed to those who insist that there can be only one "true" interpretation. The anonymous author of one *devinalh* (Provençal riddling lyric) puts the facetious troubadours' aesthetic succinctly: the more interpretations the better, as long as each one is good.[32]

One of the earliest known troubadour lyrics, Guillaume IX's "Farai un vers de dreyt nien," provokes just this sort of playful elaboration of possible meanings. "I will make a poem of strictly nothing" is not about any external reality:

> non er de mi ni d'autra gen,
> non er d'amor ni de joven,
> ni de ren au.[33]

It will not be about myself nor other people / nor about love nor about youth / nor about anything else.

Guillaume's verse is a dream poem, rhythmically, unintentionally discovered or composed (*trobatz*) while sleeping on a horse; so Guillaume claims: "qu'enans fuy trobatz en durmen sobre chevau." "I will make a poem of strictly nothing" is completely unauthoritative, even antididactic. Guillaume denies all responsibility for conveying any sort of message by it. The lyric is a reiteration of denials, of "No sai" ("I don't know") and other negatives; it is a poem made of "nothing" words and of the nothing of words, a repetitious pattern of perfectly formed strophes with no links other than formal ones, a poem that is nearly pure form, an empty figure that we, inevitably, try to fill with a conceptual sense.

Not surprisingly, this lyric has elicited a great many scholarly interpretations; everyone wants to solve its riddle. As well as allegorizing the poem (reading it figuratively or "troping" it) and trying to read it biographically, scholars have tried to imagine alternate meanings or grammatical relations of the same signs. Charles Camproux, for example, notes that "sobre chevau" ("on a horse") might also mean "super-excellent" (*sobre chebau*, a different spelling of the same sounds).[34] L. T. Topsfield remarks possible puns in the nouns "Norman" and "Franses" (Normans and Frenchmen or "rule" and "measure").[35] The adventure of Guillaume's lyric is, to steal a phrase from Roland Barthes, the "adventure of the signifier: what happens to it."[36] The adventure is ours as we try to make sense of the forms of this text. Guillaume's envoy is a call to interpretation:

Fag ai lo vers, no say de cuy
e trametrai lo a selhuy
que lo·m trametra per autruy
lay vers anjau
que·m tramezes del sieu estug
la contraclau.
(no. 4, p. 94, C ms. variants)

I have made the verse, about whom I don't know, / and I will send it to one / who will send it for me by means of others / over there, toward Anjou, / so that he may send me out of his treasury / the counterkey.

For Guillaume's *vers*, we must imagine written transmission in the irregular graphology of late-eleventh- or early-twelfth-century vernacular charters; we must imagine a manuscript that was literally hard to read. In effect, each reader would provide, out of his own intellectual resources, the "treasury" of his mind, the "counterkey" to decipher the words of and to bestow meaning on Guillaume's text. Does the sequence of letters "qu'enans fuy trobatz en durmen / sobre chevau" mean that Guillaume's verse "was discovered while sleeping on a horse" or that it "was found to be super-excellent"? Although the words are already clearly separated and defined in modern editions of Guillaume's lyric, we, too, invent the poem to the extent that we try to discover a coherent message in it. What interests Guillaume and other facetious troubadours is this adventure of signification as the text passes from hand to hand, mouth to mouth. Guillaume wants to know how the game of reading, of interpreting his text, turns out; he asks for the "counterkey," the counterpoem of subsequent interpretation; he wants to know what his fellows have discovered in his text, how they have recreated it.[37]

While reading and writing in the vernacular were relatively new and unregulated procedures, men recognized the imperfections of writing as an instrument for conveying meaning. Thus early vernacular written charters do not claim to be more than aids to living memory. Medieval people placed the responsibility for the meaning of the inscribed vernacular text on its interpreter even more than on its original author. They recognized that condensation, omission, and various idiosyncrasies in a scribe's use of signs to represent speech made the written text ambiguous. The facetious troubadours deliberately exploited these ambiguities. The emphasis on reader responsibility cut both ways and became a conventional screen—and signpost—for subversive intentions. Didactic troubadours held readers responsible for the meaning of their texts in order to absolve themselves of blame for the "foolish misinterpretations" of the "*tor*badors"[38] and the *scola neblo*. In the first strophe of "Cui bon vers agrad' a auzir,"[39] Peire d'Auvernhe points out that the merit of the lyric depends on the merit of the interpreter: a good interpreter will find his verse good; a bad one, bad. As Peire uses such terms as *good* and *bad*, they have Christian moral, as well as aesthetic, connotations, which is probably not the case when Guillaume IX makes much the same excuse for his verse.[40] With a similar admonition that the interpreter is responsible for what he finds in the text, Bernart de Ventadorn closes a lyric that is full of possible erotic puns on *cor* as heart or horn and *ric* as powerful or rigid: "Lo vers es fis e naturaus / e bos celui qui be l'enten" ("The verse is fine and natural / and he is a good man who understands it well").[41] Indeed, reading such verse is a trial of "goodness," but the meaning of *goodness* varies with the troubadour.

Before regulation of the inscription of the "natural" language of the vernacular—with the compilation of dictionaries and grammars, more widespread teaching of writing and reading, and the eventual standardization of spelling, punctuation, and letter forms after the advent of mechanical printing—the vernacular written word lacked authority to represent the intentions of an absent author. The troubadours realized what we scholars—preceded by contemporary artists—have been reemphasizing in the past few decades: that the meaning of a sign is determined by its use in a particular context, and that the most important context is the mind of the interpreter. As the Archpriest of Hita put it, words serve understanding (or interpretation) and not the reverse.

Although Provençal scholars have not yet brought themselves to revel in textual variation or indeterminacy, many have accepted the idea of a deliberate variation on the part of medieval interpreters, a deliberate *mouvance* of the text, and have renounced the hope of ever discovering the exact words Guillaume IX, or any other early troubadour, "originally" wrote.[42] More and more scholars are noting the equivocal qualities of troubadour verse (instead of trying to eliminate ambiguity) and taking aesthetic pleasure in this—as they should! Charles Camproux speaks of the troubadours' "deliberate search for the equivocal, source of the richest signification."[43] Roger Dragonetti advises that, in translation, it is best to try to leave to the expression, as much as possible, "this free play of significations";[44] on the subject of the *Conte du Graal*, he makes an observation that is equally valid for troubadour lyrics: "When one directs one's listening to the phonic substance of the words, apart from their semantic structure, something else may be understood because of these forbidden liaisons."[45] In addition to paying more attention to the texture of sounds of troubadour verse,[46] scholars have begun to discover paragrams and anagrams in the written texts;[47] as well as revealing the equivocal "etymological" senses of names,[48] they have begun to apply etymologizing interpretive techniques to other key words.[49] Tolerance for multiple meanings has even begun to extend to vulgar innuendo and erotic senses of particular words, strophes, or whole lyrics.[50] Of Arnaut Daniel's famous sestina "Lo ferm voler q'el cor m'intra," Charles Jernigan has written,

> Arnaut was certainly mocking . . . formulaic troubadour sentiments by grinding them against the most disconcerting sexual reality; and by twisting—tormenting—them into his newly invented sestina form, he also was making fun of the difficult and complex types of verse, including his own. And the form works. Certainly it is the most elaborate poetic pun-play ever devised, a poem existing on two levels, a poem compounded of *double entendres* which reoccur seven insistent times in slightly different contexts which shade the meanings accordingly.[51]

Certainly, Arnaut's is a virtuoso performance of variation and indeterminacy, but it is, as we shall see, a mainstream one. Two recent anthologies of troubadour verse, with modern translations, René Nelli's *Ecri-*

vains anticonformistes and Pierre Bec's *Burlesque et obscénité chez les troubadours*,[52] attest to a broadening of the canon, a willingness to admit more "irregular" aspects of troubadour verse. We no longer limit ourselves to interpreting "up," to sublimating as we read troubadour lyrics.

It is not so much a "new poetic" (or a new development in the visual arts) that has "reopen[ed] access to a forgotten poetry,"[53] but a change in the dominant idea of order in modern Western society, a change much too complex for discussion in this book. Gradually, over the past decades, under the impetus of scientific discoveries and technological progress, as well as political, economic, social, and moral changes, our notion of order has become more and more acentric—thus consonant with the mentality of the early troubadours. Troubadour verse is ripe now for creative reinterpretation, because now we are ready to read it in a new (but very old) way.

2

Reading Troubadour Verse
The Adventure of the Signifier

> Li mot seran descubert
> Al quec de razon devisa.
>
> The words will be discovered
> By the one who divides them rightly.
>
> —Raimbaut d'Orange,
> "Una chansoneta fera"

Restrictive modern reading and editing practices and assumptions hinder us from playing with language. We are so used to having our words already clearly divided for us in modern editions that we wonder what dividing correctly can possibly have to do with discovering the words of Raimbaut's verses. Let me begin to illustrate this, not on Raimbaut's lyric but, rather, on the two syllables represented by the letters *neblo* in thirteenth- and fourteenth-century manuscript contexts of the lyrics of three other mid- to late-twelfth-century troubadours. Marcabru was the first to use the two syllables, in a strophe that I have previously quoted from the Dejeanne edition (no. 31, p. 149), which reads as follows:

> Ja non farai mai plevina
> Ieu per la troba n'Eblo,
> Que sentenssa follatina
> Manten encontra razo;
> Ai!
> Qu'ieu dis e dic e dirai
> Quez amors et amars brai,
> Hoc,
> E qui blasm' Amor buzina.

I will never engage myself on the side / of Lord Eble's kind of poetic invention, / which maintains foolish interpretation / against reason; / Oh! / For I said and say and will say / that love is silent and false love sings loudly, / yes, / and whoever blames love slings cow dung.

When one looks at this strophe in the major manuscripts containing it, AKNR, one discovers that, for the line in question, they bear out Dejeanne's footnoted list of variants exactly, even down to word division on the page: in a conflation of two lines that ruins the rhyme scheme, the A manuscript omits "neblo" entirely and reads "Jeu per la torba a sentenssa follatina"; K, N, and R all begin with *I* ("Jeu" or "Eu" or "Yeu"), but there is a difference in the way they continue the line: K and N read "per la troba neblo," whereas R reads "per la corba neblo." Because *t* and *c* are shaped so much alike in R's script, it may be that the R scribe was writing not "corba" but "torba," just as the A scribe more clearly did.

Must we analyze the letters *n-e-b-l-o* in these lines as Dejeanne did, taking the *n* as an abbreviation for *en*, meaning "lord" or "sir," and the *e-b-l-o* as the name Eble, thus giving "n'Eblo," with reference to Viscount Eble II of Ventadorn?[1] This reading makes good sense if, as we believe, Eble of Ventadorn encouraged troubadour verse so that, in effect, his court served as a kind of "school" for vernacular verse composition and appreciation, which was marked in some way as "troba n'Eblo" or the style of Eble's court. This interpretation, based on a grammatical analysis or "division" of the grouped letters *neblo*, is probably correct, but it is not the only one a thirteenth- or fourteenth-century reader might have arrived at from reading the above-quoted lines in the manuscripts.

There is no restrictive punctuation or capitalization to prevent the medieval reader from taking *neblo* as one word, an adjective describing "troba" (verse composition) or "torba" (confusion, or a deliberate perversion or reversal of "troba"). What this "troba" or "torba" does is uphold "foolish Latin" or foolish speech against reason: "Que sentenssa follatina / Manten encontra razo." In such a context it might also be possible to understand *neblo* as "foggy," "obscuring" or "obfuscating," or "insubstantial, worthless." The feminine Latin noun *nebula*, meaning fog, mist, or cloud (figuratively "veil" or "obscurity"), developed a variety of forms in the vernacular dialects of southern and western France. Raynouard lists *nebla*, *neble*, *neula*, *nevolina*, *nivol* (or *niol* or *niul*), *niola*, *nible*.[2] Another Latin noun, this time masculine, *nebulo*, *-onis*, meaning worthless (used by Horace to designate Penelope's crowd of suitors),[3] has left no traces in the Provençal dictionaries, although it may not be irrelevant to the context of the relatively learned Marcabru's verse. Because he was dealing with so many different dialectal forms of words, some of which were shaped in new ways in order to make rhymes, the adept medieval interpreter of written vernacular verse would have to be especially sensitive to the evocations of meaning of root syllables, such as, in my example, the sounds represented by *neb* or the alternate spellings *nev* or *neu*. A medieval reader might have understood the "troba neblo" not only as the "poetic invention of Sir Eble" but also as "obfuscating poetic invention." Indeed, Marcabru may have intended, by the way he defined Eble's poetic invention as foolish, to bring out the punning sense of the name, of n'Eble as "fog."

Bernart de Ventadorn may also have played with the equivocal sense of Eble's name when prefixed by *n*. Appel edits Bernart's strophe, from "Lo tems vai e ven e vire," as follows:

> Ja mais no serai chantaire
> ni de l'escola n'Eblo,
> que mos chantars no val gaire
> ni mas voutas ni mei so;
> ni res qu'eu fassa ni dia,
> no conosc que pros me sia,
> ni no·i vei melhuramen.
> (no. 30, pp. 181–82)

Never again will I sing, / or belong to the school of Lord Eble, / for my songs [or art of singing] have no value, / neither my turns nor my melodies; / nor anything that I do or say, / do I understand how it might profit me, / nor do I see any improvement in this.

Here, in the context of Bernart's complaint about the unprofitableness of his verse, there is room for a double sense to the "escola neblo," as both the school of Sir Eble and the worthlessly mystifying school. Appel's list of variants tells us that the scribes of the DIK manuscripts all wrote two words, "ni blon," as if they understood "Never more will I be a singer, nor of the school nor blond." This seems an easy mistake, an overdoing of the repetitive structure of negation by *ni* in the strophe. However, the "mistake" is Appel's rather than the medieval scribes'. A look at two of the manuscripts discovers that the D scribe separates the two syllables only because he has no more space on the line, while the K scribe clearly writes "niblon" as one clump of letters. The DIK scribes do spell the first syllable with an *i*, but the significance of this is not clear. Hard as it is for us as modern readers, we should not regard spelling or word division in medieval manuscripts' inscriptions of Provençal lyrics as definitive and exclusive. They are approximations which can often be analyzed several ways, and their very indeterminacy may be eloquent. Thus Raimbaut d'Orange calls his readers' attention to the problem of "dividing"; how readers divide letters into groups will determine what words they discover, consequently the sense of his lyric. As to dividing "rightly," why should we assume that this means there is only *one* correct interpretation of where to divide the words?

Let me offer another example of possible play with the sense of the letters of what modern editors, and consequently modern readers, have always taken to be the name Lord Eble, this time from the first strophe of a lyric by Giraut de Bornelh:

Leu chansonet' e vil
M'auri' a obs a far
Que pogues enviar
En Alvernh' al Dalfi.
Pero, s'el drech chami
Pogues n'Eblon trobar,
Be·lh poiria mandar
Qu'eu dic qu'en l'escurzir
  Non es l'afans,
Mas en l'obr' esclarzir.[4]

A plain, low little song, / I ought to make / so that I could send it / to Auvergne to the dauphin. / However, if by the straight path / I were able to find Sir Eble, / I could inform him / that I say that in obscuring [verse] / there's no great difficulty, / but rather in clarifying the work.

The variants of the CHNR manuscripts listed by Kolsen in his edition all read "nebles" instead of "neblon" (the ABIKM reading). *Nebles* is the objective case form of *neble*, meaning cloud, fog, vapor, one of the many spellings and pronunciations deriving from the Latin *nebula*. As an instance of this spelling of *nebles*, Raynouard gives the first line of the troubadour Guilhem Adhemar's "L'aigua pueia contra mon / Ab fum, ab *nebles* et ab ven" ("The water rises against the mountain / with vapor, clouds, and wind"). This spelling on the part of the CHNR scribes may well represent their understanding of the double sense of Lord Eble's name, which is virtually explicated by the last lines of the strophe warning n'Ebles (or n'Eblon) against *obscurantism*. Modern editorial clarifications, or preinterpretations, of the medieval inscriptions of troubadour lyrics mask for us the equivocal senses of *neblo*—and of untold other combinations of letters. We play the early troubadours' word games, if at all, only with great "handicaps" that we must learn to recognize.

Troubadour lyrics survive in about thirty *chansonniers* or "songbooks" from the thirteenth and fourteenth centuries.[5] Because so few of these contain musical notation, it would probably have been more appropriate to call them "textbooks." These compilations, which we designate by letters of the alphabet, were made long after the original composition of the early troubadours' verse. Although some lyrics appear in only one manuscript, most appear in several. A relatively well-known lyric such as Bernart de Ventadorn's "Can vei la lauzeta mover," for example, appears in one form or another in twenty different manuscripts.[6] For modern editors, the problem is that the different manuscripts present slightly different versions of the same lyric. Until 1978, with Rupert Pickens' fine edition of all the manuscript versions of each of Jaufre Rudel's seven poems,[7] modern editorial practice had usually been to construct a composite version of each lyric that appears in several manuscripts. One manuscript, often either A (in Rome) or C (in Paris), generally serves as a base, but whenever the modern editor finds the base reading ambiguous—aesthetically, conceptually, or morally displeasing or confusing—he labels the base reading "corrupt" due to the scribe's fatigue, carelessness, or incomprehension of his exemplar or to some other failure of transmission. The way modern editors have been accustomed to handling textual ambiguities in the Provençal songbooks has been to avoid them altogether, whenever possible, by substituting "clearer" readings from other manuscript versions for "faulty" passages in the base manuscript. Although the composite texts that result from this editorial practice correspond to no single medieval manuscript version of a lyric, we have believed that these composite texts, purified of "corruptions," were closer to the troubadours' original compositions, which, we assumed, were not supposed to be ambiguous. For certain medieval historical texts and documents intended by their authors to be authoritative, such modern editorial practices and assumptions may be appropriate. They are certainly wrong for troubadour verse, which is, often enough, deliberately ambiguous or indeterminate and which openly or implicitly challenges its audience to a game of interpretation.

Since Paul Zumthor coined the term *mouvance* and theorized about the "movement" of medieval texts,[8] there has been a growing recognition among medievalists that variant readings should be taken seriously. In the introduction to his edition of Jaufre Rudel, Pickens argues that Provençal poets were not trying to create authoritative texts. Jaufre asks his performer to transmit his song exactly as he has composed it without changing anything; nevertheless, in the same lyric envoy he goes on to license improvements by the audience, whom he specifies as the viscount in Quercy and the count in Toulouse (and, presumably, their courts); these will "do to it whatever will make my song more pleasing."[9] The aesthetic of this kind of recreational literature called for its continuing interpretation and re-creation by its audience. One has but to look at a series of different manuscript versions of a Provençal lyric—almost any one—to see what a lot of minor variations there are, and to discover that the vast majority of these do make good sense and are clearly not the result of random errors of mechanical transcription of the text from one exemplar to another. Take, for example, one line, which I have chosen virtually at random, from the seventh strophe of Bernart de Ventadorn's "Pois preyatz me, senhor";

Amors, e que·m farai?
si guerrai ja ab te?
ara cuit qu'e·n morrai
del dezirer que·m ve,
si·lh bela lai on jai
no m'aizis pres de se,
qu'eu la manei e bai
et estrenha vas me
so cors blanc, gras e le.
(no. 36, pp. 206–7)

Love, what will I do / if I fight with you? / I believe that I will die / of the desire that comes to me / if the beautiful one, there where she lies down, / *does not make me comfortable beside her* / so that I may caress and kiss her / and strain against myself / her body, white, plump, and smooth.

This is Appel's list of variants for the italicized line:

A	No maizis pres de se	[m'aizis]
D, E, G	No maizis tant de se	
M	No maizis tant lonc se	
C	No macuelh pres de se	[m'acuelh]
I, K, N	No macuelh apres se	
R	Nos aizina de me	[s'aizina]
Q	No mallegra lonc se	[m'allegra]
S	Non ma deiosta se	[m'a]

In each case, the opening word (*no* or *non*) and, in all but one case, the rhyme word remain the same, while the central words of the line change. Although the variants do not differ very much in meaning, they differ considerably in sound ("m'aizis," "m'acuelh," "s'aizina," "m'allegra," "m'a deiosta"), creating different harmonies with the sounds of surrounding lines. To the modern ear and intelligence (at any rate, to mine) there is really not much to choose among these variants, certainly no way to detect an "authentic" line, that is, the "original" line invented by Bernart de Ventadorn. Under these circumstances, we must treat each different manuscript variation and version of a lyric as authentic in the sense that each represents a medieval interpretation of the lyric on the part of a scribe, a lyric collector, or a group of connoisseurs or "school." The great majority of these variations effect minor changes of connotation and/or changes in the harmonies of verbal sound patterns, and they make sense immediately as we read them, although I doubt that many readers do sort through the footnoted variants of most modern editions.

The kind of variation I am most interested in, however, is not of this "easy" sort but, rather, the kind that has traditionally been labeled most "corrupt," because the variants do not make immediate sense. In these cases modern editors have assumed that the scribe did not understand what he was writing or that he hopelessly bungled the spelling or the grouping of letters together on the manuscript page. If another songbook presents a version of the line that makes better sense, editors choose to print it instead of the "corrupt" one. When, as is often the case, the scribes of different manuscripts "bungle" the same line in different ways, none or few of which seem to make clear sense, modern editors assume that the line was already corrupt in the scribes' exemplars, and they correct it as they will in order to produce an unambiguous modern text that follows the rules, as we conceive them, of Provençal grammar. In my own experience of reading the songbook manuscripts, I have found that ambiguities of spelling, word division, syntax, and thus of meaning in such opaque lines may signal the medieval interpreter's perception, conscious or unconscious, of multiple meanings in the sequence of sounds of the oral text, and his reluctance or inability to choose among them and to try to eliminate all but one meaning by means of his graphological choices and grammatical analysis of the text. Some of the opaque lines and phrases in the Provençal songbooks may be deliberately so. They challenge the reader to interpretation, and this involves wordplay. In order to play the game as a medieval reader would, however, we must be aware of important differences between medieval and modern reading practices and assumptions.

For the medieval reader, the written text of a lyric was only a *semblance* or visible sign of the oral text; in order to be understood, the images on the manuscript page needed translation into sounds. The medieval reader read aloud. The early vernacular written text was audiovisual. This is why admonitions to listen (*auzir*, *escoutar*, *entendre*) appear in letters, historical compilations, and other texts that seem to be destined not for public performance but for private reading.[10] Scholars have generally dismissed such admonitions as archaic formulas meaning no more, in private reading situations, than "pay attention." This may be true in some cases, but in many others the aural admonition is appropriate. It suggests that even the private medieval "reader" read aloud and understood words by hearing himself pronounce the letters on the page. He did, indeed, need to listen well.[11] The graphology of early medieval vernacular manuscripts is irregular because of the fundamental orality of these texts. Although individual scribes had their own habitual ways of spelling certain sounds, the spelling of the same sound varied from scribe to scribe, manuscript to manuscript, and even from line to line of the same text. In an extreme example of visual variation, in English in 1324 the same scribe in the same document spells the sound represented by the stable modern orthography *hair* in five different ways: *her*, *heyr*, *hayr*, *hair*, *hoeyr*.[12] A medieval scribe did not necessarily transcribe, like a modern typist, the graphic formulas from the exemplar before him. A medieval scribe was a medieval reader. He heard the text he read, and he represented the sounds he heard according to the graphic formulas he habitually used for representing those sounds; thus his new text often differed from the text he was reproducing. Even in the case of manuscripts one of which is clearly a copy of the other or of the same exemplar, such as the I and K songbooks in Paris, there are minor differences of spelling to indicate that the scribes were not merely transferring images from one page to another; instead, they were translating images into sounds and then back into images.[13]

As long as each subsequent reader performed the text aloud, it was not entirely crucial to the meaning if a scribe used one variant spelling of a sound or another. Even if he wrote *b* instead of *v*, *bis* instead of *vis*, the medieval reader would not necessarily understand "linen" or "gray-brown" or "false" to the exclusion of "face" or "regard," because he would not react as unilaterally as we do to the configuration of letters on the page. Instead, the medieval reader would reproduce the sound, reading according to the phonics, letting the meaning arise out of the larger contextual dialectic of sounds. While the meanings we associate with *bis* would probably be uppermost, the meanings of *vis* could arise if the context allowed it. The aurally oriented medieval reader was prone to recognize—or momentarily consider the possibility of—a great many puns based on identical or similar sounds with different graphic representations, such as, in Provençal, *b/v/p* or *t/d* or *q/k/c/g*.[14] Our visual orientation toward words, the prescribed written forms of which we learn at an early age to distinguish almost like ideograms, discourages us from considering alternate meanings, from engaging in this kind of wordplay as we read. Therefore, in order to make sense of textual ambiguities involving spelling, word division, and syntax, it helps to reproduce the sequence of sounds the letters represent. By recreating the oral text as we read, we behave more nearly as a medieval reader would. We are more likely to perceive equivocal senses by reading aloud—if we listen to ourselves—than by silent reading of the grammatically preanalyzed visual configurations of modern editions.

In classical Latin inscriptions devoid of punctuation marks or spaces separating words, it was the oral performance of the text that determined its sense, not its visual appearance. Students needed the teacher's pre–reading aloud (*praelectio*) or preliminary explication in order to be able to read the undifferentiated series of letters for themselves.[15] The visual text facing the medieval reader was usually somewhat more clearly articulated, at least with respect to spacing, than a classical Latin text would have been, but, even so, the medieval reader would be more accustomed than we are today to considering the possibility of linking sounds together in ways different from those in which they appeared to be linked (or separated) by their graphic representation on the page, which was not authoritative. Like the spelling of a particular sound, the system of linking sounds (or, rather, of separating them with blank spaces) could vary from scribe to scribe. The elision of articles, pronouns, prepositions, conjunctions, and proclitics (such as *en* for "sir") was especially variable, requiring much interpretation by the reader.

For example, in the A songbook's version of Jaufre Rudel's "Lanquan li jorn," which can easily be verified in the facsimile edition,[16] the last two syllables of Jaufre's famous phrase are almost always written together in one phonetic clump, *deloing*, leaving the reader to make his own grammatical divisions, either *de loing* or *del oing*. The difference these divisions might make in the meaning of Jaufre's lyric is major. *De loing* would mean "from afar," whereas *del oing* would mean "of the ointment" and could thus evoke, depending on the specific context, connotations ranging from a quasi-sacred "anointment" to medicinal balm to sexual fluids. Marcabru, who sent at least one of his lyrics to Jaufre Rudel, had already called love medicinal: "Bon' Amors porta meizina / Per garir son compaigno" ("Good love carries medicine / to cure its companion").[17] Thus the association of love and ointment—of love's healing and even sanctifying power—is not completely farfetched. Furthermore, John Rea has presented one possible eroticizing interpretation of Jaufre's pilgrim images within the framework of which an understanding of *deloing* as "love of the [erotic] ointment" might fit.[18] In the last strophe of the A version of Jaufre's lyric, for example, Jaufre describes his desire for the "amor deloing" by using sensual terms such as "lechai" (greedy or inordinately fond), which seems to suggest a more sensual, materialistic interpretation of his love:

> Ver ditz qui m'apella lechai
> Ni desiron d'amon de loing,[19]
> Car nuills autre jois tant no·m plai
> Cum jauzimens d'amor de loing;
> Mas so q'eu vuoill m'es tant ahis
> Q'enaissi·m fadet mos pairis
> Q'ieu ames e non fos amatz.

We might enrich Pickens' translation of this strophe (p. 169) by dividing *deloing* both ways:

> He speaks the truth who calls me covetous / and desirous of love from afar [and, of the ointment], / for no other joy pleases me so much / as enjoyment of love from afar [and, of the ointment]; / but what I want is so hateful to me, / for thus did my godfather fix as my fate / that I should love and not be loved.

Nevertheless, even if the A scribe had written "de loing," medieval readers would still have been relatively free to divide the sequence of letters on the manuscript page differently from the way the scribe had done. Furthermore, Jaufre's repetition of the two syllables of *deloing* as the second and fourth rhymes of every succeeding strophe of his lyric may well have encouraged medieval interpreters to engage in division experiments that would vary and enrich the sense of the lyric or create more clever, rich rhymes.

Medieval scribes tended to elide or separate syllables according to the way they heard the phrasing of the line and according to their own graphic systems. For example, Jacques Monfrin has noted that the scribe of the fourteenth-century C songbook showed originality in using the symbol æ to link words that end in a short *a* sound with those that begin with a short *e* sound, such as "volgræn chantan."[20] The C scribe also divides words, in Monfrin's terms, according to "false cuts," in other words, phonetic cuts rather than modern morphological ones: "ab la len tir" (instead of *ab l'alen tir*) and "daquesta mor suy cossiros" (instead of *d'aquest' amor suy cossiros*). The effect of these "false cuts" is to increase the number of syllables standing alone on the manuscript page and, in cases like the division of "a-mor" above, to suggest multiple senses: "I desire this death, or this bite, or this love." Instead of defining different words, and thereby articulating the grammatical sense of the phrase, these blank spaces on the manuscript page represent vocal pauses and suggest the way the C scribe heard (or himself performed as he read) the lyric. The C scribe is by no means alone in his phonetic divisions. For example, of several hands in the N songbook (New York, Pierpont Morgan 819), the first one, like the C scribe, tends to end phonetic groups with vowels rather than beginning with them: "da mor" (instead of the modern grammatical division *d'amor*) or "bona ventura" (instead of *bon aventura*). In other cases, this scribe's divisions emphasize interior rhymes and harmonies between lines, as in the following two lines (fol. 2v, col. 1): "conoi senca esa bers / senz lar geca epo ders" (instead of *conoisenca e sabers / senz largeca e poders*). These phonetic divisions—or, for that matter, the familiar clumps of pronouns, articles, and other elided "little" words in early vernacular manuscripts—reflect the basic orality of the texts.

In order to make sense out of the irregular graphology of a medieval vernacular manuscript, the modern reader often finds himself engaging in a dialectical process of oral interpretation that is playful in nature. However, when we edit medieval texts, we change the phonetic groups into grammatical ones. In the C songbook's version of Jaufre Rudel's phrase, we change "sesta mor delonh" into *sest' amor de lonh* (wherein the apostrophe stands for the truncated vowel of the pronoun and the "a" clearly belongs to the noun *amor*, while the separation of the preposition from its object clarifies their sense). Such modern editorial practice tends to discourage wordplay by eliminating the need for an intermediate, oral stage from our comprehension of the text, an oral stage during which we are temporarily free to play, via longer or shorter pauses and intonation, with the combination of the syllables and the syntax—hence the sense—of the text. In effect, during the oral performance of the lyric, we behave like jugglers. We suspend the syllables while, in our minds, we group them into words and phrases, continually revising our groupings in accordance with the new lexical and grammatical possibilities that each additional syllable may present. During this double process of interpretation of a medieval script (from visual sign to sound, from sound to sense), alternate and often very different meanings arise—many more than when we read a preanalyzed, modern printed text. I am not advocating that we stop editing medieval vernacular texts and simply reproduce them photographically or transcribe them precisely as they appear on a particular manuscript page, or even that we print the phonetic units of the manuscript page, as Clovis Brunel did, with dashes dividing the clumps of letters into modern words. Nevertheless, we do need to recognize the effects of modern editorial and reading practices on our understanding of medieval texts. We must also examine the effects of late medieval "editing" upon the texts as we know them in their thirteenth- and fourteenth-century manuscript versions.

Although I have been emphasizing their fundamental orality, the texts of the Provençal songbooks are nevertheless relatively modern and regular in appearance compared to the earliest preserved Provençal documents. For example, in a prose charter of donation from the area around Rodez dated 10 April 1102 (contemporary with Guillaume IX), the Provençal text tends to represent speech patterns, with the basic unit being, not the word, but the phonic phrase, which is set apart on the page by blank spaces as in the following example: "alpont aselias lamitat dunamoiada devinea."[21] The Latin introductory and closing formulas of this and other contemporary Provençal charters are represented according to grammatical, rather than phonetic, units. This is in keeping with Saenger's findings with respect to the writing of Latin:

> Word separation was the singular contribution of the early Middle Ages to the evolution of Western written communication, . . . a major advance toward silent reading. On the Continent . . . it was received hesitantly, perhaps as a concession to the ignorant, and was only gradually introduced into the body of the text over the course of the ninth, tenth, and eleventh centuries.[22]

Latin grammar and the proper division of words had long been taught in the schools through writing and the analysis of classical and biblical written texts, but no such prescriptive mold yet existed for the vernacular. An early-twelfth-century written version of Guillaume IX's songs would not resemble the thirteenth- and fourteenth-century versions we know. The divisions of the twelfth-century text would be more oral and physiological (dependent on breathing rhythms and on how the tongue moves in the mouth) and harmonic. Possibly, as in certain eleventh- and twelfth-century vernacular charters, an accent mark would be used to indicate vocal expressions that would help to clarify the ambiguities of the script—to mark a hiatus and thus prevent the contraction of identical vowels, to distinguish an accented syllable, to signal whether a diphthong is increasing or decreasing, and the like.[23] By the thirteenth century, these accent marks had developed into musical signs (*punctum* and *virga*) indicating the lowering or raising of the voice;[24] they were no longer used in vernacular charters, and they do not appear in the thirteenth- and fourteenth-century songbooks that have come down to us.

Generally speaking, these songbooks represent Provençal lyrics according to graphic and grammatical conventions of word division established long after the lyrics were first composed. Nevertheless, the *chansonniers* cannot be read silently; their inscriptions of troubadour lyrics remain audiovisual, for, as we have seen in examples from the A, C, and N songbooks, the *praelectio* of their word division is not yet completely regularized and there remain many "false cuts." Furthermore, every seemingly "bungled" line reinforces the basic orality of the text by forcing the reader to pronounce the letters aloud, sort out the syllables, then the words, then the syntactical and logical relationships between words.

There is no way to capture all of the nuances of speech or song in writing. The process of writing is necessarily reductive; the process of reading, necessarily expansive. In many cases, the original graphological choices of how to represent the lyric may have been made by the troubadour-composer himself during a dialectical process of speaking or dictating, writing or having a scribe write, reading the text aloud, and beginning the process again with revisions. Many scholars now agree that the troubadours composed their verse with the aid of writing, and Dietmar Rieger has argued, against the consensus that troubadour verse was always sung, that its formal complexities would encourage reception in writing.[25] The concrete evidence Richard Rouse offers in his analysis of rolls as a transmission medium for lyrics tends to support Rieger's view and to confirm Gröber's old hypothesis that troubadour verse was disseminated on separate sheets that were cheap, portable, and not worth saving long, before finally being collected in the fine songbooks we know.[26] Rouse points to a number of illustrations of medieval poets with rolls. The Pierpont Morgan songbook (N) shows Folquet de Marseille with pen in hand and a knife for erasures seated at a writing table with an unfurled roll, his arms outstretched as if declaiming his lyric (ms. 819, fol. 63r). On folio 60 verso of the same manuscript, a dejected troubadour scatters the single sheets (*breu*) on which his verses are written. The E songbook (Paris, B.N. fr. 1749, fol. 69r) shows the troubadour Arnaut Tintinac declaiming with what looks like a small, tight roll (possibly the size of a rolled *breu*) in one hand, while the other is raised expressively.[27] (See fig. 1.) In the A songbook (Rome, Vat. lat. 5232, fol. 115r), Gaubertz de Poicibot is pictured seated in tonsure and monastic robes, and he points to the letters written vertically on the scroll that he unfurls over his knees as if explicating and displaying the text. The only marks that appear on the scroll are the capital letters F H R and some indistinct little vertical lines that might possibly represent musical notation. (See fig. 2.)

Many of the early troubadours, even those who performed their own lyrics, say or suggest that they are sending their verse in writing to someone. In "En cossirier et en esmay," Bernart de Ventadorn is quite specific:

La messatge no·l trametrai
ni ami [*or*, a mi] dire non cove;
negun cosselh en me non sai,
mas d'una re me conort be:
elha sap letras et enten;
et agrada me qu'escria
los motz e, s'a lieÿs plazia,
ligis los al mieu salvamen.
(ms. C, Paris,
B.N. fr. 856, fol. 5r)

"Letras" here may not mean Latin letters, as we usually translate the word, but, rather, the technique of phonetic spelling and reading, because what the lady is able to read is clearly a vernacular text:

I will not have the message delivered aloud to her, / and to say it to myself is not fitting; / I don't know any solution, / but one thing encourages me: / she reads and understands writing; / and it pleases me to write down / the words and, if she pleases, / she may read them to save me.

Three times in the envoy of his "Farai un vers de dreyt nien," Guillaume IX employs the term *trametrai*, which seems to have been used at the time to describe the "transmission" of a letter.[28] The C songbook's version of Guillaume's "Farai un vers, pos mi sonelh" contains an envoy in which he refers to the "pouch" in which his messenger "Monet" is to carry his verse (no. 5, p. 135): "Monet, tu m'iras al mati, / mo vers portaras el borssi / dreg a la molher d'En Guari" ("Monet, you will go for me in the morning / and carry my verse in the pouch / straight to the wife of Sir Warren"). In his "Quan lo ruis de la fontana," Jaufre Rudel calls attention to the fact that he is *not* sending his verse in writing, but only through the oral performance of "singing," as if this were extraordinary:

Senes breu de parguamina,
Tramet lo vers en cantan
En plana lengua romana
A·N Ugo Bru per Filhol.
(no. 2, p. 118)

Pickens translates, "Without any writing on parchment, / I transmit the poem singing / in the plain vernacular language / to Lord Hugo the Brown by Godson."[29] In "Cortesamen vuoill comenssar" (no. 15, p. 63), Marcabru may suggest a written medium for his lyric when he sends the "vers e·l son" (the verses with their melody or melodic notation) across the sea to Jaufre Rudel.

Because *desplegar* means, literally, to show by unfolding or unrolling, troubadours' injunctions to their messengers or singers to "display" their verse may also suggest a written transmission, and an audiovisual reading of the text by its audience, perhaps in conjunction with a "singing" performance by the messenger. Cercamon, for example, in "Assatz es or'oimai qu'eu chan," uses the pair "be·l chant ne be·l desplei" (sing or display it well) to describe the transmission of his text.[30] Marcabru, likewise, in "Hueymais dey esser alegrans" orders a messenger to display his verse before Lord Cabrieira in Urgel:

Messatge cortes, ben parlans,
Vai t'en en Urgel ses falhir,
E sias del vers despleyans
A'n Cabrieira, que lo remir.
(no. 34, p. 167)

Courteous, eloquent messenger, / go to Urgel without fail, / and display [literally, "unroll" or "unfold"] the verse / for Lord Cabrieira, so that he studies it.

The response Marcabru wants from his audience is not just a quick glance at his text but an admiring contemplation or study of his verse, as suggested by the term *remir*. In the envoy of "Lo vers comens quan vei del fau," where he challenges his critics to examine his verse closely, Marcabru uses the word *breu* not so much in the sense Dejeanne understood of "briefly" but, rather, like Jaufre Rudel, to mean "brief" in the sense of a short written document:

Marcabrus ditz que no·n l'en chau
Qui quer ben lo ver al fronzilh,
Que no y pot hom trobar a frau
   Mot de rozilh.
Intrar pot hom de lonc jornau
   En breu estrilh.[31]

Marcabru says that he's not concerned / whoever searches into the verse and breaks it [or, pleats it] up, / because no one can discover [*trobar*] there by fraud / a rusty [unpolished] word. / One can spend a very long time / going over a short document with a fine-toothed comb.

The *vers* of the early troubadours was a composition committed to writing.

Indeed, I would argue that the troubadours' linguistic play virtually required the ambiguous condensation—the brevity—of the written text, which preserved, at least in part, the phonetic groupings of speech patterns, but not the intonations, inflections, and all the other vocal and bodily signals and gestures with which men may clarify for their audiences the ambiguities in their own utterances. Ordinarily, all of the speaker's interpretive signals help us not to hesitate too long over the "correct" conceptual combination of a series of sounds, so that our erroneous combinations, due to morphological or syntactical—that is, grammatical—ambiguities, seldom reach consciousness. However, the phonetic clumps of early vernacular charters, and presumably also of the first troubadour *breu* (which have not survived), are ambiguous in their incompleteness, forcing the reader to perform them aloud and thus to replace the audible signs that have been left out of the inscription. In order to discover the words and their grammatical relationships, the interpreter of a text inscribed in such phonetic clumps had to consider the possible meanings by different combinations (cuts or elisions) of a particular sequence of letters representing sounds. This experimental, playful, and potentially highly creative process of reading the early vernacular text might even characterize the "reading back" of the text at a later time by its composer or dictator (who was not necessarily its scribe).

Rupert Pickens has pointed to Jaufre Rudel's double standard concerning the re-creation of his verse; not everyone has a right to change it, only those who are capable of refining it.[32] However, Jaufre's need for such a warning in the final strophe of "No sap cantar qui so non di" reveals the tendency to unrefined or debasing "misinterpretation." In some versions of this lyric, such as C, Jaufre cautions the person who takes up or learns his song after him (his singer-messenger, but also anyone else who learns the song on the way) from changing anything in it:

> Bos es lo vers s'ieu no·y falhi,
> Ni tot so que·y es, ben esta;
> E selh que de mi l'apenra,
> Guart si que res no mi cambi,
> Que si l'auzon en Caerci
> Lo vescoms ni·l coms en Tolza.
> (no. 6, p. 224)

> The verse is good if I made no mistakes in it, / and everything [or, every sound] in it is well placed; / and the one who will take it up [from the infinitive *apendre*] after me, / may he guard against changing anything on me, / until they hear it in Quercy, / the viscount and the count in the Toulousain.

However, once Jaufre's unchanged lyric has reached its destination, he welcomes its refinement:

> Bos es lo sos, e faran hi
> Quas que don mos chans gensara.

> The sound is good, and they will do there / whatever will make my song more genteel.

In other versions of this lyric, such as R, the composer's injunctions against changing the lyric before it reaches its destination are even more specific; Jaufre does not want the bearer of the lyric to "make mistakes or break it up": "Gart se no·i falha ni·l pessi." When it reaches Bertran and the count in the Toulousain, they will "make some words that a man will then sing": "Bons er lo vers e faran y / Calsque motz que hom chantara" (p. 236). Jaufre seems to be cautioning an oral performer against introducing his own—presumably more vulgar—interpretations before the performer has delivered the lyric with the meaning Jaufre intended. Possibly Jaufre is sending an oral composition to the court of greater lords for its initial inscription (and grammatical analysis sorting out the words). However, it is also possible that Jaufre's oral performer carried with him and delivered a written text or "breu de pargamina" for which his performance was supposed to serve as authoritative *praelectio* enabling the audience of noble readers to sort out the words of the irregularly written text—to "make" the words Jaufre intended, and then to "improve" them, recreating and reinscribing Jaufre's lyric.

The writing down of their vernacular *vers* allowed the early troubadours to imitate, on their own texts and those of their contemporaries, the audiovisual play of schoolish Latin textual exegesis, which involved not only the oral performance and amplifying interpretation of the abbreviated written text in order to discover more meanings in it, but also written imitations of model texts, using the model's words or ideas in new contexts. For example, the mid-twelfth-century troubadour Bernart Marti composed lyrics that are pastiches of earlier troubadours' phrases, especially those of Guillaume IX and Marcabru. Bernart's "Farai un vers ab son novelh" gives the modern reader a strong impression of déjà vu (or "déjà écouté") due to Bernart's combinations of the two earlier poets' words, which carry with them conflicting associations from previous contexts.[33] Bernart's line "No·m puesc mudar que no·m querelh" ("I can't stop myself from complaining") begins like the second line of Guillaume IX's "Companho, tant ai agutz d'avols conres / *qu'ieu non puesc mudar no·n* chan e que no·m pes" ("Companions, I have had such stingy entertainment / *that I can't stop myself from* singing and being concerned about it"). However, Bernart's line ends with a word and a rhyme sound ("quer*elh*") characteristic of Marcabru. "El" and "eilla" rhymes alternate in the final strophes of Marcabru's "Lo vers comenssa" (no. 32, p. 156) on the subject of the ascetic poet's status as persona non grata in the courts of great lords. By framing Guillaume's words with Marcabru's rhymes and a version of his outcast persona, Bernart contrasts the foolish license of the privileged rich troubadour with the hardship of the suffering poor one. In another strophe of the same lyric, Bernart echoes the first lines of Guillaume's

"Farai un vers, pos mi sonelh / e·m vauc e m'estauc al solelh," but with a difference:

> Si duerm trop, non er qui·m revelh,
> Ans si penran tug a gabar;
> E si stau tot jorn al solelh,
> Pauc trobarai, m'an covidar:
> Ja negus hom d'amic no vuelh,
> Si non a poder de donar!
> (no. 6, p. 21)

If I sleep too long, there will be no one to wake me, / but instead everyone will mock me; / and if I stand all day in the sun, / I will find very few to welcome me: / for no man wants a friend / unless he has the power to give!

Others of Bernart Marti's—and many later troubadours'—lyrics seem to be compilations of *sentences* or memorable phrases from Marcabru of the sort that the later medieval compilers and students of the Provençal songbooks marked in the margins with *nota* signs. Still other lyrics seem to practice the amplification or development of particular themes from Marcabru's verse. Some of the more precious rhyme schemes might also serve as playfully challenging exercises in grammatical endings. These are only a few of the schoolish composition practices evident in much troubadour verse. In effect, the transmission of troubadour lyrics in writing, instead of authenticating and stabilizing them as we might imagine, had the opposite effect of freeing interpreters to appropriate and make what they wanted of other men's signs; the ambiguous abbreviation of early vernacular writing freed interpreters to discover in the lyric whatever sort of love they desired, to recreate the text in their own images, making their own new texts, which they might render orally, write, or have written by a scribe.

Although modern editors have generally assumed that opacities in thirteenth- and fourteenth-century Provençal lyric texts of the *chansonniers* are degenerate versions of the clear and straightforward "authentic" text, these ambiguous clumps of letters may represent the multiple senses and the playful metamorphosis of meaning of the deliberately ambiguous troubadour text. The aesthetic of early Provençal lyric is one of complexity and richness of sound and sense, not of simplicity and clarity. Through irregularities of spelling, word division, and syntax—remarkable in contrast to an otherwise fairly grammatical inscription—a thirteenth- or fourteenth-century scribe could suggest his own or a tradition of double understanding of a passage and challenge the reader to interpretation. On the other hand, a scribe's "garbling" of a phrase might also result from a significant incomprehension, that is, from a conflict in meanings in the sequence of letters and sounds that the scribe is unable to resolve, so that he gives only a basic phonetic transcription of the sounds without a more sophisticated grammatical analysis. Although by no means authentic in the sense of representing the stream of sounds produced by the original composer, these phonetic transcriptions may resemble twelfth-century written texts of troubadour lyrics more closely than the grammatically analyzed and clarified versions we know. When we emend these thirteenth- and fourteenth-century manuscript versions to correct the spellings and word forms, to clarify syntax by adding punctuation, and to recombine letters and syllables into words according to later grammatical rules, we may be destroying the signs of wordplay.

Variations among the scribes of the thirteenth- and fourteenth-century songbooks in the spelling and grammatical analysis of a line, even though each scribe apparently favors one interpretation over others, may also, when we compare the variants, signal the potential ambiguity or instability of meaning—the potential for wordplay and richly equivocal understanding—of the audiovisual text, that is, of the sequence of sounds recreated from an earlier abbreviating inscription of a sequence of sounds. The scribes of the late medieval songbooks almost certainly worked from written, albeit still audiovisual, texts. The best way to demonstrate how their different determinations may indicate a potential instability or indeterminacy of meaning in the line is with an example, once again a single line chosen virtually at random from one of Bernart de Ventadorn's lyrics, "Lo tems vai e ven e vire":

> Ja no·m partrai a ma vida,
> tan com sia sals ni sas,
> que pois l'arma n'es issida,
> balaya lonc tems lo gras;
> e si tot no s'es cochada,
> ja per me no·n er blasmada,
> *sol d'eus adenan s'emen.*
> (no. 30, p. 182)

I quote Stephen Nichols' English translation of the strophe, which closely resembles Appel's German one:

> Indeed I will not part with my life / so long as I am safe and sound, / just as after the kernel is gone, / the straw flutters a long time. / And although

she has shown no haste, / she will certainly not be blamed by me, / *if only she improves by herself from now on.*[34]

The last line of this strophe does not seem to have given Appel problems in putting together his composite version, but when I look at his list of the variants from the other seven medieval songbooks containing this lyric, I cannot see that his selection of the G manuscript's line and his grammatical analysis of it are either obviously correct or incorrect. Appel's list of variants has the virtue of being unpunctuated and of representing approximately the way each manuscript version divides the letters of the line into groups:

A	Sol deus adenan emen
C	Sol mi do adenant semen
D	Sol deus adenan za cemen
G	Sol d˜s adenan semen
I, K	Sol dieus adenan camen
Q	Sol deus adenan se ment
R	Sol m do al denant si ment.

Of the four manuscripts in the Bibliothèque Nationale in Paris, Appel got the spelling and word division right in two cases (for the C and R manuscripts) and wrong in two: in both the I and K manuscripts, *adenancamen* is one clump of letters, spelled with a "c*a*men" in I and a "c*e*men" in K. The A manuscript (Rome) reads exactly the same as K; there is no division of the clump. Appel's breaks in the D manuscript (Modena) may be arbitrary as well, for the manuscript reads "adena˜za," with the second "n" abbreviated and "cemen" appearing on the next line because there is no more space above.[35] In the G manuscript's version, Appel expands the final abbreviation. Here, then, is a more accurate list of variants that reproduces the scribes' own divisions:

A	Sol deus adenancemen
C	Sol mi do adenant semen
D	Sol deus adena˜za cemen
G	Sol d˜s adenan seme˜
I	Sol dieus adenancamen
K	Sol dieus adenancemen

Q Sol deus adenan se ment
R Sol m do al denant si ment.

In spite of the differences of spelling and word division in different versions of this line, when one reproduces the sounds represented by the letters it appears that, with the exception of the CR manuscripts' reading of "mi do" instead of "deus," these inscriptions might represent nearly the same oral performance, the same sequence of sounds. The variations are of the sort that paleographers would call insignificant, the products of scribal "error"; and, yet, they suggest major differences in the scribes' understandings of the line. All variations are, as Pickens puts it, *poetically* significant. Comparison of the scribal variants shows the degree to which each inscription is an interpretation.

The last sequence of syllables in the line under consideration provoked the greatest variety of divisions. If we accept these divisions as attempts to separate words, or words plus proclitics (rather than merely transcriptions of phonetic phrasing), the different scribes seem to understand the same syllables in very different ways: *semen* as a noun would mean "seed," but *s'emen*, from the verb *esmendar*, would mean "amend or give recompense of one's own accord." *Men* or *ment*, on the other hand, would mean "lie" or, preceded by a reflexive, "break one's word." The letters *s* and *c* could both be used to represent the reflexive pronoun. As a noun, *men* could mean "mind" or "thoughts." Whereas some scribes represent the last two syllables separately on the page, others put them together, and the AIK scribes all include the last two syllables of the line in a five-syllable clump, spelled *adenancamen* or *adenancemen*. I cannot see how to make sense of this five-syllable group as one word. Grammatical analysis seems to call for further division, either in ways other scribes set forth, or else by separating *a* as a form of the verb "to have" (*aver*) from *denancamen*, which I take to mean the foresight that comes from omniscience, thus giving "only God [*deus* or *dieus*] reads minds." The D scribe's version of the line, "adenanza cemen," might mean "only God has foreknowledge of seed." Although the C scribe transcribes virtually the same sequence of sounds, he apparently interprets them differently, writing "sol mi do adenant semen" as if he understood "if only eventually it gives me seed"; the R scribe writes "sol m do al denant si ment" as if he understands "if only she gives to me eventually if she breaks her word." The G scribe, on the other hand, writes "sol deus adenan semen," as if he understands "if only of itself eventually it gives recompense."

Although each scribe has, through word division and spelling, apparently made certain interpretive choices, the scribe's interpretation was not, I have earlier argued, binding on the medieval reader, nor does it necessarily mean that the medieval scribe intended to censor all other possible meanings of a particular sequence of sounds. On the contrary, the meaning of the audiovisual text, which still had to be pronounced and heard to be understood, arose from surrounding contexts, one of the most important of which was the reader's own experience, his interpretive tendencies. Let me posit for a moment an agriculturally oriented medieval interpreter (one way of livening up a technical discussion of manuscript variants), a reader who is trying to make sense of the C version of Bernart de Ventadorn's lyric. This interpreter's problem would be, as he reproduced the sequence of sounds, not only how to combine or divide this sequence of sounds into words and how to analyze their syntactical relationships, but also how to know which of several possible meanings to attach to the same sound. For example, the C scribe's line begins with a clearly separated "sol" (as do all the other manuscript versions); however, the word *sol* in Provençal can mean not only "provided that" or "if only," as I have translated it above, but also, depending on its context(s), "earth," "penny," "sun," "alone," "only," "threshold," and "I am accustomed to." In modern French, the sounds and spellings representing these different meanings have gradually been differentiated: *sol*, *sou*, *soleil*, *seul*, *seuil*, and *souloir*. Old Provençal, as other scholars have remarked, was extremely rich in homonyms.[36] In the contexts of Bernart's extended metaphor on the ripening of grain and its eventual separation from the sheaf (a trope that deliberately calls into play Bernart's place name, for *ventador* means "winnower"), an agriculturally oriented reader's first impulse might be to take the letters "sol" as "soil" or even as "sun": "the soil [or, the sun] gives me, eventually, seed" ("sol mi do adenant semen"). But the reader might also understand "sol" as "provided that" (it gives me, eventually, seed).

Let me posit, for the sake of argument, one possible interpretation by this reader of the C scribe's text:[37]

> I will never part from my life [or, leave during my life], / as long as I am healthy and secure, / for after the spike has come out, / the grain stays a long time in the sheaf, / and if it's in no hurry, / it won't be blamed by me, / if only eventually it gives me seed [mature grain].[38]

In another strophe Bernart has threatened to leave his lady soon if she does not stop being so hard on him. Here he reverses himself, vowing never to leave her, whom he calls by the *senhal* or endearing name of "ma Vida" (my Life). What gives him patience and hope of an eventual reward is his thought that his lady is like a grain ripening within the husk. In the strophe following this one, his praise of the lady seems to continue this metaphor; he describes her body almost as if it were a plump grain ready for the winnowing: "cors be fait, delgatz e plas, / a frecha carn colorida" ("well-formed body, delicate and smooth, / with fresh, rosy flesh").

On top of the metaphor of ripening grain, one might posit at least two other interpretations: one that allegorizes about pregnancy and the other about sexual intercourse:

> I will never part from my life, / as long as I am healthy and secure, / for after the "spike" has come out, / the "grain" stays a long time in the "sheaf," / and if it's in no hurry, / it won't be blamed by me, / if only eventually it gives me "seed."

I leave the elaboration of possibilities of these procreative and erotic interpretations to the imaginations of contemporary readers. My point is that the final line and the whole strophe will support many different interpretations, from the more idealizing readings of Appel, Lazar,[39] and Nichols, who imagine a loyal, long-suffering lover-speaker, to the deliberately eroticizing reading I have just suggested, which might be spoken by a male lover boasting of his sexual prowess—by a Bernart *vantador* ("braggart"). Surrounding scriptural contexts, for all the reasons I have mentioned, do not provide *the* key to unlock the meaning of the text. That is because the text is not *closed*, but almost completely *open* to interpretation, and was even more so in the twelfth century than today.

No one scribe's graphic representations, from the thirteenth- and fourteenth-century songbooks, are correct. Neither idealizing nor debasing interpretations—nor any range of interpretations in between—are right. Yet neither are they wrong. Various interpretations coexist, contradicting and complementing one another, just as the series of separate strophes that make up the *canso* modify one another in a dynamic play of variations and contradictions that enrich the meanings of the song. The aesthetic of early troubadour lyrics is not a "feudal" one, hierarchized, subordinated, centered, stabilized, pacified, closed. It is just the opposite: the order of the *canso* is a competitive, dynamic, centerless, open order based on paratactic opposition and continually shifting configurations, an order that is always becoming. The centerless constellation of the *canso* is held together by its very indeterminacies, by the tension of deliberate oppositions and contradictions, most obviously between strophes, which are the troubadour lyric's chief organizational unit, but sometimes even between opening and closing segments of the same strophe, and even between different meanings of the same short phrases or sequences of sounds.[40]

Try as we will, it is nevertheless difficult, in accordance with *our* notions of poetic unity, to impose a consistent persona or time or place or mood or message on any *canso*, for the nature of the *canso* is to resist authority. Even more specifically, as I have argued in my opening chapter, a major "political" motivation for the early troubadours' poetic inventions and elaborations—which, from the very beginning, they had inscribed, only to recreate their texts competitively and idiosyncratically—was to challenge the authority of writing to represent the intentions of absent people, to demonstrate the unreliability of the "technology of writing." Here is a high hurdle for the modern reader.

Even if we do overcome our tendency to consider the written word as an authoritative expression of authorial intention, even if we do try to play troubadour word games with pre-interpreted modern editions of the lyrics, we are confronted with other discouragements to playful reading. Inevitably, our interpretations will involve breaking grammatical rules of the Old Provençal language as these are taught in modern universities, such as the "rule" I have broken at the beginning of this chapter, that the feminine adjectival form of *nebla* would *have* to be *neblona*, as one of my readers protested. But why not *neblosa* or a number of other forms starting from other variant forms and spellings of the noun? Should we completely rule out occasional elisions and even greater poetic license? Our participation in troubadour wordplay will also, however, entail breaking medieval rules as outlined in thirteenth-century manuals such as the *Razos de trobar* of Raimon Vidal, the *Regles de trobar* of Jofre de Foixa, the *Donatz Proensals* ("Provençal Donatus") of Uc Faiditz, and the fourteenth-century *Leys d'amors*. The purpose of these medieval grammars was to institute the rules and to police and prevent infractions, especially those encouraged by the troubadours' linguistic facetiousness. In the last line of his manual, for example, Uc Faiditz names himself as author and states that his purpose has been to teach the vernacular and to "distinguish between true and false in vernacular verse [or speech]": "Ugo Faiditus nominor qui librum composui . . . as dandum doctrinam vulgaris provincialis et ad dissernendum verum a falso in dictu vulgare."[41] Indeed, if we learn our Provençal the "right" way, following all the rules, we will not be disposed to play at all.

Another obstacle is that modern Provençal dictionaries, to an even greater extent than the brief medieval ones, censure or ignore wordplay and vulgar, erotic, or scatological expressions. The purpose of medieval Provençal dictionaries, such as the short dictionary of Provençal rhyme words with Latin definitions in Uc Faiditz's *Donatz Proensals*, was to fix the right meanings and forms of words. Uc does not exclude straightforwardly sexual terms such as *cons* and *colhz* ("vulva" and "testiculus," p. 225) and *colha* ("pellis testiculorum," p. 250). These appear as well in modern dictionaries of Old Provençal that have culled words from Uc. However, Uc generally provides only one or two definitions of each Provençal word, because his purpose is to confine the evocative power of vernacular words within limits, to restrict them to the "clarity" of Latin.[42] The anonymous author of a much longer, probably fifteenth-century, Provençal *Vocabulaire*,[43] on the other hand, seems to delight in multiplying the synonyms for each Provençal word, in every context and language he knows, mostly in Latin, but also in Greek and other Romance dialects, and in specialized or professional usages. For the Provençal word *companha* (company) he lists twenty-five cognates, including *caterva* (in Gallic dialect) and *conventa* (among monks). Such amplification goes far beyond definition into facetious play.

Modern dictionaries tend to refine language by excluding sinfully vulgar metaphoric expressions; these have been collected apart in special dictionaries such as Louis de Landes's highly inadequate *Glossaire érotique*.[44] For Provençal, there is no modern dictionary of this kind explaining erotic metaphors and images, and yet the fifteenth-century *Vocabulaire* lists many vulgar terms. For example, the *Vocabulaire* gives twelve synonyms, including the metaphoric *molo* (to grind) and *salio* (to leap) for the word *fotre* (fuck), which is illustrated with the kind of timeless sketch one finds today ornamenting washrooms and the cubicles of research libraries. Other vulgar terms and sexually metaphoric objects also receive rapid pen-and-ink illustrations: *cogul* (cuckold), *cagar* (to shit), *gola* (throat), *nas* (nose), *putan* (prostitute), *siblet* (bagpipe), *viach* (cock). Low words such as *viach* do not even appear in the modern dictionaries of Emil Levy and François Raynouard, although they supposedly draw upon the fifteenth-century *Vocabulaire*. This deserves a new edition (the last dates from 1891),[45] and more thorough analysis, because it contains some interesting definitions. For example, the first of nine synonyms for the word *bordel* is the Latin *theatrum*, probably following Isidore. While Raynouard lists *bordel*, he gives only the most common sense, a house of prostitution; Levy, whose dictionary is just what it calls itself, a supplement to Raynouard's, does not list the word at all. The deficiencies of modern dictionaries—often deliberate—make it impossible for us in many instances to turn to them for authoritative corroboration of playful interpretations of troubadour verse.

In the *Vocabulaire*, the word spelled *joy* means "yoke," especially with reference to cattle. Levy lists this meaning under the spelling *jo* and gives a number of helpful examples, among them the spellings for the same word of *joi*, *jou*, *jouc*, and *joui*. Is it possible that different regional dialects might cause confusion between the two words meaning "joy" and "yoke"—that a more northern spelling, *joi* or *joy*, read aloud in the south, could produce a vulgar, and implicitly sexual, pun? Would a Gascon reading a Limousin phonetic spelling—or a Limousin mimicking a Gascon pronunciation—bring out punning senses? Joy of love? Yoke of love? Game (*joc*) of love?[46] Which it is in any particular situation may well depend on the interpreter/performer's accent. This suggests that we should pay more attention to dialects—and dialect dictionaries—than we have previously done in interpreting troubadour texts.

Judging especially from the rhyme words, Max Pfister calls Guillaume IX's language a "hybrid . . . characterized by phonetic, morphological, and lexical doublets."[47] One member of the doublet (or the pun) may be a Poitevin form, while the other is Old French. Poitiers, the capital of Guillaume's domain, was near the linguistic border between *oc* and *oil*, which Guillaume's lands spanned. Roger Dragonetti has discussed the medieval expression *parler poictevin*, which meant "to speak without saying anything" or "to speak ambiguously."[48] To the speaker of a more southern—or northern—dialect, Poitevin speech may have sounded like *barbarolexis* or a stream of sounds mixing the familiar and the strange to equivocal effect, evoking many senses difficult to resolve into one. Guillaume IX seems to have deliberately played on such dialectal ambiguities. In the sole surviving N manuscript versions of Guillaume's "Compaigno, non puosc mudar qu'eo no m'effrei," which will be discussed later at greater length, the last line is repeated in nearly the same form to bring out a double, possibly triple, pun in the last two syllables, "que·s laisses morir dessei" ("than to let oneself die *dessei*"). As one word, pronounced and spelled in Poitevin fashion, *desse* would mean "immediately"; as two words, with the final vowel pronounced as a diphthong as in Old French, *de sei* would mean "of thirst"; or possibly, without the diphthong, the *se* could be understood playfully as a reflexive pronoun, giving the sense "all by oneself." In this context, the "foreign" French diphthong produces an erotic innuendo, "thirst" for *vit*. Old French *vit* (penis) sounds the same as the *vi* (meaning "wine") of the preceding line: "s'om li vedava vi fort per malavei" ("if one were forbidden strong *vi* due to its ill effects").

The problem with trying to imagine such a dialectic of dialectal play is that we do not have the original *breu* of the early troubadours. We have only much revised thirteenth- and fourteenth-century compilations whose provenance is usually not very precisely known. When I use the name of a particular troubadour in discussing the wordplay in a lyric, I am very probably giving credit to the original composer for subtleties introduced by later interpreters. In many cases, as well, the attribution to a composer may be wrong. Different songbooks attribute the same lyric to different troubadours, and sometimes the same songbook attributes the same lyric to different troubadours. The C songbook's double attributions have often been remarked, usually as a sign of its unreliability.[49] Near the end of the first index (an alphabetized list of opening lines), there is a series of triple attributions that seems to have gone unnoticed. Beginning with Aymar de Roca Ficha's "Tan doussamen me ven al cor ferir," the rubricator gives two other attributions for the lyric in the margin: "Giraut de Calenso" and "Arnaut de Maruelh." He links these two names in red ink to the title "Tan doussamen." In this and the ten following cases, alternate attributions are not corrections, but acknowledgments of other interpretive traditions with respect to particular lyrics. This multiplicity of interpretations did not bother the C scribe or compiler as much as it does modern scholars; he seems to have been more interested in the formal aspects of the verse than in presenting it as biography. There are no *vidas* in the C songbook.

I have based and will continue whenever possible to base my interpretations of troubadour lyrics on the fourteenth-century editions of the scribe of the C songbook (Paris, B.N. fr. 856). This is not because the C songbook's inscriptions are any more "authentic" than those of any other songbook—for they are all composite texts drawn from earlier medieval written and perhaps also oral sources—but, rather, because it is preferable, for reasons I have already given at length, to quote from a medieval composite edition than from a modern editor's composite, more rigidly pre-interpreted text. The C songbook is a very large fourteenth-century collection written in one hand and was copied, according to Jeanroy, in the area northeast of Toulouse (between Cahors, Rodez, and Béziers), while Monfrin locates its origin more southerly, in the Narbonne area.[50] I believe that the fourteenth-century C songbook, Jeanroy's favorite, better preserves the playful tradition of interpretation of troubadour verse than do songbooks copied in the mid-thirteenth century in Italy, but written with more seriously historicizing—rather than playful—intentions. More detailed comparisons of the songbooks I must save for a later chapter.

3

Sentenssa Follatina

Facetus est, qui facit verbis quod vult.
He is facetious who makes what he wants out of words.
—Donatus, commentary on
Terence's *Eununchus*

The early troubadours' word games draw upon both schoolish Latin and jongleuresque vernacular traditions of playful interpretation. Evidence of schoolish, goliardic play survives from as early as the seventh century in the *Epitomies* of one Virgil, known today as Virgil of Toulouse. This specific identification appears in a tenth-century citation by Abbo of Fleury; Virgil himself, in his *Epistles*, claims to write in Gaulish: "in quibusdam Gallorum nostrorum scriptis invenimus canno."[1] In another passage, he is slightly more specific, claiming to speak a dialect of Bigorre, that is, of Gascony: "bigerro sermone clefabo." Michael Herren has remarked a possible play here on *bi-gerus*, Latin meaning "twofold" or "double," that is, ambiguous.[2] Such play would not invalidate the Gascon identification but would suggest the equivocal nature of Virgil's Gascon speech. A similar etymological pun is probably intended in the Gaulish identification, because the syllable *gal* in words such as the later vernacular *galiar* or *galier* (Old Provençal or Old French) means "trick" or "mock."[3] In any case, the name Virgil is almost surely a pseudonym, as is the name of Virgil's teacher, Aeneas (note the parodic role reversal), and all the other grammarians Virgil names, such as Donatus and Virgil of Troy (the latter the author of a work on the "Twelve Latinities"), Primogenus of Cappadocia, Estrius the Spaniard, Gregory of Egypt (author of three thousand books on Greek history), Balapides of Nicomedia, and the three Vulcans, one of Arabia, one of India, one of Africa.[4] Either these names are sheer comic inventions, or they are the playful pseudonyms of participants in a sort of burlesque literary academy (one thinks of Charlemagne's) formed for the amusement of Latin scholars, perhaps a youth group licensed to contest the authority of the masters on special festive occasions.[5] Later, in the fifth chapter of his *Epitomies*, Virgil warns that proper names should never be taken at face value but always be given a much more subtle interpretation (p. 42): "propria ergo nomina non secundum simplicem sonum sonanda sunt, sed secundum subtiliorem quandam interpretationem."

Virgil's *Epitomies* is a hilarious burlesque of Latin grammar instruction, with Isidore of Seville's teaching methods and assumptions as its chief target. In his *Etymologies* and his briefer *Differences*, Isidore's purpose is to purify corrupt Latin word usage, to return words to their proper paths, their "original" meanings. His method of untangling the knots of language and distinguishing words confounded in poetic and common Latin usage is to uncover their different roots or origins.[6] To Isidore, both poetic and barbarous linguistic license is decadent and witnesses to the moral corruption of the speaker or writer. His *Etymologies* begins with the word *disciplina*: "*Disciplina* a *discendo* nomen accepit; unde et *scientia* dici potest. Nam *scire* dictum a *discere*, quia nemo nostrum scit, nisi qui discit. Aliter dicta disciplina, quia discitur plena" ("*Discipline* takes its name from *learning*; from whence it may be called *knowledge*. In fact, *to know* can be said to come from *to learn*, because no one knows ours unless he learns it. In other words, a discipline is said to be full of learning"). Virgil's burlesque grammar, on the other hand, begins with an etymological definition of the word *sapientia* that emphasizes sensual delectation over intellectual knowing:

> *Sapientia* autem ex *sapore* sic nominatur, quia sicut in corporis fit gustu, ita et in animae motu quidam sapor est, qui artium dulcedinem gustet, qui verborum sententiarumque vim discernat amara quaeque refutans, suavia vero consectans.
>
> (p. 2)

> The name of *knowledge* comes from *taste*: analogously to what occurs in the physical sensation of taste, there is, in the function of the soul, a taste that appreciates the suavity of the arts, which experiences the force of words and phrases; it rejects the bitter, but adheres to the sweet.

This sensual emphasis turns medieval pedagogy on end. In his chapter on "Metrical Composition," Virgil uses sensational, carnivorous metaphors to describe the "mordant" art of interpretation, which he calls "dialectic"; according to Virgil, dialectic "draws out into broad daylight and extracts, in a way, the entrails of each thought, the marrow of each sense, the veins of each word." In conclusion, he remarks that some have called dialectic "sophistic," meaning "subtle," or else "savory" because of its good taste (pp. 30, 34). The purpose of Isidorian exegetical dissection is just the reverse: to discover the ruling idea, the truth of words, not their taste. Furthermore, Virgil carries Isidore's division of words and speculation on their roots to ridiculous lengths, ending up, in some cases, "back in the womb." Thus, Virgil's explication of *terra*:

> The earth is called *terra* because men strike it with their feet [*teritur*]; but it means otherwise, if separated, because in philosophical Latin *ra* is interpreted as "bearer" or "genitor," from whence also cargo ships are called *rates*; thus, *terra* is thrice *ra* [*ter-ra*], first, because we are born from it, whence man is called *homo*, from humus; second, because we are nourished and restored by its fruits; third, because, once dissolved by death, we retire in it as in the mother's womb.
>
> (p. 148)

To the modern reader, Isidore's etymological definitions often seem ridiculous, but Virgil's are even more so; they are deliberately foolish Latin explications, "sentenssa follatina."

Instead of one correct Latin language, as Isidore would have it, Virgil describes no fewer than twelve Latins, all equally correct, although only one is written. He explains that the very name *Latin* comes from and reveals the great richness of choice or "latitude" its lexicon and grammar give the speaker or translator (p. 4). Virgil illustrates the twelve kinds of spoken Latin with twelve different words for *fire*, all but the first invented out of meaningful roots, mostly Greek, that suggest various characteristics of fire. Surely these imaginative neologisms are a witty reversal of Isidore's etymological practice and authoritarian purpose. In the first kind of Latin, fire is called *ignis*, because of its nature of burning everything; in the second, *quoquihabin*, for its cooking power; in the third, *ardon*, because it blazes; in the fourth, *calax*, because of its heat; in the fifth, *spiridon*, because of its subtlety; in the sixth, *rusin*, because of its red color; in the seventh, *fragon*, because of the crackling of the flame; in the eighth, *fumaton*, because of its smoke; in the ninth, *ustrax*, because it consumes; in the tenth, *vitius*, because with its vigor it brings life back to half-dead members; in the eleventh, *siluleus*, because it sparks out of flint; in the twelfth, *aeneon*, because of the god Aeneas, who lives in it (p. 6). Later, in his "Catalogue of Grammarians" (pp. 164–66), Virgil defines the "twelve Latinities" in a different way, quoting the work of "Virgil of Troy": the first kind of Latin is called *usitata* because of its current use in speaking and writing; the second, *assena*, the abbreviated language of notaries; the third, *semedia*, archaic, half out of use; fourth, *numeria*, with special names for numbers; fifth, *metrofia*, the language of intellect; sixth, *lumbrosa*, the language of amplification; seventh, *sincolla*, of brevity; eighth, *belsavia*, of inversion; ninth, *presina*, of reduced lexicon; tenth, *militana*, of increased lexicon; eleventh, *spela*, vulgar; twelfth, *polema*, highbrow.

In order to mock both the method and the idealistic assumptions behind such dissection, Virgil exaggerates Isidore's exegetical method of dividing, naming, and defining. "On Cutting Up Words" ("De scinderatione fonorum," pp. 128–44) is Virgil's burlesque lesson on the art of cutting up, reversing, scrambling, or reweaving the original order of whole lines, words or syllables, or letters on the page. The "Art" begins with a rationale that sounds like the traditional Christian apology for the use of enigmatic language, especially God's use of it in the Bible. Virgil recounts that his master, Aeneas, the first to develop the practice of cutting up words, explained its uses to the young Virgil thus:

> My son, there are three reasons for cutting up words: the first is to test the subtlety of our students when they have to search out and discover what is being obscurely presented; the second is to give the language a certain pomp and eloquence; the third is in order not to make it too easy for petty men or the first stupid person who comes along to understand our secret doctrines, in other words, to prevent the pigs from trampling on precious pearls, as the old proverb says.

"De scinderatione fonorum," then, is an art of enigmatic composition—or of deciphering such compositions. Into the mouth of his master, Virgil puts a prediction that his own burlesque *Epitomies* best fulfills. Aeneas warns that, in the hands of the ignorant, the art of cutting up words will be turned against the masters: "In effect, if they study according to these principles, not only will they have no more reverence for their masters, not only will they cease to show them any respect or deference, but, worse still, like real pigs, they will tear to pieces those who have equipped [ornamented] them." Rather than abbreviating and abstracting the core of previous grammar texts, Virgil's *Epitomies* fragments and explodes grammar theory; it dissects and rearranges, but puts nothing back together again. Instead of one art of speaking correctly, one law, Virgil gives us our choice of a dozen. This is variation with a vengeance. Nothing could be more facetiously disrespectful of the idealistic principles of pedagogy—except, perhaps, the troubadours' later interpretive *disciplina*[7] or the open-ended collection of late seventh-century texts known as the *Hisperica Famina* (*Western Speech*), in its highly wrought, "amplified" style and with its macaronic word choice that mixes barbarous with erudite Latin.

The first word of the *Hisperica Famina* is *ampla* (copious, sonorous, full). According to Michael Herren, the texts' most recent editor, the chief characteristic of Hisperic Latin is its fanciful, extraordinary lexicon, which he catalogues as a mixture of "specialized or obscure words in place of general or well-known words, some of which result from metaphor; ordinary words used in exceptional senses; words used in their etymological sense; words formed on the misunderstanding of a gloss; words resulting from a confusion of forms [ignoring the rules of Latin word formation]; and metonymy."[8] This Hisperic Latin vocabulary, like the early troubadours', is meant to challenge interpretation. The result of such deliberate Hisperic deforming and reshaping of the classical Latin lexicon is a text that puts masters of Latin grammar on about the same footing as novices. The reader who knows his barbarisms, his slang and vulgar expressions, and who has a good imagination has as strong an advantage as one who knows his Greek and Latin roots. An authoritative pinning down of this metamorphic text is virtually impossible. Different readers will interpret—have interpreted—its enigmatic language differently. Although he does not use the term *mouvance*, that is what Herren is describing when he writes that "the manuscripts that contain the strange compositions known as *Hisperica Famina* are not exemplars of a single, unified work, but rather are representatives of four separate recensions of versions of 'faminations,' each manuscript being the *codex unicus* for the version that it represents" (pp. 7–8).

The fragmentary structure of the *Hisperica Famina* troubles classicists almost as much as their bizarre vocabulary. Comparing the four surviving manuscript versions of the texts, Herren remarks, "The most striking—and disconcerting—aspect of all the versions of the *Famina* is the absence of any cohesiveness among the parts" (p. 11). The *Hisperica Famina* articulates itself (like later troubadour verse) in a cumulative fashion by means of paratactic structures. Not only does nearly every line of verse of the *Famina* encapsulate a thought, but the separate sections of verse seem to be unconnected: first there is the Hisperic challenge to classical Latin scholars; then a list of the faults of speech; then a "rule of the day"; then a series of riddling descriptions of natural objects. There is no authorial voice holding these fragments together in a narrative fiction, no subject, and the style is such a promiscuous mixture of erudition and vulgarity as to seem completely out of control. In short, the *Hisperica Famina* is deliberately insubordinate. The controlling idea is outside the text, and this idea is to burlesque and overthrow the rigidities of Latin pedagogy and of the classical aesthetic. With the "scepter of rude Hisperic speech," which allows the speaker to reshape words at will, the author(s) break the "Ausonian chain" of classical Latin (vv. 54–60). With outlandish tropes, deliberate barbarisms, and every other "vice" of speech, the Hisperic author(s) mock the strictures of "urbanity."

A contestatory intention is evident, as well, in the *Hisperica Famina*'s parodic subversion of the pedagogical composition practice of imitating authoritative, model texts. Herren notes that Virgil's *Aeneid* and *Georgics* are "a source of topoi that become, as it were, molds for Hisperic filling" (p. 24). This "filling" (*farce*) is often extremely earthy in nature. The writer(s) constantly subvert our idealistic expectations with exceedingly materialistic fulfillments. For example, the section entitled "Lex diei," "The Rule of the Day," which we might expect to contain the monastic rule of an early Irish scholar's day and which begins with extremely aureate diction ("The Titanian star inflames the ceiling of heaven"), turns out to deal mainly with brute necessity, with the satisfaction of the physical hunger of birds, beasts, fish, men—the "rule of the day" indeed. This is hardly Virgil's *Georgics*. The lines on birds, for example, begin with the pleasing melody and harmony of the "winged court" (vv. 146–48), but then the flock descends on a freshly manured field: "they pierce the clods of the fields / and swallow bits of worm with their beaks; / they peck through the smelly mixten, / and glut their hungry innards with succulent food." Such are the fruits of piercing the riddle of Hisperic Latin words:

> va(m)paneas aculeant glevas,
> vermia sorbellant picis frustra,
> oleda pungunt stercolinia,
> fameas esciferis replent vesiculas sucis.

The "truth" we discover in this enigmatic text is the most basic "rule" of hunger, of mastication, and of the devouring of one species by/after another: "Huge dolphins sweep the foamy deep, / they suck in salty particles through open jaws / and devour scaly fish" (vv. 175–77). The scholars' own supper ends the day:

> We munched on crusts of bread with toothy movements, / for which there abounded a delicious smearing of Irish oil. / We chomped down joints of meat with compressed teeth.
>
> (vv. 298–300)

How can this Hisperic text be anything but a burlesque of the idealistic presumptions of Christian exegesis, which inevitably found a spiritual truth beneath the opaque body of the word? Our efforts at interpreting the *Hisperica Famina* (as in interpreting some early troubadour verse) lead in exactly the opposite direction, to the discovery of physical compulsions. There is even a deliberate play in the title *Hisperica Famina* on the syllable *fam*, as in the Latin word for hunger, *fames*, out of which the fictitious Latin word *famina* was derived (Provençal *famina*, Old French and English *famine*). The Hisperic faminators are famished. A similar kind of provocative materialism is at times discernible beneath the troubadours' difficult coinages.

Virgil's *Epitomies* and the *Hisperica Famina* are early examples of a learned, goliardic tradition of linguistic play that mocks the rules of grammar instruction and the rites of the Christian religion. Such play was institutionalized on certain topsy-turvy feast days, when the lowest members of the ecclesiastical hierarchy, such as choir boys and students, "ruled" in foolish fashion, performing burlesque masses, liturgical songs, and plays.[9] We have come to identify the goliards, rather too exclusively, as "wandering scholars," those, for example, whom the Council of Treves in 1227 forbade to sing light, and doubtless burlesque, verses to the melodies of the sacred songs of the *Sanctus* and *Agnus Dei*.[10] In medieval usage, anyone with some Latin education who mocked the rules with facetious or barbarous Latin could be called a goliard, even if he did not "err" literally, but only figuratively. Hugh Primas (the "first" or the "subtle"), the "Arch"-poet, Walter Map, Walter of Chatillon: all were goliards, although they held offices. The "family of Golias" was huge and widespread, because it was spawned by the authoritarianism of the medieval religious hierarchy, from the grammar schools on up. The goliard deliberately pronounced or deformed classical or biblical words in rustic fashion (*barbarolexis*) or combined words and syllables in irregular ways (*solecism*) to produce punning senses, especially erotic, scatological, or otherwise vulgar and materialistic meanings (*cacemphaton*) that contrasted with and subverted the "correct," ideal reading of the text. In addition to deforming and travestying authoritative or sacred texts through relatively small changes in his interpretation or performance of these texts, the goliard also invented texts that were loaded with such puns and innuendos, "new" texts that were pastiches or parodies, varying in degree of fidelity to authoritative, "sacred," textual models.[11] This kind of goliardic play required an initiated audience, a relatively elite group of reader/interpreters who could recognize and appreciate various degrees and kinds of truancy from the correct forms of the learned languages (classical and biblical Latin) and who knew the standard biblical textual models well enough to appreciate parodies of them. Nevertheless, the mentality behind even this kind of goliard play seems "popular" because of the way it uses barbarism and materialism to overturn the ideal ordering of things, especially of the Latin language, which was the official, legal basis for other social orders.

The medieval Church allowed a certain amount of insubordinate goliardic levity at feasts and even in office, especially if the writer did not perform his works *in propria persona*. Nevertheless, the Church seems also to have lost to the entertainment circuit many of those it educated to read/sing. It regularly threatened to shave off their tonsures and defrock them (if they had already taken vows) and to verbally eject them from the clergy so that they would lose the clerical immunities and privileges that, generally speaking, were the right of any man who had learned to read his psalter. The Council of Cahors, Rodez, and Tulle, in 1287, for example, attacked the problem of clerics who misused their "clergy" to spend part of their time as professional comic entertainers: "We command that clerics not be jongleurs, goliards, or buffoons, declaring that if they exercise this disreputable art during the year they are divested of all ecclesiastical privileges and, even more serious in this world, if, albeit warned, they do not desist . . . , they are excluded from all rights of clergy."[12] Troubadours such as Peire Rogier, who left his canonry to become a jongleur, witness to the problem. Other troubadours managed to retain their ecclesiastical posts, perhaps by circulating their works in writing or by leaving the performance itself to others. The Provençal *vidas*, which combine medieval interpretations of the troubadours' verse with surviving traditions about them, explain that the Monk of Montaudon specialized in *sirventes* and *coblas* (occasional, polemical verse) while remaining in the monastery; Giraut de Bornelh, who taught *letras* in school in winter, spent his summers going around to courts with two singers (called *cantadors*, not jongleurs) to perform his works; Arnaut de Maroill, who could not support himself with his learning, "went out into the world," but, like Peire Cardenal, who had been a canon of Le Puy, Arnaut had a personal jongleur to accompany him and perform his songs.[13] The main difference between the goliard and the verbal jongleur seems to have been in the language of performance, consequently in the audience. The goliard composed, interpreted, but could also perform, texts in Latin; the jongleur performed, but could also compose and interpret (*trobar*), in the vernacular.

According to their Provençal *vidas*, many troubadours and jongleurs profited from early instruction in Latin letters (which included instruction in religious song) to learn to compose, that is, to write, vernacular verse. Arnaut Daniel, for example, "amparet ben letras e delectet se en trobar. Et abandonet las letras, et fetz se joglars" ("learned his letters well and took delight in composition, and abandoned letters to become a jongleur," no. 9, p. 59). The case of Uc de Saint Circ is even clearer. As the son of a poor knight, Uc was intended for the clergy. His parents "manderon lo a la scola a Monpeslier. E quant ill cuideront qu'el ampares letras, el amparet cansos e vers e sirventes e tensos e coblas, e·ls faich e·ls dich dels valens homes e de las valens domnas que eron al mon, ni eron estat; et ab aquel saber el s'ajoglari" ("and they sent him to school at Montpellier. And while they thought he was learning letters, he was learning *cansos* and *vers* and *sirventes* and *tensos* and *coblas*, and the deeds and words of the valiant men and women who lived or had lived in the world, and with this knowledge, he became a jongleur," no. 33, p. 239). Arnaut de Maroill, a cleric of low birth, turned to the entertainment circuit because he could not make a living as a cleric: "clergues de paubra generacion. E car no podia viure per las soas letras, el s'en anet per lo mon" (no. 7, p. 32). Another cleric-turned-jongleur was Uc Brunet, who was learned in letters and clever at composing, also in the vernacular: "e fo clerges et enparet ben letras, e de trobar fo fort suptils, e de sen natural; e fez se joglars" (no. 21, p. 199). Guiraut de Calanso, a jongleur from Gascony, likewise knew his letters well and composed cleverly: "Ben saup letras, e suptils fo de trobar" (no. 25, p. 217). Elias Cairel, the jeweler-turned-jongleur, was an excellent scribe: "ben escrivia motz e sons" (no. 35, p. 252). Peire d'Auvernhe was a learned and lettered man, "savis hom fo e ben letratz" (no. 39, p. 263), as were the troubadours educated as canons: Peire Cardenal "apres letras, e saup ben lezer e chantar" ("learned letters and knew how to read and sing well," no. 50, p. 335); both Daude de Pradas and Peire Rogier were learned in letters and in the vernacular ("savis de letras e de sen natural," no. 30, p. 233, and no. 40, p. 267). A late jongleur of Italian origin, Ferrari de Ferrara, not only knew letters well but was an excellent scribe and compiler of books: "E sap molt be letras, e scrivet meil ch'om del mond e feis de molt bos libres e de beill" (no. 101, p. 581).

Many of the early troubadours whose *vidas* do not mention their Latin studies must, nevertheless, have been lettered. For example, a ruler such as Guillaume IX needed some Latin training, and in "Pos de chantar m'es pres talenz," in the C and R manuscript versions, he prays to Jesus in both "romans" (the vernacular) and in Latin (no. 11, p. 279).[14] The scholarly etymological wordplay in Marcabru's verse witnesses to his Latin learning. Four of the troubadours' *vidas*, those of Giraut de Bornelh, Uc Brunet, Daude de Pradas, and Peire Rogier, state that they were learned ("savis"), not only in Latin letters but also in "natural sense" ("sen natural"), which means the vernacular language, and not merely proverbial wisdom, because "savis" connotes knowledge gained through formal instruction. In order to be able to compose verse in writing, or to read what they dictated to a scribe, or to interpret or perform a written text, twelfth-century troubadours and jongleurs had to learn Latin grammar first; and then, probably in secular circles from older troubadours and jongleurs, they had to learn to use the Latin alphabet to transcribe and read back the sounds of everyday speech, "sen natural." The only troubadour whose *vida* distinguishes him as "savis . . . de sen natural" without reference to any knowledge of Latin letters is Bertolome Zorzi, a mid-thirteenth-century Venetian (no. 100, p. 579). It was not until the end of the thirteenth century, and for the Catalan court of Sicily, that Jofre de Foixa wrote his *Regles de trobar*, the purpose of which was to instruct "clever men who had not studied Latin grammar" but nevertheless wanted to be able to appreciate troubadour verse.[15]

With their Latin letters, the schoolboys who later became troubadours learned exegetical techniques and practiced these on literary texts in a competitive, game-like way, one scholar vying with another at demonstrating his analytical, explanatory expertise before the master.[16] Certain troubadours' *vidas* remark their ability at understanding and explaining their own or others' verse. The public explanation of lyrics seems to have been an integral part of the performance context; perhaps, in court as earlier in school, the performance of the verse was the "pretext" for competitive debate displaying and asserting the explicators' intellectual prowess and wit—the more explications the better, as long as each was found to be good. A. H. Schutz translates the word *entendre* in the *vidas* as "to imagine creatively," and he understands it as part of the original composition process, whereas I see it as a part of the re-creative process. The distinction is perhaps moot. The *vidas* sometimes couple *entendre* with *trobar* and sometimes with *dire*. Arnaut de Maroill, a cleric-turned-jongleur, was good at composing and understanding ("sabia ben trobar e s'entendia be," no. 7, p. 32). The jongleur Aimeric de Sarlat, whose *vida* attributes to him the invention of only one *canso*, was very clever at explaining and understanding, presumably other men's words ("fort subtils de dire e d'entendre," no. 19, p. 196). The Dauphin d'Auvergne's *vida* uses another formula to praise his judgment and understanding of verse: "e·l plus conoissenz e·l plus entendenz" (no. 42, p. 284). One of the most interesting cases is that of Richard de Berbezill, a poor but worthy knight who was good at composing verse, but not at understanding or explaining it in public. Richard always got stage fright at explaining time and had to be helped, although he sang, declaimed, and composed lyrics well:

> Bons cavalliers fo d'armas e bels de la persona; e saup mielz trobar qu'entendre ni que dire. Mout fo pauros disenz entre las genz; et on plus vezia de bons homes, plus s'esperdia e menz sabia; e totas vetz li besoingnava altre que·l conduisses enan. Mas ben cantava e disia sons, e trobava avinenmen motz e sons.
>
> (no. 16, p. 149)

> He was a knight skilled in arms and handsome of his person; and he knew how to compose better than to understand or explain. He was extremely timid at explaining in company; and the more worthy men he saw listening, the more he got lost and the less he knew; and every time it was necessary for another to lead him on. But he sang and spoke the sounds well, and he composed graciously the words and melodies.

The jongleur Guillem de la Tor had just the opposite problem. He knew plenty of *cansos* and understood them, as well as singing and composing well. However, when it came to explaining his *cansos*, Guillem bored his audience by making a longer sermon of the reasoned explication (the *razo*) than the song itself:

> E sabia cansos assatz e s'entendia e chantava e ben e gen, e trobava. Mas quant volia dire sas cansos, el fazia plus lonc sermon de la rason que non era la cansos.
>
> (no. 32, p. 236)

In his initial vignette in the I manuscript (Paris, B.N. fr. 854, fol. 131v), Guillem himself appears lethargic. His right hand hangs down, lacking animation, while his left hand supports his head. The vignette illustrates the *vida*, and contrasts sharply with the iconography of other illuminated capitals, where the troubadours declaim or explain their verse with animated faces and extend their arms in expressive gestures.[17]

The *vida* of the early-fourteenth-century troubadour Ferrari de Ferrara describes a kind of explication trial or contest among jongleurs on feast days at court. Other jongleurs who understood Provençal well would pose questions on their own (or on Ferrari's) verse or on that of other troubadours, and Ferrari would answer, proving his mastery, in effect teaching the other jongleurs, turning the court into a school:

> E qan venia qe li marches feanon festa e cort, e li giullar li vinian che s'entendean de la lenga proensal, anavan tuit ab lui e[·l] clamavan lor ma[i]stre; e s'alcus li·n venia che s'entendes miel che i altri e che fes questios de son trobar o d'autrui, e maistre Ferari li respondea ades; si che li era per un canpio en la cort del marches d'Est.
>
> (no. 101, p. 581)

> And when the marquis held a feast at court, and jongleurs came who understood the Provençal language, they all gathered around him and called him their master; and if one came who understood Provençal better than the others and asked questions about his own or others' compositions, master Ferrari responded immediately; so that he was like a champion in the court of the Marquis of Este.

Furthermore, as his *vida* tells us, Ferrari demonstrated his interpretive ability in the book of extracts from troubadour verse that he compiled and wrote, selecting only the pithiest strophes from each *canso* (those that expressed the *sentence* or idea of the lyric most succinctly), and selecting or separating (*triar*) the words (analyzing them grammatically by their spacing on the page):

> E fe[s] un estrat de tutas las canços des bos trobador[s] del mon; e de chadaunas canços o serventes; tras .I. cobla o .II. o .III., aqelas che portan la[s] sentenças de las canços e o son tu[i]t li mot triat. Et aqest estrat e scrit isi denan.

> And he made an extract of all the songs of the good troubadours of the world; and from each *canso* or *sirventes* he drew one or two or three strophes, those that express the main points of the songs and in which all the words are separated. And this extract is written hereafter.

Ferrari's *vida* prefaces a copy of these extracts, bound today as part of the D songbook in the Estense Library in Modena (Estense 45 [α, R, 4, 4], fols. 243r–261v).

The information the thirteenth- and fourteenth-century *vidas* give us about twelfth-century troubadours cannot be relied upon completely. Nevertheless, remarks that early troubadours make in their verse concerning its understanding or interpretation also point to a schoolish performance context involving competitive exegesis. Guillaume IX requires his "companions" to interpret lyrics such as "Companho, farai un vers covinen." He reviles anyone who does not listen to and try to understand the verse ("E tenguatz lo per vilan qui no l'enten"), and at the end he requests a judgment from his listeners in the form of "counsel" ("Cavalliers, datz mi cosselh d'un pessamen," no. 1, p. 17). His riddling "Farai un vers de dreyt nien" Guillaume also closes with a request for interpretation, figuratively, a "counterkey" to unlock the verses' meaning: "que·m tramezes del sieu estug / la contraclau" (no. 4, p. 94).

Marcabru's verse is rich in criticism of the troubadours for their false interpretations. Some of these passages I have already mentioned, such as his refusal to uphold the "troba neblo" (obfuscating, "nebulous" composition or explication) that maintains "sentenssa follatina" against right reason (no. 31, p. 149). Elsewhere Marcabru calls the troubadours "disrupters of true friendship" ("torbadors d'amistat fina") and "mixers of base doctrine" ("mesclador d'avol doctrina," no. 36, pp. 175, 176). For Marcabru, as for Isidore, linguistic corruption is a sign of moral corruption and social decline. Sometimes Marcabru complains that the troubadours do as they please with his verse, mixing it up and making a mockery of what he has composed in a natural way, that is, in the vernacular and according to what he considers to be the proper forms:

E segon trobar naturau
Port la peir' e l'esca e'l [*or*, peiræléscaæl] fozilh,
Mas menut trobador beriau
  Entrebesquilh
Me tornon mon chant en badau
  En fant gratilh.

(no. 33, p. 159)

And according to natural [or, vernacular] composition, / I bring the stone and the mortar and the file, / but destructive minor troubadours / mix it up, / turning my song into a mockery, / doing just as they please with it.

At the end of the same lyric, however, Marcabru challenges the troubadours to do any damage to his perfectly constructed poem:

Marcabrus ditz no·n l'en chau
Qui quer ben lo ver al fronzilh
Que no·y pot hom trobar a frau
  Mot de rozilh.
Intrar pot hom de lonc jornau
  En breu estrilh.

Marcabru says that he's not concerned / whoever searches into the verse and breaks [or, pleats] it up, / because no one can discover [*trobar*] there by fraud / a rusty [unpolished] word. / One can spend a very long time / going over a short document with a fine-toothed comb.

Elsewhere, Marcabru claims to compose by means of a "pure" understanding or meaning that protects his verse from dismemberment, presumably by those whose intentions are not pure:

Auiatz de chan cum enans' i meillura,
E Marcabrus, segon sentenssa [*or*, s'entenssa] pura,
Saup la razon e·l vers lassar e faire
Si que autr' om no l'en pot un mot traire.
(no. 9, p. 37, A ms. variants)

Listen to how the lyric grows and improves; / for Marcabru, with his pure understanding [or, according to a pure *sentence*], / knows how to lace together the meaning and the verse form and make it / so that other men can't remove [or, betray] a word.

In spite of Marcabru's claims, his text is not stable. The E manuscript version of this very strophe, for example, reads "raire" ("to rub out" or "to erase") as opposed to A's "traire" ("to remove" or "to betray"). Has a *t* been erased from *traire* or has a *t* been added to "betray" the word *raire*? It is impossible to tell if either of these are the words that Marcabru originally "laced together"—but by no means so permanently as he pretended. Although Marcabru avows that he himself has trouble explicating obscure words and admits to the difficulty of understanding the syntax (how the reason unfolds) and the grammatical forms of the words (how each word is declined) in his "chant" (his verse as it is read or sung), he criticizes the troubadours for their infantile games of interpretation, which fragment the words by guesswork and turn into a discipline what "truth" granted:

Per savi·l tenc ses doptanssa
Cel qui de mon chant devina

So que chascus motz declina,
Si cum la razos despleia,
Qu'ieu mezeis sui en erranssa
D'esclarzir paraul' escura.

Trobador, ab sen d'enfanssa,
Movon als pros atahina,
E tornon en disciplina
So que veritatz autreia,
E fant los motz, per esmanssa,
Entrebeschatz de fraichura.
(no. 37, p. 178)

For a learned man I take him, without doubt, / the one who in my song guesses / how each word is declined / and how the intellectual sense unfolds, / because I myself err / in clarifying obscure words.

Troubadours, with their infantile sense, / cause the worthy difficulty, / and turn into a discipline / that which truth grants, / and they make the words, by guesswork, / riddled with breaks.

On one level, what Marcabru is complaining about here is that the troubadours ignore the most obvious, literal meaning of vernacular words to play with the fragments, the meaningful roots, turning understanding of the vernacular into an Isidorian *disciplina*. Their guessing, infantile-minded interpretations destroy the integrity of words and falsify the "truth," instead of uncovering it. Like Guillaume IX, Marcabru challenges his audience to interpretation; however, he insists that it be the "right" kind.

Bernart Marti, a contemporary and imitator of Marcabru, took a similar stance. In "Companho, per companhia," he complains about the debasing interpretation of his verse by a foolish group of "apostate" or artificial, false lovers. The echo of Guillaume IX's lyrics addressed to his "companions" designates the group Bernart is criticizing for their verbal follies (or *foudatz*) and for adultery:

Companho, per companhia
  De folor
Soi d'amor en gran error.
Laidament romp e deslia,
E·l jovens qu'en leis se fia
  Vai marritz
Pels amadors apostitz.

Ma part ai en la folia,
  Chantador,
Quar anc fui proatz d'amor,
C'al comensar me fon pia,
Mas era·m torn' en bauzia

Tot quan ditz,
Per que·m tenc per avelitz.[18]

Companions, through the companionship / of folly, / I am in great error concerning love. / In an ugly fashion she [folly] breaks and unbinds, / and the youth who trusts in her / goes saddened / because of false [or, artificial] lovers.

I have my part in the folly, / singers, / because once I was esteemed by love, / which, at the beginning, was sympathetic to me / but now [love] turns into trickery on me / everything I say, / so that I consider myself to be brought down.

On one level, Bernart's second strophe is about the fickleness of love; on another, it may refer to the deliberate misinterpretation of his verse by false lovers, a foolish company that encouraged Bernart's song only to break it up and unbind it.

Peire d'Auvernhe seems to voice a similar complaint against a deliberately debasing and foolish kind of interpretation. In the first strophe of "Cui bon vers agrad' a auzir," he points out that the merit of the lyric depends on the merit of the interpreter: a good interpreter will find his verse good and a bad one, bad. As I have earlier suggested, for Peire these value words have moral connotations as well as aesthetic ones:

Cui bon vers agrad auzir
de mi cosselh be qu'el escout
aquest c'ara comens a dir;
que pus sos cors li er assis
per ben entendre sos e motz
ia non cug digua que anc auzis
melhors motz trobatz luenh ni prop.

De ben non fai az escarnir
qui l'au, ans deu escoutar mout,
si tot l'outracujat albir,
ab lur nesci feble fat ris
tornon so a q'es d'amon de sotz
mas lo ben vens que s'enantis
e l'esquerns resta de galop.[19]

Whoever takes pleasure in hearing good verse, / I counsel him to listen well / to this one that I am just beginning to pronounce; / for as soon as he has his heart set / on understanding in a good way the sounds and the words, / he will never say that he has ever heard / better words composed far or near.

It doesn't do any good to mock. / Whoever praises must listen well beforehand, / although the extravagant interpreters, / with their ignorant,

> feeble, self-satisfied laughter, / turn that which is high down low. / But the good wins when it advances, / and the mockery stops its galloping.

On the subject of the misinterpretation of his verse in "A be chantar," Giraut de Bornelh uses the same axiom. Love (and the love lyric) seems good to the good interpreters, who reason the right way, and treacherous to the tricksters, who interpret the wrong way:

> Era no par
> Que chastiars
> Me valgues ni clams ni tensos?
> Pero no cuich c'anc Amors fos
> Plus fina, s'amadors trobes;
> E qui per drech la razones,
> Totz iorns se melhur' e val mais?
> Mas si com par fin' als verais,
> Sembla trefan' als trichadors
> E lor enjans fa·l nom chamjar;
> Que, pos falh, non es fin' Amors.[20]

> Now it appears / that neither criticisms / nor complaints nor debates get me anywhere. / Yet I do not believe that love has ever been / more refined, if only lovers found it so; / and whoever reasons [interprets] rightly / always improves and is worth more. / But just as it [love] seems refined to the true [lover-interpreters], / it seems treacherous to the tricksters, / and their deception changes its name, / so that, because it is faulty, it is no longer refined love.

In the envoy of "A be chantar," Giraut reinforces this moral with an analogy between verbal texts and colored textiles. Just as, in buying colored cloth, one would make a mistake to buy the least beautiful color, so, in interpreting his text, one would make a mistake to choose the worst "colors," that is, to focus, in the tissue of the text's sounds, only on the vulgar syllables:

> Seyngne Sobre-Totz, de colors
> Son li drap, e qui·l sap triar,
> Falh, si compra los sordeiors.
> (p. 72)

For both Peire d'Auvernhe and Giraut de Bornelh, the goal of the schoolish, courtly interpretation of the lyric should be to improve and refine the text, not to mock and debase it.

On one level of meaning, though by no means the only one, Giraut de Bornelh's verse frequently treats the problem of textual interpretation. For example, in the third strophe of "Si per mo Sobre-Totz no fos," he reproaches great lords (among them, probably, Raimbaut d'Orange) for interpreting in the worst way, pecking to pieces ("becilhet" in the A songbook) or debasing or biasing ("baysset" in the C version), fragmenting the verse and reversing its meaning so that the bad seems good, and the good bad:

> Mas fo apellada razos,
> Desc' om tenc per pros los savais,
> E·ls fracs e·ls leyals e·ls verais
> Apelet om per sordeiors,
> E moc la colpa dels alsors,
> Des qu'anc vers baysset ni frais.
> (no. 73, p. 464, C ms. variants)

Henceforth it was called reason / when men took the worthless for the worthy / and the generous and loyal and true / men called the worst, / and laughed at the sins of the great ones / whenever they debased or broke to bits the verses.

In "De chanter" (no. 41, p. 238, C ms. variants), Giraut defines a courteous "foolishness" that involves a free and easy troping (in rhetorical terms, a changing of time and place) which enhances and refines meaning through figurative expression:

> E no·m par
> Qu'om sia cortes
> Que tot jorn vol esser senatz.
> Trop m'agrada bela foudatz,
> Lonhdana de retenguda,
> Si com temps e loc si muda
> Que·l sen
> Fai pareissen
> E l'enans' e l'esmera
> Qu'eu eis, que chan, esquiuera
> Per ver enans
> Que chantes, si jois fos afans
> Ni trebalhs cortezia.
> Ja Deus sos pro no sia,
> Qui laissa joi ni bel semblan
> Per malvestat ni per engan.

And it does not seem to me / that a man may be courteous / who always wants to be crafty. / Beautiful foolishness pleases me very much, / far removed from restrictions, / [beautiful foolishness] such as when time and place are changed / so that it makes / the meaning appear / and enhances it and refines [or, ornaments] it. / Because I myself, who sing, would have refused / for sure, rather / than sing, if joy were painful labor / or disputation courtesy. / May God do him no good / who abandons joy or beautiful seeming / for meanness or falsehood.

In the last few lines of this strophe, Giraut seems to be disparaging those who reject the beauty of figurative language, *bel semblan*, for a laborious, sententious ingenuity in interpretation of the sort that breaks up and pierces through words in search of hidden senses.

The target of some of Giraut de Bornelh's criticism is probably Count Raimbaut d'Orange, with whom Giraut jousts in one *tenso* (Kolsen, vol. 1, no. 58, pp. 374–78), and also Raimbaut's court, which Giraut elsewhere calls the "escolh Linhaure" (no. 29, p. 164). Raimbaut carried on the tradition of facetious interpretation of the *scola neblo*. In the opening strophe of one lyric, he admits to such "rich" understanding, such ingenuity at discovering meaning in the audiovisual text of vernacular verses, that he is unable to bring his verse-game to a conclusion; the multiplicity of senses overthrows the sense:

Un vers farai de tal mena
On vuelh que mos sens paresca,
Mas tant ai rica entendensa
Que tostz n'estauc en bistensa
Que no poc anc complir mon gaug;
Ans tem c'un sol jorn no viva
Tant es mos desirs del fag lonh.[21]

I will make verse in such a way / that I want my meaning to appear, / but I have such rich understanding / that I am soon suspended by hesitation [between meanings?], / so that I cannot bring my pleasure [or, game] to completion. / Thus I fear I will not live a single day, / so far is my desire from the deed.

Raimbaut's wordplay involves many of the same old vulgar puns used by Guillaume IX, Jaufre Rudel, and Bernart de Ventadorn, in addition to some clever new ones concealed in rich rhymes. In the first strophe of "Una chansoneta fera," Raimbaut suggests a key to the interpretation of this *vers* which "seals sense" ("sen sela"): the words will be revealed to the one who guesses (or divides) rightly:

Una chansoneta fera
Voluntiers laner'a dir;
Don tem que m'er a murir
E fas l'ai que sen sela.
Ben la poira leu entendre
Si tot s'es en aital rima;
Li mot seran descubert
Alques de razon devisa.
(no. 3, p. 75, R ms. variants)

> I would gladly have made a little *canso* / easy to say, / but I fear I would die, / and I have made it so that it conceals the meaning. / Yet it may be easily understood, / even though it is in such rhyme. / The words will be discovered / by the one who divides them rightly.

In his *tenso* debate with Giraut de Bornelh, Raimbaut defends *trobar clus* (Kolsen, vol. 1, no. 58, pp. 374–78), that is, relatively "closed" performance and appreciation limited to fellow troubadours and connoisseurs who compete at explaining the verse, and especially at discovering multiple senses in the audiovisual text in imitation of grammar-schoolish Latin exegesis.[22]

Giraut de Bornelh had a wider and in some respects more serious use for vernacular lyrics. Unlike Raimbaut, Giraut was of humble social origin.[23] He used his knowledge of Latin and the vernacular ambitiously to better his social position. As he went from court to court in the summers with his singers and explained his lyrics, Giraut seems to have assumed the role, not of an entertainer (the singers did that), but of a vernacular language teacher who, like the religious cantor, taught reading through *singing* inscribed texts. Just as he may have used the Latin texts of religious songs to teach school in winter, so the "master troubadour" may have used his own—and, probably, other troubadours'—vernacular song texts to demonstrate and teach vernacular grammar: reading, writing, and fundamentals of composition and interpretation. This needed doing. The Church was not alone in needing a stable written vernacular to bind men to contracts of donation or to preserve their testimony under oath. Lettered laymen, especially troubadours and jongleurs, seem to have served informally as vernacular language teachers for the lay public from as early as the mid-twelfth century. The *vida* of Uc de Saint Circ, who was himself a composer of explications of other troubadours' verse,[24] tells us both that he learned vernacular verse in Montpellier when his parents thought he was learning Latin letters and that, later in life, Uc gladly shared his learning by teaching others: "Gran ren anparet de l'autrui saber e voluntiers l'enseingnet ad autrui."[25] This may refer to Uc's didactic *razos*.

Trobar clus and *trobar leu*, the relative merits of which Raimbaut and Giraut debated, involved two different kinds of interpretation, two different attitudes toward the inscribed text. For us, Giraut's "open" verse is no easier to understand than Raimbaut's "closed" verse. Raimbaut, like Guillaume IX before him, challenged his relatively elite audience to discover and invent rich senses, to play with the language of his lyrics, whereas Giraut castigated those who interpreted otherwise than he intended and, according to his later *vida*, himself traveled from court to court supervising the performance of his lyrics by his singers and explaining them in "masterful" fashion. The composition of Provençal lyrics must have been greatly stimulated by this contest among twelfth-century troubadours over the purpose and use of the text. On the one hand, the more pious and didactic troubadours, such as Marcabru and Giraut de Bornelh, insisted on the permanent authority of the inscribed text to represent its author's intentions; on the other hand, the facetious, and often deliberately impious, troubadours deauthorized inscription by treating the written text of vernacular verses as a malleable matter to be reshaped according to the desire of each new interpreter, re-formed either by means of equivocating, jongleuresque performance techniques or by the more imaginary duplicity of figurative or etymologizing interpretation. The facetious troubadours tended to treat the inscribed texts of vernacular lyrics as riddling objects composed of constantly changing configurations of signs—marks on hide or wax—objects upon which they themselves bestowed meanings, the more the better, as long as each was clever. The didactic troubadours, on the contrary, tried to treat the inscribed lyric text as a *representation* of the intentions of its author. Much was at stake in this contest between *sentenssa follatina* and *razo*.

4

Razo

Ja mais bon vers non er auzitz
ni cansos per razon complida.

Never again will good verse be heard
nor lyrics completed with explication.

—Daude de Pradas, "Ben deu esser solatz marritz"

The evidence of the Provençal songbooks suggests that by the mid-thirteenth and the fourteenth centuries, the game of schoolish exegesis of vernacular lyrics had, for the most part, been turned to earnest, that is, to discovering the real historical situations and the moral ideas expressed by the words of the lyrics. This censorship of verbal *foudatz* may be attributed, not only to the thirteenth-century Inquisition, but also to the need to regulate and stabilize the vernacular for commercial and legal purposes. Not surprisingly, there is much more surviving evidence of this later, idealizing appreciation of troubadour verse than of the earlier, more facetious aesthetic. There was nothing foolish about master Ferrari de Ferrara's explications. Serious, didactic exegesis, which aimed at being authoritative and at uncovering the "true" meaning of the lyric text, was written down in the form of the *vidas* and *razos* we know. Facetious exegesis, on the other hand, was an oral performance, a social game of finding and inventing meanings—the more the better. Consequently, facetious exegesis was not usually written down,[1] except in the form of the lyrics themselves, as clever, creative interpretations were incorporated into "new" lyrics. The early troubadours' practice of facetious interpretation is indirectly reflected in several other ways as well: in the outright or veiled warnings against misinterpretation in the verse of troubadours such as Marcabru, Peire d'Auvernhe, and Giraut de Bornelh, which I have already discussed; in the precautions that the opponents of *sentenssa follatina* took against it in their *razos*, grammar books, and rules of composition; and in the textbook format of certain songbooks, as well as in their interpretive marginal markings and illuminations.

Our perspective on troubadour verse is very much biased by the serious, historicizing intentions of the compilers of the majority of surviving songbooks. Most of these were written in Italy by men such as Ferrari de Ferrara, for whom the troubadours' language was a learned language almost as different from their native vernacular as Latin. Of the major songbook collections of Provençal verse, only three (C, E, and R) were copied in Languedoc.[2] The B songbook, although written in Provence or by a Provençal scribe, draws heavily upon the Italian A songbook. The late-thirteenth-century M songbook, whose readings often correspond to those in C and R, seems to be of hybrid execution; its text and alternating red and blue decorative capitals are written in an Italian style, but the large vignettes of the troubadours and the grotesques in the lower margins seem to be of northern French execution.[3] Although, as I have already explained, we may perceive traces of earlier, facetious wordplay in the variants and textual ambiguities of these songbooks, the purpose of their thirteenth- and fourteenth-century (and chiefly Italian) compilers was to preserve clear, authoritative versions of the lyric texts and, in most manuscripts, to provide some glossatory framework as well. Thus the finest Italian songbooks, such as A, I, and K, preface each troubadour's verse with his *vida*. As Margarita Egan has demonstrated, the "lives of the troubadours" are vernacular equivalents of the *vitae poetae* in the classical tradition of didactic textual commentary: "Theoretically, the Old Provençal *vida* corresponds to the *vita poetae*, and the *razo* to the rest of the *accessus*. But 'lives' and 'explanations' are not always distinct genres: sometimes *razos* are biographical, *vidas* exegetic."[4] As we have seen, the *vidas* do contain some information about certain troubadours' education and social background that must have come from oral tradition or other lost sources.[5] In the main, however, the thirteenth- and fourteenth-century *vidas* and *razos* are serious, historicizing interpretations of the lyric texts that provide little additional information.

Although a *vida* was invented to preface the verse of nearly every troubadour in the textbook format of the mid-thirteenth-century Italian songbooks (AIK), *razos* were written out for relatively few troubadours. The only *razos* in the A songbook treat two of Raimon Jordan's lyrics. In addition to these, the IK songbooks give a relatively long series of prose *razos* interspersed with quotations from Bertran de

Born's *sirventes*. In both these cases, the *razos* treat the lyrics as truthful representations of autobiographical and historical events. In the *Biographies* Jean Boutière has remarked that the "number and length of the *razos* are not in proportion to the notoriety of the poets" (p. vii). Looking through the whole corpus of *razos*, we find that almost none were invented to explain the verse of the early, facetious troubadours. There are none for Guillaume IX, Jaufre Rudel, or Raimbaut d'Orange. There is only one *razo* called such for Bernart de Ventadorn, and that in the sixteenth-century N^2 songbook. What Boutière and Schutz extract from Arnaut Daniel's *vida* in the R songbook and label *razo* is not an *explication de texte*, but a narrative, based on non-lyric sources, of the historical situation that lay behind the composition of a particular lyric attributed to Arnaut Daniel. In a composition contest sponsored by Richard the Lionhearted, Arnaut stole his competitor's lyric, much to the delight of Richard and the rest of the audience and to the chagrin of the other jongleur. For his good joke, Arnaut was awarded authorship of the stolen song.[6] This story from a songbook written in Languedoc seems to take verse composition in game; it prevents us from reading "Arnaut's" lyric autobiographically in the usual serious way of other *razos*.

The general lack of *razos* for the verse of the more facetious twelfth-century troubadours is probably not due to a loss of documents. The fourteenth-century Catalan Sg songbook presents six historicizing *razos* for Giraut de Bornelh in front of his *vida*. The number of *razos* extant for the more didactic troubadours is much larger than for their facetious contemporaries. This is not surprising. Marcabru, it will be remembered, castigated the "scola neblo" for maintaining "sentenssa follatina" against "razo," *foudatz* against *sen*. When used by the teacher-troubadours, *razo* was a morally and ideologically loaded term; for these men, the purpose of verse composition was to express a *razo*, a serious message or *sentence*. The composer sought words to express the prior idea of the *razo*, and the purpose of the form was to convey the content. For the founders and followers of the *scola neblo*, on the other hand, the formal aspects of the verse were more important than content. In their eyes, every lyric was about "dreyt nien," in other words, about as many things as its interpreters were able to invent or discover (*trobar*) in its tissue of letters and sounds, in the forms of the text. Whereas the facetious, anti-authoritarian exegesis of *sentenssa follatina* was not committed to writing, the historicizing, moralizing, and spiritualizing glosses of the teaching troubadours and their followers were written down and collected, even more systematically during the fourteenth century than during the thirteenth. The lack of either *vidas* or *razos* in the C songbook (or in the hybrid M songbook) and their grouping apart from the lyric texts at the beginning or end of the two other songbooks written in Languedoc (E and R) suggests that these southwestern compilers were not as intent upon putting troubadour verse into a seriously didactic framework as were Italian compilers. The tradition of facetious exegesis—or *gay saber*—was not entirely dead in Languedoc in the fourteenth century. This tradition may also have prevented later interpreters from inventing reductive, didactic *razos* inappropriate to the more licentious aesthetic of early troubadours such as Guillaume IX, Bernart de Ventadorn, or Raimbaut d'Orange.

The desire to stabilize the written forms of the vernacular and to make it into an authoritative medium of expression is perhaps most strikingly demonstrated by the testimony appended to the *razo* of Guiraut Riquier, which he composed in rhymed couplets sometime between 1280 and 1285 to "clarify" an earlier lyric by Guiraut de Calanso known as the "menor ters d'amor" ("smallest third of love").[7] Guiraut Riquier explains that he wrote this explication at the request of Count Henry of Rodez who, in January of 1280, set several troubadours gathered at his court for the holidays the task, individually, of clearly explaining Guiraut de Calanso's ambiguous lyric. According to Riquier, the count chose him among all the rest to write down the *canso* "exactly as he heard it, without changing any words in it" ("e·m det / escricha la chanso / que motz camjatz no·y fo, / aisi com l'auziretz," p. 274, vv. 52–55). Presumably the designated exegetes took written copies of the lyric away with them for further study. Riquier's strophe-by-strophe explanation also quotes or reinscribes the entire lyric. None of the other three troubadours seems to have come through with an interpretation. Perhaps they did not take the count's request as seriously as Guiraut did. After a delay of five years, Count Henry and a high council of interpreters decided that Guiraut Riquier's interpretation was worthy, that it "touched the heart of understanding." Consequently, the count authorized this interpretation (both reinscribed lyric and gloss) by turning the written document of Riquier's exegesis into a kind of charter witnessed to, dated, localized, and sealed with the count's seal:

E nos entendem pro que·l cors
de l'entendemen a tocat,
e prestam li auctoritat.
E per so qu'el crezut en sia,
volem li·n portar guerentia,
e mandam, que·y sia pauzatz
nostre sagel, so ès vertatz.
L'an c'om comta M.CC.
LXXXV., ni may ni mens,
.VI. jorns a l'intrada del mes
de juli, aisi vertat es,
que fon fag ab gran alegrier
ins el castel de Monrozier.
(pp. 299–300, vv. 24–36)

And we understand [it to be] worthy, for he has touched / the heart of understanding, / and we lend him authority. / And so that he will be believed, / we want to give him a guarantee, / and we order that our seal / be placed there; this is the truth. / The year, as counted, 1285, / no more nor less, / six days from the beginning of the month / of July, in truth, / this was done in great happiness / in the castle of Monrozier.

The exaggerated earnestness of Guiraut's quest for authority in exegesis seems almost ludicrous—unless we stop a moment to think and compare. Here is the late-thirteenth-century equivalent of a diploma in vernacular letters, the guarantee of interpretive authority. The worth and veracity of Riquier's "definitive edition" and exegesis of an earlier troubadour's lyric are first approved by the count and his council of interpreters and then sealed with the count's seal. When political power "guarantees" interpretive authority, as in this instance, there is a reduction of many possible meanings to one and a fixing in place of this one.

In the expressions that Raimon de Cornet finds ambiguous and chooses to gloss from a fourteenth-century lyric by Bernart de Panasac, on the other hand, we may see the reflection of the tradition of facetious interpretation. These two late troubadours were not minor in their own times. Bernart de Panasac was the only nobleman among the seven founders of the Toulouse Consistory (to be discussed later), and Raimon de Cornet, a Franciscan, was the author of many lyrics, both pious and impious.[8] In his long verse *razo*, Raimon's avowed purpose is to disclose the true spiritual meaning (praise of the Virgin) that Bernart de Panasac has disguised as praise of a temporal lady:

Be par, segon albire
D'ome que trobar sab,

Le vers, senes tot gab,
De la mayre de Dieu.
(p. 56, vv. 20–23)

That is: According to the interpretation of men who know *trobar*, the verse, "all joking aside," is about the Mother of God. At the end of a line in rhyme position, the expression "senes tot gab" is often filler; here, however, it may deny the facetiously eroticizing interpretations earlier troubadours have attached to conventional expressions praising the lady. The first passage Raimon singles out as a "little obscure" is the last part of Bernart's first strophe, where the poet expresses his desire to present his verse to his lady on his knees (in the traditional attitude of textual presentation to a patron) as a servant serves (or makes a present to) a good lord, because she is so great: "Soplegui vos que prengatz aquest vers, / Qu'ieus vuelh servir de ginolhs, cum fay sers / Som bo senhor, car etz de grans afars" (p. 56). There is really no problem in applying these lines of Bernart's to the Virgin, unless Raimon imagines that service on one's knees carries with it inappropriate erotic connotations from the earlier use and facetious explication of the conventional expression in troubadour love lyrics. To avoid such innuendos, Raimon emphasizes that the *verse*, and the effort of composing it, is the service the poet offers:

Mas un pauc es escurs,
Quan ditz que prengal vers,
Que de ginolhs, cum sers,
Li vol de grat servir.
Certamens el volc dir
Que la Verges humils,
Car es tan senhorils,
Sos digz no mesprezes,
Per que ja non perdes
Lo vers ni son esfors.
(p. 57, vv. 28–37)

But he is a little obscure / when he says that, taking the verses, / on his knees, like a servant, / he wants very much to serve her; / certainly he means / that the gracious Virgin, / because she is so exalted, / will not disdain his words, / so that he will not lose / the verses or his effort.

Nevertheless, in Raimon's explication the possibility of a conventional pun on the feminine Provençal nouns *verga*/*verge* or Latin *virga*/*virgo* (rod/virgin) arises in the line "Que la Verges humils," which might sound like "Que la verg' es humils." Thus Raimon's lines might be understood: "Certainly he wanted to say / that the 'rod' is humble; / because it is [or, you are] so excellent, / do not disdain [or, mistake] his words / so that you will not lose / the verse or his 'effort.'" Other "obscure" epithets, metaphors, and phrases that require Raimon's "clarifying," and often allegorizing, explanation also suggest the possibility of more physical, materializing interpretations. The didactic troubadours, from Giraut de Bornelh on, constantly called attention to the obscurity of earlier or contemporary verse in order to magnify their own authority and convince audiences of the necessity for their clarifying *razos*. Thus Raimon de Cornet, in his burlesque exegesis, keeps announcing the success of his interpretation: "Assatz vos ay ubert / Lo sieu entendemen" ("Thus I have opened up for you / his intention") or "Tot son entendemen / Vos ay demostrat clar" ("His whole intention / I have clearly demonstrated to you," p. 58, vv. 56–57, and p. 60, vv. 120–21).

Although three songbooks written in Languedoc have survived, all using a somewhat less didactic format than their Italian counterparts, this small number is to be compared to the fourteen surviving manuscripts of Matfre Ermengaud of Béziers's supremely didactic, and anything but brief, *Breviari d'amor* (*Breviary of Love*), which he says he began writing in 1288. The purpose of Matfre's "compilation," as he himself announces, is to clarify the obscure, to open up the understanding and clarify the thinking of those who are not subtle, learned interpreters:

> E vueilh la present obra far
> Per obrir los entendemens
> E declarar los pessamens
> De cels que no son aprimat,
> Ni fort entendut, ni fondat
> En las Sanctas Escripturas
> Ni en leys, ni en naturas.[9]

> And I want to write the present work / in order to open up the understanding / and clarify the thinking / of those who are not clever at letters, / nor very experienced, nor grounded / in Holy Scripture / or in civil law or in natural science.

Matfre depicts himself as a master troubadour who has been asked by lovers and diverse troubadours to clear up their doubts concerning the nature and origin of the love that the troubadours sing (vv. 55–79).

Matfre's amplifying exegetical methods are the traditional ones of division and definition. It is not until line 27,791 that he begins the section that most resembles other didactic troubadours' *razos*: the "Perilhos tractat d'amor de donas segon que han tractat li antic trobador en lors cansos" ("The Perilous Treatise on the Love of Ladies such as Earlier Troubadours Have Treated in Their Lyrics"). This 20,000-line verse *razo* quotes selections from many troubadour lyrics, explaining and placing them in a Christian moral context. Whereas the "truths" that the songbooks' *razos* aim to disclose are mainly biographical ones, Matfre reads for moral *sentence*. (See fig. 3.)

Also belonging to the tradition of serious troubadour exegesis is Dante's *Vita nuova*, the technical, formal meaning of which is surely "new-style *vida*."[10] Dante's quotations of his earlier lyrics alternating with prose exegesis of them resembles the alternation of verse, *vidas*, and *razos* in contemporary Provençal songbooks of the sort Ferrari of Ferrara compiled, or the even more extensive exegesis (verging on the *novella*, as Boutière remarked)[11] of the fourteenth-century Italian H and P songbooks. Dante's *vida* is "new" in that it is written in Italian, and also in that the poet himself compiles a textbook of his own verse. While didactic troubadours such as Giraut de Bornelh seem to have explicated their own and others' lyrics orally, and may even have committed these *razos* to writing (as Guiraut Riquier later did), the didactic troubadours almost certainly did not compose their own *vidas*. These were probably invented with the textbook format of the thirteenth- and fourteenth-century songbooks. Dante's *Vita nuova* resembles the Provençal *vidas* in that it treats his verse as autobiography. Not only does Dante explain the life situations that motivated his lyrics, but, like a medieval grammarian, he explains the logical order of the argument (the *razo*) *per divisionem*. Dante's views are those of earlier didactic troubadours. He insists that the poet should be able to clarify his own verse in prose explication, "for it would be a disgrace if someone composing in rhyme introduced a figure of speech or rhetorical ornament, and then on being asked could not divest his words of such covering so as to reveal a true meaning."[12] In his *Vita nuova*, and also in his Latin prose treatise on vernacular eloquence (*De vulgari eloquentia*), Dante assumes the role of a vernacular language teacher.

In his explications, Dante respects the integrity of individual words; his pursuit of "truth" stops short of dividing words into component syllables. This suggests that he was aware of and wanted to avoid the kind of facetious troubadour interpretation that played with Isidorian etymologizing dissection and, even more fundamentally, fooled around with combining the syllables of the inscribed text into words. In his explanation of his *canzone* beginning "Donne ch'avete intelletto d'amore," for example, Dante "divides" at greater length than usual, but not as far as he could: "Certainly to uncover still more meaning in this *canzone* it would be necessary to divide it more minutely; but if anyone has not the wit to understand it with the help of the divisions already made he had best leave it alone" (pp. 58–59). With the *Vita nuova*, Dante tries to prevent people from taking his love lyrics in game; he insists on his authority as poet over the meaning of his verse. By writing his own "new-style" *vida* and explaining the real-life situations that motivated his lyrics, Dante insists that the voice of the lyric is his own voice, and that he is not pretending. Nevertheless, his earnestness may also discover the conventional troubadour game of interpreting love lyrics facetiously.

Like Dante in *De vulgari eloquentia*, where he condemns formalist games such as the "useless equivocation" in rhymes "that always seems to detract from the meaning" ("inutilis equivocatio, que semper sententiae quicquam derogare videtur"),[13] the Provençal grammars and the *Leys d'amors* combat playful linguistic laissez-faire and insist on responsible interpretation. In the earliest of these, the late-twelfth-century or early-thirteenth-century *Razos de trobar*, Raimon Vidal regards the troubadours as vernacular language teachers. The purpose of his book, he claims, is to make known which troubadours composed and taught (that is, explained) verse best: "voill eu far aqest libre per far conoisser et saber qals dels trobadors an mielz trobat et mielz ensenhat."[14] Raimon specifies that the audience for his *Razos de trobar* (*Explanations of Poetic Invention*) is everyone who wants to compose, understand, explain, or listen to verse: "Totas genz . . . q'en volon trobar o q'en volon entendre o qu'en volon dire o q'en volon auzir" (p. 2). According to Raimon, the audience of troubadour verse has a responsibility to judge it wisely, and this requires understanding and technical expertise. He castigates listeners who understand nothing, but are too proud to admit their ignorance by posing questions publicly, and who, in consequence, bestow praise and blame unjustly. The audience's refusal to participate in the public exegesis or "teaching" of the lyric shortchanges both listeners and composers:

> En aqest saber de trobar son enganat li trobador, et dirai vos com ni per qe: li auzidor qe ren non intendon, qant auzon un bon chantar, faran senblant qe for[t] ben l'entendon, et ges no l'entendran, qe cuieriant se qe·lz en tengues hom per pecs si diz[i]on qe no l'entendesson. En aisi enganan lor mezeis, qe uns dels maior[s] sens del mont es qi domanda ni vol apenre so qe non sap. Et sil qe entendon, qant auziran un malvais trobador, per ensegnament li lauzaran son chantar; et si no lo volon lauzar, al menz no·l volran blasmar; et en aisi son enganat li trobador, et li auzidor n'an lo blasme.
>
> (p. 4)
>
> In this knowledge of poetic invention the troubadours are deceived, and I will tell you how and why: the listeners, who understand nothing when they hear a good song, pretend that they understand it very well when they don't understand it at all, because they believe they will be considered stupid if they say they don't understand. And thus they deceive themselves, because one of the most sensible things in the world is to ask and to want to learn what one doesn't know. And those who understand, when they listen to a bad troubadour, they praise his singing as instructive, and if they don't want to praise him, at least they do not want to blame him, and in this way the troubadours are deceived, and the listeners have the blame.

When Raimon chastises troubadours for faults, he often includes "entendedors" with them, because the two activities are inseparable. Indeed, the troubadours were often their own "entendedors," not only in the written/oral dialectic of the "individual" composition process, but also in the re-creative dialectic of courtly performance and explication of one another's verses. Thus Raimon recommends his manual to all clever composer/interpreters (p. 24): "totz homs prims s'en porria aprimar en aqest libre de trobar o d'entendre o de dir o de respondre" ("Every subtle man will be able to refine himself in this book concerning composition or understanding or explicating or answering").

The reflection of earlier facetious wordplay may be evident in the corrective, disciplinary intention of another such grammar, the late-thirteenth-century rhymed *Doctrina d'acort* of Terramagnino of Pisa,[15] who insists that a clear, continuous presentation of an idea is more pleasing than an intricate rhyme scheme—in other words, that content should be preferred over form. Terramagnino particularly warns against barbarisms and solecisms, which troubadours disclaim by blaming performance practices:

> Car may mi play e agrada
> Razos ben continuada

Que mot qan alcus los entresca
Ab rimas e entrebesca.
. . . .
Eu voil qe visi, barbarism
No·y meyta ni solecism,
Tot qe mant trobador preza[t]
H[a]ian en lur chantar pauzat;
Mas per aqo s'en escuzon
Qar, qan alcus i fai lo son,
Chantan lo pot abreuiar
Si con se tayn, e aluoygnar:
Eu voill qe en la scrichura
Meta primamen sa cura.[16]

Because more pleasing and agreeable to me / are continuous arguments / than words when someone weaves / and interlaces them with rhymes. / . . . I do not want vices, barbarisms / or solecisms, thrown in, / such as many highly praised troubadours / have put in their songs; / but for this they excuse themselves / because, when someone puts sound to it / in singing, he may shorten it, / just as when he slows down and lengthens it. / I want [the troubadour] to put his attention / first and foremost into the inscription.

As insurance against deformation of their words in performance, Terramagnino insists that the troubadours should pay more attention to how the words are written out. He seems to mean that the troubadour should preanalyze and preinterpret his text for the performer/reader by writing or having it written unambiguously and grammatically, separating words properly.

The *Flors del gay saber*,[17] large parts of which were incorporated a few years later into the *Leys d'amors* of the Toulouse Consistory, was compiled sometime before 1341 by an anonymous author who explains that his purpose is to teach "sabers de trobar," that is, vernacular composition, as earlier troubadours had done, but more clearly than they, arranging and putting in order their scattered teachings and adding some new ones:

Et aquestas leys damors fam per so que ayssi hom puesca trobar plenieiramen compilat e ajustat tot so que denan era escampat e dispers. . . . Per so quel sabers de trobar lo qual havian tengut rescost li antic trobador et aquo meteysh quen havian pauzat escuramen. puesca hom ayssi trobar claramen. Quar ayssi poyra hom trobar motz essenhamens. e motas doctrinas. las quals degus dels anticz trobadors non han pauzadas. jaciayso que sian necessarias ad trobar.

(vol. 1, p. 1)

I have made these laws of love so that one will be able to find here fully collected and fit together everything that previously was scattered and

> dispersed . . . , so that knowledge of poetic invention which the early troubadours kept hidden, and even that which they set down obscurely, one will be able to find clearly [set forth] here; because here one will be able to find much teaching and much doctrine that none of the early troubadours set down, even though necessary to poetic invention.

The third reason for the compilation of the *Flors* is to "bridle lovers' base desires and dishonest movements and to teach them how they should love" (vol. 1, p. 4). Like other authors of Provençal grammars and composition manuals, the compiler of the *Flors* assumes that there is an intimate connection between correct grammar and correct morals. In teaching one, one teaches the other. Nevertheless, in his fine focus on form and in his desire to be comprehensive in collecting earlier troubadour teachings and techniques, the compiler of the *Flors* gives us some valuable information about various kinds of poetic license used by the facetious troubadours.

Especially helpful for recognizing puns and near-puns (*équivoques*) is the *Flors'* section on phonetics and orthography. The writer tells us, according to fourteenth-century conventions of the Toulouse region (roughly those of the C songbook), what letters represent the same consonant sounds, especially at the ends of words (rhyme position). The letters *p* and *b*, for example, are interchangeable, as are *g* and *c*, although it is more common to write *c* than *g* at the end of a word; *k* and *q* sound like *c* but are not often written in terminal position; according to correct opinion, *c* really should be sounded more than *s*: such are some of the *Flors'* prescriptions (vol. 1, pp. 32–34). In a later section (vol. 2, p. 194), the author discusses certain regional differences in pronunciation (which may produce puns and ambiguities when a text written in one region is read aloud elsewhere). The Gascons, for example, employ an aspirate *h* instead of *f*, pronouncing (and also sometimes writing) *hranca* for *franca*, or *hilha* for *filha*; they pronounce *r* for *l*, *bera* instead of *bela*; and *b* for *v*, *bertat* for *vertat*. The author of the *Flors* takes account of these multiple ways of writing words or pronouncing them in his role as grammarian, mainly for the purpose of trying to regulate and clarify confusing conventions of vernacular orthography and pronunciation of written words. He would prefer that the Gascons made a distinction between the sounds of the letters *b* and *v* and that they observed it in reading and writing. For the purpose of such clarification, the author of the *Flors* probably sometimes makes distinctions where none actually existed in common usage.

Yet these very ambiguities—which grammarians tend to regard as flaws in the language—are poets' treasures. Some parts of the *Flors* acknowledge the troubadours' quest for multiple, "rich" senses in their verse. On the subject of equivocal rhymes (vol. 1, p. 196), the author points out that different spellings of the same sound do not destroy the highly prized equivocation in pairs such as *cap/gap* (head/boast) or *quar/car* (because/precious). He notes that both synonyms and equivocal words are helpful in composition; synonyms enable easy composition and equivocal words enable subtle composition: "E saber motz sinonimatz et equivocz. ajuda fort a dictar. li sinonimat. a leu dictar. li equivoc. a subtilamen dictar" (vol. 2, p. 36).[18]

In the *Flors'* section on rhymes and "variable" words, we seem to have entered a game world of language reminiscent of Virgil of Toulouse's "Art of Cutting Up Words" (with its various ways of separating, reversing, scrambling, or reweaving words, syllables, or letters) or of the imaginative coinages of the Hisperic Latin vocabulary. The troubadours' art was one of equivocation, of finding different meanings in the same texts. The multiple senses of their playful interpretations depended, as I have already suggested, on capturing a sequence of sounds in the abbreviated and, as we have seen, in many respects highly ambiguous form of writing, and then considering possible variant interpretations of the sequence of letters on the page. The various reading practices described by the *Flors* would probably seem much less extravagant to us if we silent modern readers of words as ideograms regularly had to puzzle out the grammar of early vernacular texts as medieval readers did, if we, like they, read as though we were solving a riddle, as though reading were an adventure in signification.

One playful medieval technique of interpreting was called retrogradation, reading backward, either by letters or by syllables, so that the word produced was either the same as or different from that read conventionally, from left to right. The *Flors* (vol. 1, p. 182) gives a number of examples: read backward by syllables *tafata* and *remire* mean the same as when read forward; *ama* and *tot* produce the same sense read in either direction letter by letter. On the other hand, *amor* read backward letter by letter produces the word *roma* (an anagram Arnaut Daniel played with)[19] and *amar* read backward makes *rama* (branch), while reversing the syllables of *cava* (cave) produces *vaca* (cow). The same group of letters or sounds evokes different meanings when read in different sequences according to different assumptions about the direction of reading. This can even change from the horizontal to the vertical, as in strophes that the *Flors* calls *rescosta* or *cluza* ("hidden" or "closed," vol. 1, p. 314), wherein one reads downward "by the first or the last or middle letters, syllables, or words of one or more strophes in order to separate, read, and learn the name of a certain person or thing or a certain *sentensa* or *doctrina*." In accentual rhymes (vol. 1, p. 196), how we choose to accent the same combination of letters or syllables changes their meaning: "moving the accent moves the signification of the words, while the letters remain the same." The *rim equivoc contrafag* (equivocal counterfeit rhyme) also depends on the way we read, that is, on the way we combine or separate the letters or syllables of a sequence grammatically into words. As examples, the *Flors* gives *luna* (moon) and *l'una* (the one), *semena* (sows seed) and *se mena* (conducts himself), *coms* (count) and *qu'oms* (that the man). From the grammarian's point of view, such rich rhymes are deliberate solecisms, licensed only by their poetic context, and the same is true of the other irregular composition and interpretation techniques, such as reading backward.

In other passages of his compilation, the author of the *Flors* specifically warns against equivocal expressions that allow different grammatical and expressive liaisons or separations of letters and words. He dubs any kind of verbal ambiguity involving "doubtful sense" *amphibolia* or *amphibologia*, and his first example involves two different possibilities of punctuating and understanding a series of words forming a couplet: "Cel que ses am mi dinatz / Mal pro li fassa" (vol. 3, p. 106). When we pause before the word *mal*, the lines mean "He who dines without his friends / Evil profit it him!" and the *mal* modifies *pro*; but if we pause after the *mal* (enjambing the line), then the *mal* modifies *dinatz*, and the couplet means "He who dines without his friends / poorly, does so for his own profit." Although he does not enumerate them, the grammarian tells us that there are as many kinds of amphibologies as there are ways of mistaking the sense, that is, thirteen ways, six involving the word itself and seven "outside" it (vol. 1, p. 108). One kind of amphibology may arise from the awkward linking of words ("enpost liamen de las dictios") so that a person may understand the sequence of letters on the page in a way other than it was intended. An example the *Flors* gives of this awkward linking is the couplet "Lerguelh del monges / No pretz un poges." If we read "del monges" as "of the monk," then the line is missing a syllable (in the *Flors*' terms, an "accent"), although the couplet does make sense. However, dividing the letters of *monges* into two words, *mon ges*, also makes sense in the context and gives the right number of syllables: "I don't give a whit for worldly pride." This latter division, at least in the opinion of the writer of the *Flors*, does not destroy the rhyme.

To show how the combination of one word with another can produce a different word, the *Flors* cites the couplet "Quar be volia Mantelina / Aytant quo fazia Martina" (vol. 3, p. 110). In the first line *quar* may be joined to *be* to form the word *carbe*, or *be* may be joined to the first syllable of *volia* to give the word *bevo*, or the last syllable of *volia* may be joined to the first syllable of *Mantelina* to give the word *aman*. According to the grammarian, this line is defective because these different, meaningful elisions not only "trouble" the sense, but also the *sentence*. The entire couplet can be read two different ways: "Mantelina wanted as much hemp as Martina did" or "I wanted Mantelina as much as [I wanted] Martina." The difference depends on how one interprets the two syllables represented by the letters *quarbe*, either as one word, *carbe*, meaning "hemp," or as two, *quar be*, an emphatic introductory phrase.

Equivocation that can result in two different sentences is to be avoided (vol. 3, p. 110): "Aquest vici deu hom esquivar qui vol obra neta. quar en qualque maniera torbe la sentensa o la veda doptoza. vicis es" ("This vice one ought to avoid if he wants to make a clear work, because in whatever manner it disturbs the *sentence* or renders it doubtful, it is a vice"). Nevertheless, the author admits that it is difficult to avoid the possibility of equivocal elisions in many cases, as with the prepositions *quar* and *can* ("because" and "when"), which are often followed by words beginning with a *q* or *c* or by *per* or *so*, all of which may produce equivocal combinations (such as *c'anc*, meaning "for never," or *canso*, "song"). He counsels avoiding, if possible, the use of *quar* followed by *be* or *bo*, and he considers it preferable to use an article of the wrong case, *lo* instead of *le*, to modify words that begin with a hard *c* sound, such as *cabas* or *cas* or *camis*, in order to avoid ambiguities (vol. 3, p. 110):

> Alcunas vetz labitutz se lia enpostamen am son cazual coma. *le cabas. le cas. le camis. le capitols.* perque en est cas es miel dig *lo* que *le.* canque sia de nominatiu. coma *lo cabas. lo camis* et en ayssi des autres lors semblans.

> Sometimes the article links itself awkwardly with its object as in *le cabas*, *le cas*, *le camis*, *le capitols*, which is why in this case it is better to say *lo*

than *le*, even though it is nominative, as in *lo cabas*, *lo camis*, and so on with similar words.

The author of the *Flors* does not need to explain the cacemphaton involving the words *lec* (lecher) or *leca* (lick) that these combinations could produce: *lec-as*, *leca-bas*, *lec-amis*.

These kinds of equivocal liaisons are of precisely the sort that the early troubadours—whom Marcabru (no. 36, p. 175) labeled *torbadors* (troublers)—played with in their compositions and explications. They depend, as I have already explained, on an audiovisual, rather than strictly visual, approach to the written text. For the author of the fourteenth-century *Flors*, it was evidently not enough to separate the words "correctly" by blank spaces on the page or to spell "quar be" with a *q*. He advised avoiding the awkward liaison altogether. The visual configuration did not yet have final authority in the vernacular. The voice did, that is, the phonetic, expressive interpretation of the series of letters noted on the page. The *Flors* compares the reading of accentual verse to singing. Indeed, the author says that such reading is called song (*cans*) by analogy to the vocal performance of a melody (vol. 1, p. 58). In both cases, the voice interprets a visual text whose abbreviated form allows much room for performative variation.

In the faults the *Flors* proscribes, we may see the reflection of earlier troubadours' facetious wordplay—their making what they wanted of the forms and meanings of words. The "variable" words that the *Flors* says are "permitted neither in reading nor speaking" recollect the peculiarities of the Hisperic vocabulary and also Marcabru's complaints against troubadours/*torbadors* for deforming words. The *Flors*' list of variable words (those used or formed irregularly) begins with foreign and nonsense words and "counterfeit" words made from Latin; then the author names various ways of deforming preexisting Provençal words. "Presumptuous" (*prezomtiu*) words, such as *displicina* instead of *disciplina*, "transport a syllable or a letter from one place to another in a word"; "overweening" (*outracujat*) words replace one part of a word with an extraneous part, and they are "proud" if the replacement occurs in the beginning of the word, "exaggerated" if in the middle, and so forth. Words can retain their original meaning in spite of additions, in which case they are *destargugat* (slowed down), or change their meaning, becoming *biaysshat* (biased or turned aside). When something is subtracted from the beginning of a word, it becomes *de-*

fectiu (defective); from the middle, *romput* (broken); from the end, *troncat* (cut off, vol. 2, pp. 202–6). With such names, distinctions, and definitions, the *Flors* takes account of, and tries to regulate, the troubadours' verbal license. We seem, almost, to be back in the game world of the "Twelve Latinities."[20]

The practical advice the *Flors del gay saber* gives on how to compose verse is also so completely formalistic that it seems facetious. The author begins with an artisanal comparison between composing rhymed verse and weaving: "Just as a weaver must first prepare and warp the threads and then weave the cloth, so a man who wants to make a *canso* or a *vers*, and has not yet thought of or imagined any *sentence*, must first search for four different kinds of rhymes" (vol. 3, pp. 376–80). The methods the *Flors* suggests for finding words with the desired rhyme endings involve running through the letters of the alphabet to stimulate the memory of words with different beginnings, but the same rhyme ending. For those who are really dense, the *Flors* suggests two methods of using the alphabet to construct artificial words that, if they "make sense," can then be used for rhymes (vol. 3, pp. 380–82). This preliminary process of finding and setting down rhymes the author calls "setting in place a warp of rhymes" ("Pauzat havem nostre ordimen dels rims," vol. 3, p. 384). Upon the framework of the rhymes, the text of the lyric will be woven (*tresat* or *entrebescat*).[21] The last advice the *Flors* gives troubadours is how to fill up space or plug holes:

> Vist havem quaysh pedas. perque cove que viram de pedas. et es pedas ajustamens de paraulas vueias que no fan re cant a la sentensa e fay se pedas per una dictio o motas o per tot un bordo.
>
> (vol. 3, p. 390)

> We have considered semi-chevilles; so that now it is fitting to consider chevilles. These chevilles [literally, worthless, stopgap pieces] are extra, empty words that have no effect on the sense, and they are composed of one word or several or an entire line.

Although the *Flors* counsels against the use of *pedas* in the *canso* or *vers*, it finds them useful in longer rhymed narratives. Is it by accident that the *Flors del gay saber* breaks off on the subject of how to say nothing with words?

Joseph Anglade has set 1358 for the date of completion of Guilhem Molinier's final version of the *Leys d'amors*, "laws of love," of the Toulouse Consistory.[22] The *Leys* considerably abbreviates the vernacular language instruction of the *Flors* and prefaces it with historical documents announcing the foundation of the Toulouse Consistory and outlining its regulations for membership and rules for participation in the annual May Day lyric competition it sponsored. According to the initial contest announcement of 1323, in the form of a circular letter in verse, the seven troubadours who founded the consistory, "following the practice of earlier troubadours," had been meeting Sundays in an enclosed garden in order to read their own compositions and correct one another's "errors":

Perque nos set, sequen lo cors
Dels trobadors qu'en son passat,
Havem a nostra voluntat
.I. loc meravilhos e bel,
On son retrayt mant dit noel,
El pus dels dimenges de l'an.
E no y suffrem re malestan,
Qu'essenhan l'us l'autre repren
E·l torna de son falhimen
A so que razos pot suffrir.
(*Leys*, vol. 1, pp. 10–11)

This is why we seven, following the spirit / of bygone troubadours, / have at our pleasure / a marvelous and beautiful place / where many new poems are performed [or, repeated, exposed, retraced] / most Sundays of the year; / and we do not allow there anything incongruous, / for one corrects the other, teaching, / and turns him from his error / toward that which right reason is able to permit.

Of the seven founders of the consistory, only one was noble, Bernart de Panasac, "donzel"; the others were bourgeois (a burgher, two bankers, two merchants, and a notary). Yet their Sunday "school" seems to have imitated the schoolish appreciative situation of earlier troubadour verse performed within the circle of the court: Guillaume IX and the companions he challenged to interpret his verse, Marcabru and the critical audience whom he dared to find any flaws in his texts, the *scola neblo*, and the "escolh Linhaure" of Raimbaut d'Orange.

As they institutionalized the consistory more and more from 1323 on, the seven Toulousain founders substituted the university for the grammar school or *schola cantorum* as a model for their secular imitation. Anglade has noted many similarities between the structures and intentions of the Toulouse Consistory and the University of Toulouse, which was founded in 1229, and, in 1245, forbidden by Innocent IV to use the vernacular ("language of the Philistines") in its theological teachings (vol. 4, pp. 33–39). Both the university and the consistory comprised an inner circle of masters who met in a particular place to teach, examine, and dispute; both had written regulations and officials such as a beadle and a chancellor; both granted degrees of bachelor and doctor involving similar ceremonies and conferring similar privileges. Most important, both university and consistory were organized for the study of texts: in one case, Latin texts; in the other, vernacular ones. The consistory authorized Guilhem Molinier, a lawyer by profession, to compile and draw up its official rules and the authoritative version of its teachings for reference in correcting and debating the fine points of vernacular composition during its annual contests. Whereas the ecclesiastical institution of the university taught theology, the secular (bourgeois) institution of the consistory taught its vernacular "gaya sciensa."

The *Leys d'amors* appear to regulate and sanctify troubadour verse. The earliest version of the rules for an annual May Day poetry competition describes a multistaged contest beginning with the singing of the composition and then the reading (*legir/vezir*) of it in writing, followed by correction of any misplaced word or other scriptural flaw, provided that the correction is consonant with reason:

> Et adonx auziretz chantar
> E legir de nostres dictatz;
> E se y vezetz motz mal pauzatz
> O tal re que be non estia,
> Vos ne faretz a vostra guia,
> Qu'a razo no contradirem.
> (vol. I, p. II)

And then you will listen to our poems / sung and read, / and if you see there words badly set down / or anything that ought not to be, / you will handle it after your fashion, / so that it does not contradict reason.

After this the troubadour was to be questioned and to defend and explain his verse in the course of a debate that would demonstrate his knowledge and prove that he had indeed composed the verse and not stolen it:

> Mas ben crezatz que sostendrem
> So qu'aurem fayt, en disputan;
> Quar responden et allegan
> Es conogut d'ome que sap,
> Can gent razon' e tray a cap
> So q'us altres li contraditz;

E cel que reman esbahitz
Tant que so qu'ades ha retrag
No sab razonar, l'autruy fag
Par que vol per sieu retenir,
Et enayssi fasescavir [*or*, fa ses cavir],
Car l'autruy saber vol emblar.
(vol. 1, pp. 11–12)

But you may well believe that we will defend / what we have done in debate, / because in answering and making justification under oath, / what a man knows becomes evident, / when he reasons nobly and draws to a conclusion / that which another contests in debate; / and he who remains dumbfounded / and does not know how to explain / what he has just performed, it seems as though / he wants to claim another's composition for his own, / and he does so without achieving it, / because he wants to steal another's knowledge.

The model for this contest is scholastic, but the earliest competitions may not have been as serious and pious as the rules make them out to be.

In the *Leys*, Guilhem announces that no awards will be given to men who write verse to deceive women or to sin in any other way. Composers of love lyrics that do not apply as well to love of God and the Virgin will be interrogated under oath about the object of their verse:

Ni aytan pauc no jutja hom ni dona degunas de las ditas joyas ad home que fa dictat per decebre femna o per autre peccat, per que cel que fa dictat d'amors que no·s pot applicar a l'amor de Dieu o de la sua mayre, sobre aysso deu esser enterrogatz et am sagramen, segon que sera la persona et als senhors mantenadors sera vist.
(vol. 2, p. 18)

Nor will a man award or give any of the aforesaid gifts to a man who makes a poem in order to deceive a woman or for any other sinful purpose, because he who makes a poem about a love that cannot apply to the love of God or of His mother should be interrogated under oath concerning this in accordance with his rank, and this will be witnessed by the assisting lords.

Scholastic debate turns, here, into a mini-Inquisition by the panel of seven "mantenador" judges, founders of the consistory. Furthermore, Guilhem advises that the verse be written in a clear way, with pleasant, open words, "am bels motz plazens et ubertz," and not in such a way that one has to engage in a never-ending labor of "constructing" (or construing, in the grammatical sense) the words, so that the lyric seems empty, like a bell without a knocker:

Quar del tot nos appar dezertz
E coma squila ses batalh
Dictatz que de bos motz defalh,
O cant lo cove costruir
Tant qu'om non pot a cap venir.
(vol. 1, p. 40)

> Because [it] seems completely empty to us, / and like a bell without a knocker, / a poem lacking in wise words [*sentence*], / or [a poem] that has to be construed / to such an extent that one is not able to reach a conclusion.

Guilhem, like Marcabru long before him, insists that the integrity of words must be respected. However, he recommends that the poet use obscure words, such as figures of speech and other metaphoric language, because these give pleasure to subtle interpreters, as long as they make "good sense":

Empero paraulas escuras,
O per semblansas o figuras,
Fin cor e subtil fan alegre,
Mas que sens bos s'en puesca segre.
(vol. 1, p. 41)

> However, words obscured / either by images [metaphoric language] or figures [of thought] / give pleasure to refined and subtle minds, / as long as the good sense can be followed.

The first of the eight criteria Guilhem lists for judging the best lyric is its high *sentence*; the fifth, how well the lyric can be applied to praise of God and Mary; the sixth, the *sciensa* of the composer, as demonstrated by his explanations. Formal considerations—such as the difficulty of the rhyme scheme and of the rhymes themselves, and the appropriateness of the melody—are sandwiched between these moral considerations (vol. 2, pp. 25–26). The rules of the consistory give every appearance of high seriousness.

5

Lo Gay Saber in Words and Pictures

Dire vos vuelh ses duptansa
daquest vers la comensansa.
Li mot fan manta semblansa.
Escotatz.
Qui ves proeza balansa
semblansa fay de malvatz.

I want to tell you unequivocally
the beginning of this verse.
Words take on many appearances.
Listen.
Whoever wavers in regard to valor
makes himself seem worthless.

—Marcabru, R songbook
(my italics)

Modern scholars have missed the gaiety in the "gaya sciensa." Joseph Anglade, for example, remarks that the preambles to several of the consistory's documents "seem to announce, sometimes, a Rabelaisian conception of life and even of poetry."[1] Nevertheless, he can find only one text, and that not in the *Leys* but in the earlier *Flors del gay saber*, that seems to satisfy such expectations, "La Porquiera" ("The Lady Swineherd"), an extremely vulgar burlesque of the *pastorelle* and *canso* genres that the *Flors* cites as an example of a particular rhyme scheme.[2] Alfred Jeanroy laments the monotonous conventionality of the lyrics crowned by the consistory, especially those praising the Virgin: "many of these compositions are frankly ridiculous, and the best do not rise above a barely respectable mediocrity. The lyrics to the Virgin, banal paraphrases of litanies, are nothing but monotonous *kyries* of sonorous substantives and epithets, often 'amphigorical' [obscure or equivocal]."[3] Jeanroy attributes the banality of the verse the consistory promoted to the tyranny of the Inquisition in Toulouse, but he questions the necessity for such extreme piety:

> Meridional poetry, in order to save its own life, believed it had to dress itself in the pious livery that it was so ill-prepared to wear; not only the

> *canso*, but the most frivolous genres, displayed the Cross; the Queen of Heaven became the only "lady" it was permitted to sing about. Was there really an absolute need for this? Like their predecessors at the end of the thirteenth century, the Guiraut Riquiers, the At de Monses, the Cerveri de Gironas, could not the poets of the fourteenth century have purified the expression of love, insisted on commonplaces of morality and the depiction of contemporary life, in order to lull the suspicions of the Church by means of a respectful neutrality and prudent abstention? Was the Inquisition in Toulouse really tyrannical enough to require this total confiscation?[4]

I think not. Compared to a century earlier, Inquisitorial activity in Toulouse was not very important in the mid-fourteenth century, when the consistory began to sponsor its annual competitions. For the most part, the consistory's teaching of grammar and composition in the vernacular seems to have been serious. The consistory was a bourgeois institution supported by the city, and it fulfilled the need, as troubadours had done for a long time, for secular language teaching and regulation of the vernacular. Bankers, merchants, notaries, and a great many other laymen needed to know how to write and read the vernacular; for legal purposes, they needed a writing that was both clear and authoritative. Nevertheless, the consistory's May Day lyric competitions seem to have mixed much game with the earnest. Almost every medieval institution, secular or religious, saw periodic festive reversals of a burlesque, dramatizing nature. The Inquisition does not seem to have stopped them; indeed, it may have had a stimulating effect. For example, at Pamiers, sometime before 1327, when the bishop took the punitive action of excommunicating participants, these festive burlesques seem to have mocked the clergy and also religious attempts to spiritualize love. According to the bishop's descriptive censure,[5] both clerics and laymen of Pamiers and Foix put on an open play ("ludum cenicum") in which members of the clergy were burlesqued in a procession with phallic candles, banners depicting male and female genitalia, boys disguised as women, and the singing of lewd songs. The name of this festivity, in the vernacular, was Cent Drutz, "the Hundred Lovers." The first day of May, which the consistory chose for its contest, was a traditional time for overturning the everyday rules of the social order, a time for festive license, for overthrowing *sentence* with *solas*.[6] The superficial piety of the winners of the consistory's May Day contests is, I believe, part of the verbal game in which, on this one weekend every year, the consistory revived the contestatory verbal facetiousness of the earliest troubadours.

In the first two contests, of 1324 and 1325, the lyrics that won the "joya d'amors," the prize of the golden violet (a reification of the *joi d'amors*), both seem to balance precariously between an apparently pious message and a thinly concealed obscene one involving conventional erotic puns and metaphors. The first winner, Arnaut Vidal's "Mayres de Dieu, verges pura," for which he was also honored with a "doctorate in *gaya sciensa*,"[7] ostensibly praises the Virgin Mary for redeeming the flesh, that is, humankind, by giving birth to Christ; but the lyric also seems in certain passages to supplicate the poet's own "rod," using the same metaphors, puns, and near-puns that Arnaut Daniel had made famous in his highly equivocal sestina "Lo ferm voler qu'el cor m'intra" ("The firm desire that enters my heart/body"): *arma* (soul/weapon), *verga* or *verge*(*s*) (rod/virgin), *cambra* (chamber/Venus's chamber).[8] The finesse of Arnaut Vidal's lyric lies in the way it suggests, but will not finally allow, obscene interpretation, as, for example, in the second strophe and the tornada:

Verges, ses par de par de plazensa,
Per nostr' amor, fos plazens
A Dieu, tan que'n pres nayshensa,
D'ont pueys per nos fo nayshens.
  Humilmens
Vos prec que m siatz guirens,
E que m portetz tal guirensa,
Qu'ieu an lay, ses defalensa,
On gaugz non es defalhens:
Car yeu, de cor, soy crezens
Que qui'n vos ha sa crezensa,
No mor perdurablamens,
Ans er ab gaugz revivens.

Si, cum soy lay autreyatz
On vertutz es autreyada,
En vostra cambra ondrada
Duzesca, car lay ondratz
  Mans desfagz,
  Si qu'els refatz.
Prec vos que de la re fada,
Verges, per qu'om es damnatz,
Si us plats, guirens no siatz.

Beneath the clichéd praise of Mary lie several possible erotic subtexts:

> Virgin ["rod"], without peer in regard to "pleasure," / for love of us you were "pleasing" / to God, so that you were born, / whence, for us, he was born. / Humbly / I pray that you will be my guarantor, / and will bear me such assurance / that I will go there, without fail, / where "joy" never fails; / because, in my heart, I believe [because, in my "horn," I am grow-

> ing or "swelling"][9] / that he who places his belief ["swelling"] in you / will not "die" eternally / but will "revive" in "joy."
>
> May it be granted me there / where "virtue" is recognized, / in your "chamber," honored / and soft, there where "honored" / are many "undone" men / until they are "restored." / I beseech you that, concerning the "foolish thing," / Virgin ["rod"], for which man is damned, / it may please you to be my guarantor.

This lyric seems to play not only on the virgin/"rod" pun, but also with the folk belief in the rejuvenating effects of the virgin vagina.[10] Erotic puns and metaphors in Arnaut Vidal's lyric are not the result of unconscious associations but, rather, of convention, of a tradition of deliberately facetious interpretation. The prizewinning lyric of 1325, Raimon d'Alayrac's "En amor ay mon refugi" ("In love I have my refuge," pp. 7–9), also seems to oscillate between piety and obscenity. The interpretive play here once again involves conventionally equivocal terms such as *cor* ("mind" or "spirit"/"body" or "horn") and extended metaphors that may be interpreted either "up" or "down," spiritualized or eroticized: seeking refuge in a castle (str. 1 and tornada), beating against the walls of a prison-box (str. 1), turning in circles like a millstone around a fixed center (str. 2), and so on. An eroticizing interpretation might produce the following innuendos in the third strophe:

E, no m don Dieus be, si m doli
De lies servir, ni se voli
Autramen morir ni viure;
Car ab lies tan m'acossoli,
Que de mals me te deliure:
Per qu'es dregtz donx que la m liure,
E fort e ferm m'i encastre.

> And may God never give me any good if I complain / about "serving" her, nor if I desire / otherwise to "die" or "live"; / because I "*con*sole" myself so well with her / that I am "unburdened" of discomfort, / whence it is right that I should go ["abandon myself"] there, / and, "strong and firm," "shut myself in."

From 1325 to 1345 there is a break in the collection of winning lyrics, but perusal of the winners from 1345 to 1484 leads to the conclusion that the interpretive game of the consistory's annual May Day poetry contest continued. Hypercorrect graphologies such as "quonquerir" instead of "conquerir" ("to conquer") avoid possible puns on *con* in a revealing fashion. Interpreting such verse is like playing a game of peek-a-boo; now we see the pun, now we don't. In order to appreciate more fully the game of these innuendos, we have to imagine the dramatic situation of the lyric's performance and of the examination of the composer, according to the contest rules, by a panel of troubadour inquisitors in order to make sure that the verse was not meant to serve any sinful purpose. As the composer tried to prove that his lyric was *really* about the Virgin Mary (much as Raimon de Cornet did for Bernart de Panasac's lyric), ambiguous images and expressions would come to the fore, probably much to the delight of the audience, although the pious interpretation alone would be officially sanctioned by the consistory. In this game of transgression, the range of possible connotations of key terms, such as *verges*, is constantly changing with the context of each new strophe, in order to keep the interpreter off balance. Sometimes strophes seem to divide down the middle, the first half praising the Virgin, the second the "rod," as in the following example from Huc del Valat's "Per l'amistat, on fort mon cor se fiza," a winner in 1372 (p. 18):

Sus totas etz coronada,
Gentils flors d'umilitat,
Amb excellent castetat,
  Que us dat
Lo pretz que nos enluminada;
Car vos etz de gaug la vena,
D'on cascus deu vos lausar,
Creyser e multiplicar
  E pensar
Quom dreg d'amor determena.

The first five lines describe the Virgin conventionally: "You are crowned above all, / noble flower of humility, / excellent in chastity, / who gave us [or, which gave you] / the high regard that enlightened us." The epithet and the praise of the next five lines, however, seem slightly odd: "because you are the vein of joy / whereby each ought to praise you, / to increase and multiply / and consider / that the custom of love requires it." In his edition of *Les Joies*, Jeanroy placed a question mark after the phrase "creyser e multiplicar." Indeed, these lines seem to evoke the context of May Day fertility rites; they seem to apply better to the *verga* than to the *verge*, to the "rod" as "vein of joy" (or of pleasure) whereby people increase and multiply. Such playful—and profound—worship of the Virgin / "rod" extended beyond the Toulouse Consistory's verbal May Day games. Pictorially, the punning conflation of virgin and "rod" (Latin *virgo* and *virga*) was represented in late medieval and Renaissance art, especially in images of Madonna and Child in which, as Leo Steinberg has argued, the Christ Child's phallus is deliberately central.[11]

But what evidence do we have that medieval interpreters actually did perceive specific puns in specific passages of troubadour verse, that they did play with the language of these lyrics? Most of the songbooks were conceived, compiled, and used as textbooks for serious study; yet some show marks of facetious interpretation, especially in pictures, but also in marginal annotations. All of the major songbooks except A have some sort of medieval or Renaissance marginal markings. In the M songbook (Paris, B.N. fr. 12474), for example, there is much underlining of Provençal words in the texts and definition of them in the margins in Italian. Sketches of pointing hands, brackets, or abbreviations for the word *nota* call attention to specific passages in many songbooks. Modern editors almost never mention these markings in their editions, for the reason that it is nearly impossible to be sure who the annotators were and exactly when they studied the texts. Generally speaking though, as the editor of the S songbook (Oxford, Bodleian Douce 269) remarked, these marginal *nota* signs indicate "proverbial or apocryphal" passages,[12] that is, what the readers perceived as the moral *sentence* or main ideas of the lyrics or else their autobiographical or historical content. In several songbooks, such as K, which is supposed to have been annotated by Petrarch and Bembo,[13] *senhals*, or code names, are underlined in the text and/or copied in the margins. Although the majority of marginal annotations, along with the *vidas* and *razos* collected in the songbooks, testify to late medieval attempts to read troubadour lyrics as autobiography or exemplum, there are a few marginal indications of playful interpretation.

In certain songbooks there are wavy bracketing lines (as in K and M) or lines (as in C) broken by crosshatches running alongside textual passages that seem to sustain both spiritualizing and eroticizing interpretations. Sometimes a pointing hand and a wavy line mark the same passage rich in *sentence* and *solas*. This happens, for instance, in the K songbook on fol. 91, col. 2, beside the most erotically suggestive passages of Arnaut Daniel's sestina "Lo ferm voler qu'el cor m'intra." The *senhal* "conort" that the same K annotator wrote three times in the margin beside Bernart de Ventadorn's "Lonc temps a qu'ieu non chantei mais" (fol. 17v) calls attention to the possible erotic undersenses of adjacent lines of the text such as "mas con li fos bons servire. E s'ieu n'ai pen' e martire." *Con* and *fos* (from *fotre*) are classic troubadour puns, and love "service" is too. The phonetic word division of the phrase "pene martire," as it appears in the manuscript, suggests phallic martyrdom as well as the grammatical sense, "pain and martyrdom" (*pen' e martire*). The *senhal* the annotator supplied (for it does not appear in the adjacent strophes) is in itself highly ambiguous, as are several other early troubadour *senhals* such as "genz conquis" (noble "conquest") and "bels" or "francs cavaliers" (beautiful or free-spirited "rider"). *Conort* means "welcome"; but, if divided and explained in a facetiously etymologizing way, it could mean "cunt place" (*con-ort*). Alongside the serious study of troubadour lyrics ran a facetious interpretive tradition. The marginal markings of the Provençal songbooks, some apparently in the same inks as the texts or illuminations, deserve closer scrutiny than they have yet received, or than I am willing to give them here, because they give evidence of reactions to troubadour verse that are, although not precisely datable, more nearly contemporary with the verse than our own interpretations.

It is hard to argue convincingly that a wavy line or a crosshatched one (as opposed to a straight line or another linear form) signals wordplay in the text it marks. Manuscript illuminations and marginal and *bas-de-page* sketches are more explicit signs of facetious interpretation. Before discussing the playful illuminations of the R and M songbooks and the medieval Gallic tradition of rebus-like illustrations of textual puns, I will describe, briefly, for comparative purposes, the didactic, historicizing iconographical tradition of the Italian songbooks. The Provençal marginal instructions for the illuminator of the A songbook, never erased, have been edited by D'Arco Silvio Avalle; these instructions briefly detail what the pictures in the initials should represent: for Marcabru, "a male jongleur without an instrument"; for Raimbaut d'Orange, "a knight on horseback"; for Giraut de Bornelh, "a master on a chair," and so on.[14] Often the execution went beyond the instructions. For example, Giraut is seated on a low couch, as he is supposed to be, but he also has a long gray beard and is pointing to an open book to signify his masterly status.

The illuminations in the A songbook are similar in principle, and also in many particulars, to those in other Italian songbooks, such as I, K, and N. Following the rubricated *vida* of each troubadour, within the frame of the initial letter of his first lyric there is a miniature representation of the troubadour illustrating something said about him in his *vida*. Generally speaking, if the *vida* notes his nobility, the troubadour is pictured on horseback; if the *vida* states that he was a cleric or a monk or that he entered a religious order, the figure has appropriate robes or a tonsure; if the *vida* says he was a good jongleur, he may play an instrument; if nothing is said about an ecclesiastical or noble status, or if the *vida* remarks his learning or verbal expertise, the troubadour figure is often represented in a declaiming or teaching pose, with arms outstretched, as if persuasively presenting or explaining the text of his lyric to an audience. For example, the K songbook (and also I, from the same atelier) illustrates Giraut de Bornelh's *vida* with a miniature of him declaiming with his two singers directly behind him. (See fig. 6.) In the same songbook, Marcabru and Bernart de Ventadorn also appear in frontal and profile versions of this same pose, with arms raised in expressive gestures. (See figs. 7 and 8.) In the I songbook, Arnaut de Maroill appears in ecclesiastical robes reading at a pulpit from a book, reflecting the remarks in his *vida* on his clerical status and his ability to sing well and "read the vernacular" ("lesia romans," Paris, B.N. fr. 854, fol. 46r). "Reading" here means reading aloud.

In the AIK songbooks, the form of the initial letter often serves as a kind of stage for the troubadour figure, who steps over the base of the initial or reaches beyond it with his hand. In the N songbook, the initial letter is more often interposed between the figure and the viewer, although the troubadour may reach an arm over the crossbar of an E, for example, or extend his foot beyond the base of the letter. The implication of either of these variants of the same iconographical structure—with the initial letter of the lyric text framing a full-length figure of the troubadour—is that the words of the lyric represent a historical truth having to do with the life of the poet. The N songbook (Pierpont Morgan 819) carries its realistic (or reifying) illustrations the furthest, by means of a peculiar system of pictorial "footnotes" at the base of the page or beside the columns of the text. These colored illustrations of proverbial expressions and actions described in the lyrics are keyed by red markings to the textual passages. When Giraut de Bornelh says in one *canso* that he does not "give two needles" for anything except serving his lady, the marginal note presents a drawing of two needles. (See fig. 9.) In several footnotes Love appears as a winged creature resembling religious images of angels or seraphim (as on fol. 58v). Such interpretive illustrations take the words and phrases of the lyric text as representations of real things and events.

In contrast to the historicizing illuminations of the Italian songbooks, the initials of the R songbook (Paris, B.N. fr. 22543) are very playful and innovative. This songbook, written in Languedoc, is oriented more toward performance and role-playing than toward scholarly exegesis of the lyrics. Although it contains *vidas*, it groups them together at the front of the compilation, and it places near the end the large, chronologically ordered and dated collection of Guiraut Riquier's verse (including his *razo* on the "menor ters"). The bulk of the R songbook is devoted to presenting the texts of the lyrics and to giving musical notation for about 160 (out of 1,110) of them.[15] R is the only major songbook, and the only one written in Languedoc, to include music, although one annotator of a songbook written in Provence, E (Paris, B.N. fr. 1749), gives some marginal indications concerning the melodic performance of several lyrics.[16] The performative focus of the R songbook is mirrored in its initials. These often picture, on the back leg of the letter, facing away from the text, a jongleuresque, masklike face with outstretched tongue tipped by a gold ball. (See figs. 10–12.) Elsewhere in the R songbook, in a very light ink drawing emanating from the extension of a letter at the base of fol. 21v, a series of small circles comes out of the mouth of a head in profile wearing a long, pointed cap. These circles probably represent a sequence of sounds or syllables. This is the meaning, as well, of the small gold balls touching, or at a short distance from, the tips of the tongues of the jongleuresque faces on the backs of initial letters. It is as if a word—or sound or syllable—had just left the jongleur's tongue. Other gold, red, and green balls appear at other places within and without the space of the initial letters, and the illuminator juggles with their placement so as to vary the configuration of the balls with each new initial. The formalist aesthetic of these initials in the R songbook—with their carefully studied variation of a limited number of colors and shapes—corresponds to and perfectly illustrates the aesthetic of early troubadour verse, with its infinite variations on a limited set of topics, key terms, and verse patterns. The R songbook's initials bear very close attention.[17]

I will focus, for now, on the noses of the jongleuresque masks, which, by their varying sizes, shapes, and inclinations, sometimes seem to comment on the lyrics by suggesting the opening tone or mood of performance. In medieval (and modern) folk belief, the size of the nose, as Bakhtin reminded us, signals the size of the penis.[18] The bigger the nose, the bigger the penis, and the more lascivious (or less spiritual) the nose's owner. This belief is reflected, for example, in the saying that the author of the *Art of Love*, Publius Ovidus *Naso*, was so named for the size of his nose ("pour quantité du nez").[19] Like modern clowns, and Roman mimes and actors of farce, whose masks displayed huge, grotesque noses,[20] some medieval jongleurs played with the imagined resemblance between noses and penises; they assumed burlesque names. Guillem Mita ("Big-nosed Trickster") was the name of the jongleur who was proclaimed "universal king of *histriones*" in 1174 at a great feast of reconciliation and merriment at the court of Beaucaire;[21] and the vituperous troubadour Guillem de Berguedan conflated two phallic metaphors by calling his jongleur by the name Nas-de-corn ("Horn-nose"). The R songbook's initials display every possible shape for a human nose and many shapes of birdlike beaks, the latter probably because, in Provençal, *bec* was slang for the nose and also for the penis.[22] These bird beaks are wide open in song, tongues outstretched with gold balls at the tips, just as for the jongleuresque faces. While some of the noses in the R songbook are strikingly elongated or pointed, others droop expressively, and a very large number seem to be smashed in or flattened. How these short noses got to be that way is suggested by an image at the top of fol. 52v. (See fig. 10.) There, standing on an initial *L* backed by an orange-beaked, birdlike face, a blacksmith or *fabre* dressed in an apron with his hair tied back by a kerchief holds up a hammer in one hand and with the other uses long-handled tongs to pinch the nose of an angry-looking, chimerical creature. The lyric by "Fabre d'Uzest" that this scene illustrates seems to begin on the subject of *gay saber*: "It is time to rejoice, and, although I am not boastful, / I want to be a singer and demonstrate my knowledge." The orange-beaked mask suggests the joyful mood of the opening lines. If one reads further into the lyric, one finds that it is really about "measure" (a proper time and place for everything) and about reining in folly. This is what the pinching of the chimera's nose probably signifies: the suppression of verbal *foudatz*, which had so much to do with phallic bravado, and the "forging" by Fabre d'Uzest of good "usage" or manners.

I would not go so far as to claim that every form of nose in this songbook represents an interpretation of the facing lyric, because the illuminator's main interest is in variation; but occasionally he does use the form of the nose on the outer face of the letter to suggest the mood of the lyric. Let me give a few examples. On fol. 69r, the very long, needle-shaped, down-pointing nose of the mask suggests the biting criticism and negative tone of Peire Cardenal's *sirventes* beginning "Falsedat e desmezura an batalh enpreza." (See fig. 11.) On fol. 53v, a mask with a long, flat nose that droops below the level of the outstretched tongue illustrates the depressed mood of the first lines of Aimeric de Belenoi's "Ailas perque vieu loniamen ni dura / sel que tot jorn vei creisser sa dolor" ("Alas, why does the man live long and endure, / who every day sees his suffering increase"). Likewise, the long, droopy nose of fol. 45r illustrates the "sadness" and "brokenhearted" state Gaucelm Faidit mentions near the end of the first strophe of his "Pel joi del temps qu'es floritz." For the famous lyric in which Bernart de Ventadorn requests counsel over the problem of his lady's unfaithfulness to him with other lovers, "Ar m'acosselhatz senhors" (fol. 57v), the lips of the jongleur mask protrude beyond the nose, which is so flat that it almost seems to have been cut off. (See fig. 12.) The initial letter of Bernart's very next song, "La dossa votz ay auzida," features a mask with a swollen, uplifted nose and intense, forward-staring eyes that suggest possible erotic senses of the word *cor* in the first strophe in proximity to words or phrases such as "salhida" ("leaped"), "cossirier" ("desire"), "me levia" ("lifted me up"), and "m'assazona" ("ripened" or "softened").

In addition to the jongleuresque faces on the back sides of the initial letters—or, occasionally, replacing the flower or leaf terminals of extensions of letters—the R songbook's initials sometimes contain the head of a troubadour, as on fol. 20v, where the initial *P* of a *sirventes* by Bertran de Born frames a head in helmet and neck guard representing the bellicose Bertran. (See also fig. 12.) Such double-faced initials, with the jongleur mask looking out from the text and the head within the letter usually looking toward the text, may suggest the relationship between poet and persona. However, many of the interior heads are not realistically depicted; there are glowering green faces, heads with balls emanating from their mouths, animal and bird heads, and, even more frequently, stylized filler of flower and leaf forms and colored balls against variegated backgrounds. Never does one find, as in the Italian songbooks, a full-length figure of a troubadour framed in the initial letter. Although it is difficult to be certain of this, the illuminator's depiction of the head (Provençal *cap*) alone in the space of the initial letter may be based on a playful analogy between the position of the head with respect to the human body, and the position of the first initial with respect to the body of the following text.[23] If so, even the more realistic heads within the R songbook's initials are not depictions of individual troubadours as men, but playful commentaries on the forms of the text. The illuminator of the C songbook, which was also written in Languedoc, may be playing a slightly different game with the notion of "heading" when he depicts various colors and shapes of hats on a series of heads within initial letters, as, for example, on fol. 364v, fol. 366r (see fig. 13), and also on fol. 363v, where a tonsured male head with a bird's hooked beak in place of a nose and ostrichlike legs and feet in place of a neck wears a long hat that curves upward and forward to terminate in a hooded feminine head. A similar sort of playful formal analogy between the position of *A* at the head of the alphabet and the position of the head on the body may explain the tendency in the Italian S songbook (which contains no illuminated capitals) for the initial letter *A* to terminate in an ink sketch of an animal, bird, or human head (on pp. 190, 208, 217, 230, and 241, for example).

Comparison of the Italian and southern French traditions of illuminating songbooks is made difficult by the ablation of so many of the illuminations in two of the southern French songbooks, E and C. Nevertheless, the French illuminations seem much more deliberately playful, irregular, and eclectic than the Italian ones—as if to illustrate the dictum "the more interpretations the better, as long as each is good." Whoever cut the pictures out of the C songbook tired near the end of the massive manuscript. In the remaining illuminated initials, there is a little of every iconographical tradition. There are several initial *I*s (fols. 258r, 326v, 340r) filled with various woven or knotted patterns reminiscent of much earlier woven initials that played on the idea of the text as textile. (See fig. 14.) There are full-length figures of several of the troubadours in persuasive, exegetical poses similar to those in the AIK songbooks, but much larger. On fol. 202v, for example, Arnaut Daniel stands on the base of the letter *L* beginning his sestina "Lo ferm voler qu'el cor m'intra"; in his right hand he holds a small book, half concealed by his robes, and he points with the index finger of his upraised left hand at the facing text. (See fig. 15.) Near the end of the manuscript, instead of full-length troubadour figures we find the heads or busts previously mentioned; although larger, these somewhat resemble the heads within the initials of the R songbook. Inside several initials, there are birds and beasts; many of these are the same animals one finds in the *bas-de-page* sketches of the M songbook: peacocks, rams, dogs, lions. On fol. 214r in the C songbook, for example, there is a lion with a forked, foliagelike tail in the initial beginning a lyric by Jaufre Rudel. (See fig. 16.) Most interesting and, once again, most similar to the *bas-de-page* grotesques of the M songbook are the chimerical creatures that the C illuminator depicts within the spaces of the initial letters, especially in symmetrically divided letters such as *B*, *E*, *M*, or *S*, as if the bilaterality of the letter suggested the chimerical creature composed of two or more species.

Just as I treated in greater detail the R songbook's nose play, I will dwell for a moment on the C songbook's chimeras. These seem to suggest, by their various combinations of the human and the bestial, the two "sides" to early troubadour verse. Many of the C songbook's chimeras have a sacred-looking top and a profane bottom. Monastic robes and hoods cover the torsos, or at least the heads and necks, and human heads emerge from the hoods, while the denuded bottom parts exhibit bestial rumps, hooves, or paws and terminate in serpentine tails. Such is the case, for example, in the initial *L* on fol. 212v, where the eyeballs of the hooded head look upward in a pious way, while the bestial hindquarters end in a knotted and double-pronged tail. (See fig. 17.) On fol. 238v, the hooded man's head looks upward at the end of a flamingolike neck; the torso is ostrichlike, with small wings, and the tail is serpentine. Versions of this same chimerical model with a human top and an obscene bestial bottom also appear on fols. 253v, 344v, and 363v. In the two vertical compartments of an initial *M* on fol. 210r, there are complementary chimeras. On the left side, the creature has a pious top and bestial bottom; on the right side, the order is reversed, and a beak with a long, leafy-tipped tongue emerges from the hood, while a human face appears on the nude beast's rump. (See fig. 18.) Likewise, on fol. 365r in an initial *T*, the order of things is reversed, and the beast appears on top, the human on bottom; the chimera's head is a dog's, the neck and body are swanlike, with wings; the legs and feet are human, and the tail is a serpent's. In the bottom horizontal compartment of the initial *E* on fol. 344v, there is a particularly pious chimera in monastic robes with an upraised gaze and more than the usual amount of the bestial hindquarters concealed; in the top compartment, directly above the praying head, appears a large, front-facing male head attached directly to a pair of outspread legs with foliage sprouting in place of a phallus. (See fig. 19.)

Such chimeras, in themselves, are not as original as they might seem. Jurgis Baltrušaitis gives an antique example of a crouching chimera (or *grylle*) closely resembling that in the top space of the *E* just described. Likewise, he gives examples, from late-thirteenth- and fourteenth-century books of hours and psalters, of chimeras that combine bestial bottoms with robed and hooded, pious tops, some even in poses of supplication or devotion.[24] However, the prior or contemporary use of similar chimeras in other contexts does not excuse us from trying to understand more specifically how and why they are used in the context of the C songbook and, in different forms, in other Provençal songbooks as well. Medieval men did not borrow as blindly as we often like to think.

The different ways different songbooks use chimeras suggest different traditions of interpreting the letter and the lyric. In the C songbook, chimeras appear *inside* the initial letters, framed by the letter in much the same way as the full-length troubadour figures in the AIKN songbooks. The iconographical difference is significant. For the serious, didactic illuminator/reader of the Italian tradition, the letter—or the lyric—represents a historical or moral truth; it represents life. For the facetious, playful illuminator/reader, on the other hand, the letter is an enigmatic sign, the lyric a puzzle represented by the chimerical beast, an unreal, nonsensical creature composed of such diverse parts that it is impossible to construe or define, a shape-shifter.[25]

The Italian manuscripts of the late Middle Ages are not as rich in chimeras as are French, English, and German manuscripts. Nevertheless, the Italian songbooks are not completely devoid of changeling creatures. The AIKN manuscripts' initials commonly sprout into fanciful combinations of foliage. Sometimes a chimerical beast is part of this growth, which evolves out of the illustrators' play with the shape of the letter or, rather, with the letter's extensions. In Italian manuscripts, the foliage, and sometimes with it the chimera, grows at the place where the letter begins or ends; the basic shape or body of the letter (its distinguishing common form) is not affected by such flourishes, but remains enclosed within its regularizing square frame. For example, a dragonlike creature grows out of the extension of an initial *S* in the I songbook. (See fig. 20.) More rarely, the entire initial may be drawn in the shape of a chimerical beast, as in the N songbook, where an *S* sometimes appears with two serpentine heads.

In the R songbook, from Languedoc, the illuminator's playful variation of the forms of the letter goes much further than in the Italian songbooks. Chimerical creatures sprout everywhere from the extensions of the letters, each chimera slightly different from its predecessor, and some nearly detaching themselves into anecdotal marginal illuminations (as with the pinching of the chimera's nose on fol. 52v, fig. 10). Furthermore, the chimeras of the R songbook are not relegated to the fringes and outermost boundaries of the letter, but make up its very body. With a grotesque jongleuresque head on the back leg of so many initials, and considerable variation in the basically square shape of the body of the initial, the letter itself in the R songbook seems chimerical. The M songbook's chimeras, on the other hand, are entirely detached from the letter in *bas-de-page* illuminations that burlesque the idealism of the vignettes and lyrics above. These I will treat more thoroughly later.

The tradition of playing with the form of the letter, turning its body or extensions into chimerical beasts, is just as old as the shapes of the chimeras or *grylles* that the C songbook encloses within some of its initials. In the *Book of Kells*' carpet pages illustrating biblical texts such as "Liber generationis" or "Christi autem generatio" or "In principio erat verbum," chimerical letters suggest the enormous generative power and vitality of the divine word, which defies containment. Illustrating the texts of troubadour lyrics in the Provençal songbooks, such play suggests the difficulty of controlling the letter or, more precisely, of controlling the significations of the letter, symbolized visually by its shape-shifting, chimerical form. In the didactic Italian songbooks, chimeras are relegated to the extensions of the letters; in the R songbook, they proliferate everywhere, thereby suggesting that playful interpretation of troubadour verse was still practiced in southern France in the fourteenth century. Such letters are, in Bakhtin's terms, carnivalesque (rather than classical) bodies.[26] The meaning of these chimerical letters depends partly on what we are looking for in them; different people will see different things, just as one reader may understand the letters *neblo* on a manuscript page as "Sir Eble" and another may understand "foggy." In the surviving initials of the C songbook, enigma is even more central. Instead of framing an image of the troubadour as a man, many of the initial letters frame a chimera, image of equivocation, of the ambiguity of the letter as sign, and of the playfully foolish aesthetic of early troubadour verse. The chimerical letters of the Provençal songbooks suggest medieval men's awareness that the meaning of the letter depends on its interpreter and on how he perceives its context.

The illuminations of the M songbook (Paris, B.N. fr. 12474) illustrate both the seriously historicizing, idealizing tradition and the facetious, burlesque tradition of interpreting troubadour verse. The northern French format of the historiated initials is different from that in any other Provençal songbook. The initial itself is rather small, and its interior space is always filled by stylized vegetal motifs. Resting on the top of the initial's square golden frame is a larger square frame approximately equivalent in width to the column of letters of the text. Within the unobstructed space of this large frame, against a solid gold background, a full-length figure of the troubadour is depicted.

The first vignette is exceptional; it sets a didactic tone for the collection. In this vignette, Giraut de Bornelh appears as a master sitting in a high chair with his legs graciously crossed. He has lifted his right arm and points upward with his index finger, as if explaining the text of the book that lies open in front of him on the high-pedestaled lectern. (See fig. 21.) After this first vignette, most of the rest present the different troubadours, no matter what their social estate or profession, as courtly riders in garden settings. These vignettes, each with its gold background, tree to the side, and tuft of grass under the horse's hooves, seem to represent the courtly ideal of the *loc aizi* or *locus amoenus*. They frame an image of perfection. In the Italian songbooks, it is conventional to present Folquet de Marseille as the bishop he later became; an image of him in episcopal robes opens the I songbook, for example. However, in the M songbook there is nothing to distinguish Folquet (fol. 25r) from Aimeric de Peguilhan. (See fig. 22.) Both appear as handsome young men holding green wands and dressed in blue robes trimmed with fur. The horses in these vignettes vary more than their stylized riders. Among the few iconographic variations is the mirror Peire Cardenal holds up (emblem of his didacticism) instead of the usual green wand. (See fig. 23.) Both Bertran de Born (fol. 227r) and Peire Vidal (fig. 24) are pictured in arms on chargers riding at full tilt, probably in illustration of the knightly verbal bravado of their lyrics. Jaufre Rudel kisses his lady—and does not seem to be on the verge of fainting—in a garden. (See fig. 25.)

At the bottom of the columns headed by these idealizing vignettes of the troubadours appear unframed grotesque figures and scenes. These are not realistic renditions of words or phrases in the lyric texts, like the "footnotes" of the Italian N songbook, but, rather, subversive burlesques that may witness to the facetious tradition of interpreting troubadour lyrics. For example, Bernart de Ventadorn often vaunts his personal refinement or pure heart (*fin cor*) in his verse, yet in some contexts a baser understanding of Bernart's *cor* (as "horn," meaning anus or penis) works as well. Pierre Bec has noted that several scatological parodies of Bernart's verse seem to have been stimulated by punning etymological interpretation of Bernart's place name as *Ventador*, "one who blows or breaks wind."[27] Below the vignette of Bernart as courtly rider in the M songbook is a colored sketch of two dogs, one blowing, with much fanfare, a long horn with a banner on it into the rear of the other dog. (See fig. 26.) This picture also calls to mind the blatantly vulgar expression "cornar al cul" used in the three-way debate among "Raimond de Durfort," "Turc Malec," and Arnaut Daniel.[28] However one chooses to interpret this *bas-de-page* scene, it is subversive of the ideal courtly scene regularly framed in the vignette above.

In the same M songbook, at the top of the first column of fol. 51r, Peire Vidal swings his sword on his charging war-horse; at the bottom of the column, a small dog pounds with a very long pestle in a mortar. (See fig. 24.) Under the figure of Jaufre Rudel embracing his lady in the garden (fol. 165r) is a chase scene over rough terrain in which a man sticks a long-poled spear through the flesh of the hindquarters (or into the anus?) of a fleeing wild pig. (See fig. 25.) Is this a vulgar burlesque of Jaufre's most famous expression, *amor de lonh*, love from afar? The most debasing of these *bas-de-page* scenes occurs on fol. 89r below the vignette of Aimeric de Peguilhan. (See fig. 22.) A chimerical creature (top half man, bottom half serpentine) plays a flute and tabor (oral and percussion metaphors for sex),[29] while a small human figure sitting on the chimera's head with bared buttocks urinates or defecates in a stream of red over the chimera. Raimbaut d'Orange (fol. 135r), Raimbaut de Vaqueiras (fol. 103r), Raimon de Miraval (fig. 27), and Peire Cardenal (fig. 23) all have chimeras with human tops and fishy or serpentine tails below their idealized vignettes. The aggressiveness of these chimeras, armed with clubs or swords and bucklers, contrasts with the grace of the courtly riders in the garden scenes above; furthermore, the changeling nature of the chimeras may suggest the troubadours' interpretive combats.[30] In addition to chimeras, there are also a number of regular beasts—lions, birds, and the like—illuminated in gold in the lower margins beneath the larger vignettes. I see no burlesque intention behind these, although they may be more closely related to the works of particular poets than first appears. Daude de Pradas, for example, author of a treatise on hunting birds (*Dels auzels cassadors*), has a hunting bird beneath his vignette on fol. 167r. Below the large unfinished vignette for Bertran de Born on fol. 229r, at the base of the column, a wolfish creature stands with two long horns stuck through a tree trunk, perhaps in mocking commentary on Bertran's bellicose verbal posture.

In the illuminations of the M songbook, the "high" and the "low" interpretations of troubadour verse have their separate places and relative values. The highly serious icons have a larger and more important space linked to the initial letters heading the columns. Grotesque and chimerical creatures do not, in this songbook, grow out of the form of the letter itself or appear framed within the interior space of the letter. Rather, they are detached and relegated to the lower margin, from which they make their subversive commentary. In the M songbook, burlesque interpretation seems to be an occasional option, while high seriousness is the rule. The letter per se is not perceived as enigmatic or unpredictable.

Without analyzing them in great detail, we have generally attributed the grotesques and drôleries of medieval pictorial representation, as well as the monstrous capitals and gargoyles of medieval sculpture, to the survival of pagan superstitions (belief in the efficacy of frightening "power" symbols or the practice of ritual obscenity)[31] or to the flights of fantasy of daydreaming monks and artisans engaged in the monotonous labor of exacting reproduction or copying. These explanations of the origins of medieval grotesques are surely correct in many cases, although there may be consciously playful or contestatory motivations as well. To St. Bernard, in his famous letter to the Abbot of St. Thierry after 1120, representations of ridiculous and deformed creatures in cloisters and other religious contexts profaned and undercut the authority of the religious structure (text or temple) and detracted from its gravity:

> But in the cloister, under the eyes of the Brethren who read there, what profit is there in those ridiculous monsters, in that marvelous and deformed comeliness, that comely deformity? To what purpose are those unclean apes, those fierce lions, those monstrous centaurs, those halfmen?[32]

Bernard does not seem to have been placated by the conventional apology that such monstrous creatures were representations of sin and evil and served to teach moral lessons. Rather, Bernard was concerned about the burlesque and risible effect of such "irregular" shapes—obscene apes, centaurs, and chimerical collages of man and beast. He seems to have read a sinful or destructive intention behind such forms.

In *Images in the Margins of Gothic Manuscripts*, Lilian Randall attributes grotesque figures to "the medieval propensity for juxtaposition of contrasting elements," to a "provocation by contrast," the sacred text evoking the profane "context" of the marginal commentary. She notes that liturgical books are much more copiously illustrated in the margins than secular texts and argues that marginal drôleries in medieval manuscripts are not gratuitous:

> In a surprising number of instances a *raison d'être*, even for totally inappropriate motifs, does exist. The problem for the iconographer is dual, namely recognition and interpretation. It is most easily solved when the subjects in the margins are directly related to their adjoining text or miniature. Allusions to a more remote frame of reference such as local usages, prejudices, or current events are obviously far more difficult to fathom, particularly since they are often cloaked in absurd or amusing disguise.[33]

Randall gives the example of a manuscript produced under the aegis of the Abbot of St. Germain d'Auxerre, which has a playful "heraldic" *bas-de-page* sketch of an ape dressed like an abbot holding a skull up in the air with its hands. Abbot Guy de Munois (1285–1309) commissioned a seal with just such a representation and the punning inscription, "abbe de singe air main d'os serre."[34] Thus the illustration of the monkey aping an abbot is a complex riddle or rebus; it is a figurative representation of a series of verbal puns that involve the rearrangement of a sequence of syllables into different words meaning different things: the monkey with its hands in the air = "singe air main" = Saint Germain, and the holding up of the skull = "d'os serre" = D'Auxerre. This visual drôlerie identifies the provenance and patron of the manuscript; the relationship of the *bas-de-page* illustration to the text is clear only to those who can solve the riddling rebus. Such punning play is purposeful, and it somewhat resembles the concealment of a medieval author's or scribe's name in an anagram, a series of beginning or final letters of verse lines, or in another figure or pattern of letters woven into the text in such a way that, to discover it, the interpreter must read the text in a different direction or manner than he conventionally would.[35]

It is my impression that many of the grotesques and drôleries that ornament the borders of the pages of medieval religious or strongly idealizing secular texts are signs of facetious interpretive *jonglerie*, visual representations of the manuscript-makers' playful oral and manual performance of the sounds and syllables and the visual signs of the text. Language, spoken and/or written, is not a perfect instrument for conveying meaning now and was even less so before mechanical printing and universal vernacular education. Interpreting spoken texts and, even more so, medieval written ones involves many false combinations and associations, most of which never reach consciousness or are extremely quickly forgotten once censored and discarded in favor of the "right" or appropriate interpretation in the particular context. To eliminate multiple, conflicting meanings is the work of the grammarian and lawmaker; to evoke them, the work of the poet, the dreamer, and sometimes even the medieval manuscript illuminator. There is something to the theory that medieval marginalia of a grotesque or fantastic nature, like the doodles in student notebooks today, are the signs of daydreams. The dream world is a play world divorced or distanced from reality, outside its bounds; the marginal space is likewise a free space outside the bounds of the central textual space, ruled off from it. The dream is a kind of commentary on regular thought, a metatext that expresses, mainly in images but also in words, all sorts of puns and verbal connections and combinations that would be—indeed, probably have been—censored in the serious text of waking thought.[36] Likewise, the marginalia of medieval manuscripts may express, in "disguised" visual form, puns and other associations and alternate meanings that have arisen during the oral and manual performance of the text on paper but have had to be censored as inappropriate to the serious intention of the sacred liturgical or idealizing secular text. In this respect, marginal drôleries, like dreams, restore the wholeness or richness of possible senses to the interpretive process, and yet they do so in a well-ordered—ultimately stabilizing rather than subversive—way that takes account of alterity without undermining the authority of the central text. Chimeras and grotesques relegated to the margins are far less subversively relativizing than those that make up the very shape of the letter, as they do in the R songbook.

There is, however, a difference between the individual person's idiosyncratic dream and the more conventional and consciously playful marginal illustrations of a medieval manuscript illuminator. This difference probably results from the social (as opposed to private, individual) situations of textual performance and interpretation in the Middle Ages. A popular proverb expressed the relativity of interpretation with the phrase "so many heads, so many meanings" ("tant ciés, tant sentences").[37] Nevertheless, medieval marginal drôleries are not usually the product of a lone illuminator's daydreams, but, rather, of linguistic performances and games played in small groups, games like the troubadours', that involved the deliberate or chance discovery of equivocal senses of the text.

The condition for much of the wordplay illustrated in the margins of medieval religious or idealizing secular texts seems to have been the slow-motion performance or oral re-creation of the verbal text during the course of writing it in a scriptorium or atelier, or of singing it with elaborate vocalizations. Liturgical song often involved suspending syllables for lengthy periods, thus breaking up words; such performance, as also the scribal writing of texts, required a formalistic concentration on the parts, with consequent loss of awareness of the meaning of the whole or of a controlling idea—concentration on the senses rather than on the sense. The visual figure in the margin—or, sometimes, growing out of the letter into the marginal space—is often a playful interpretation of selected syllables of the text, not a representation of the text's general meaning or *sentence*. For example, on several successive pages of a thirteenth-century Provençal catechism written in Languedoc (Paris, B.N. fr. 2427), the illuminator turned the usual foliage appendages of the initial letters into hands holding ejaculating penises, and then he lightly disguised these with the outlines in white ink of foliage. (See fig. 28.) Leaves are, of course, the usual biblical and statuary cover for the private parts, but that does not exclude a trilogy of macaronic puns from motivating the visual association as well: *folias* meant "leaves" (also of a book); *folhas* meant "folly" or "sin"; and an educated man might also be aware of the Greek *phallos* (taken over into Latin as phallus and linked visually with foliage, as we have seen, in the case of ancient and medieval chimeras that sprout foliage in place of a phallus). When we turn to the Provençal text opposite, we discover that certain words in the text have inspired this eroticizing visual play. On fol. 45v, for example, the lines preceding the initial contain a number of words that can be understood, quite apart from the general sense of the passage, in an erotic way: "Vertutz fa hom ardit . . . fort . . . ferm . . . durable" ("Virtue [or, virility] makes a man ardent . . . strong . . . firm

. . . long-lasting"). In the passage on fol. 47r, the wordplay is based on the evocative syllable *cor*: "Vera nobleza ven a hom de cor franc gentil & debonaire" ("True nobility comes to a man from having a heart [or, 'horn'] that is generous [or, free], genteel, and from good stock"). On fol. 40r, the principal suggestive syllables are the *con*s of the words *conquerir* and *conoisser*, and the *vi* of *vida*, and the word *vertutz*, once again meaning "virility": "Comensament de parvenir a bona vida e conquerir vertutz es conoisser." While reading the religious text (or while writing it, if he was also the scribe, not impossible in this case), the illuminator engaged in a bit of juggling with the sense of the syllables. He reproduced his playful experience of the text and commented on the hidden, erotic sense he had discovered in it by means of an analogous visual play with penises and leafy covers. A "horny" illuminator? Perhaps, but individual desire is not the only motivation for his play; his word games, down to the very puns he discovers and covers, are conventional ones of troubadour and jongleuresque entertainment.

The wordplay illustrated in the margins of medieval manuscripts is not always profanatory in a vulgar or erotic way, but it often does involve a deliberately contradictory, materialistic interpretation of the ideal or abstract. We have already mentioned "head" play in initials heading lyrics and larger segments of the Provençal songbooks C and R. There is comparable play with the divisions of the text in a twelfth-century Cistercian manuscript of Gregory's *Moralia in Job*. A series of initials heading sections of the *Moralia* shows monks at work cutting down a tree, chopping wood, cutting grain. These miniatures have always been assumed to bear no relationship to Gregory's message, but to be realistic, humorous depictions of everyday life in an early Cistercian monastery.[38] Although these images do not comment on Gregory's text, they may comment playfully on the text as artifact, the text that the illuminator is articulating with his designs, working to shape, while his brothers work outside cutting and clearing and shaping the land.

With figurative initials, like the capitals that top the columns of a Romanesque religious building, the illuminator marks the divisions of the text. The Latin word for chapter or paragraph, that is, for the divisions of the text, is *capitulum* and derives from the same root as *caput* ("head"). A capital letter "heads" or "caps" the text; but it also divides the text into parts, and this function links the "capital" with the verb *capulare*, "to cut," especially "to cut wood." Thus, the illuminator of the *Moralia* presents a capital *I* in the form of a tree whose height matches that of the adjacent column of a new chapter.[39] In the treetop, a lay brother has just sawed off the branches that would exceed the height of the rubric of the new section, and, at the base of the column and of the tree, a monk hacks away at the trunk. This image may be a playful representation of the illuminator's and scribe's own activity of dividing the text (*capulare*) with capitals into *capitula*. The visual play rests on verbal play with the possible meanings of the syllable *cap* in various combinations. In other situations artists play with the manuscript page as "leaf" (Latin *folium*, Provençal *folh* or *folha*) to imagine a visual analogy between the column of letters and the tree trunk. In the right margin of the R songbook, for example, a thick branch grows out of the "trunk" of a column of letters on fol. 21r (see fig. 29); in another variation of the same playful analogizing, the *incipit* of the next folio is written on the topmost green leaves of a tree whose uppermost twigs alone we see at the bottom right of fol. 30v, but whose trunk we must imagine stretching down the column of fol. 31r, the next folio page (see fig. 30). The illuminator juggled with visual and aural forms. Etymologizing play with the same root syllable may be the reason for the differently shaped and colored hats (Provençal *capel*) on the heads in the C songbook, mentioned earlier. Likewise, the elaborately woven initials that we find, for example, in Bibles from St. Martial of Limoges, a lectionary from Montmajor, a gradual from Albi,[40] and other eleventh- and twelfth-century religious texts contemporary with the earliest troubadour verse, as well as in the C songbook, all illustrate the old "textual" analogy between ruling the page and warping, writing and weaving, and the playful perception of the text as textile. (See figs. 4, 5, 14.)

Other songbooks in the large St. Martial collection are a fecund source of initials that figuratively represent the illuminator's—or his monastic fellows'—juggling with the syllables and the meaning of the song text. The acrobatics of the letter are analogous to and illustrative of the illuminator's *jonglerie* with the letters, syllables, and words of the text he is ornamenting and, in so doing, commenting upon. A mid-eleventh-century St. Martial trope collection (Paris, B.N. lat. 1119), for example, forms a *Q* with the body of a man contorted until his bright red, outstretched tongue faces his own buttocks on fol. 69r. (See fig. 31.) In this manuscript, figures with open mouths and outstretched tongues illustrate joyous song. On one level, the illuminator may be playing with the sound of the letter *Q* and of a vernacular slang word, *cul* ("tail"). Similarly, on fol. 70v of the same songbook we find a *Q* in the shape of a dog biting its tail. However, the human *Q* may also illustrate the last word of the adjacent text of the Latin song, "collaudant," an expression of communal praise. When intoned slowly with separation of syllables, this might sound much like *cul laudant*, which seems to be what the human *Q* is doing, praising his tail.

The image of a dog biting its own tail may have been suggested by playful interpretation of the words "refertis potentes" from the adjacent text on fol. 70v. To the speaker of Provençal, *f/v* and *d/t* seem to have been virtually indistinguishable sounds. Thus the illuminator—or other monastic fellows engaged in playful interpretation—may have understood the phrase, quite apart from its religious context, as "in a reversed position" (*revertis*), "eating its tail" (*pudent-es*, from the Provençal verb *escar*, "to eat"). Animals biting their own limbs or tails are common ornamental motifs in medieval manuscripts. However, this St. Martial dog is one in a series of initials formed by dogs (Latin *canes*) with open mouths and bared teeth beside song texts that contain the word *canendo* ("singing") or forms of it.[41] During religious celebrations, the monastic illuminators of the St. Martial songbooks must have themselves performed or listened to others perform the songs whose texts they copied or "performed" on parchment. Thus they would have been aware of puns or innuendos that might arise from the prolongation of syllables during singing performance of the text, as well as from their audiovisual copying in the scriptorium.

On fol. 107v of another songbook that once belonged to the abbey of St. Martial of Limoges (see fig. 32), there appears a multicolored drawing of two secular figures that do not seem to belong in a tonary (a manual that classifies religious songs, usually for teaching purposes, according to the Psalm tones of the Gregorian chant).[42] The smaller man juggles four balls with his hands while dancing. Beside him, an armed knight (of higher social status than the juggler, hence greater size) plays a long, straight, flutelike wind instrument with his mouth and hands. The position and shape of the knight's sword hilt are decidedly phallic. Two of the juggler's balls rise into the text to underscore, like *nota* signs, the two syllables *haec* and *con* from the Latin text, "Haec est Ecce concipies Seculorum" ("Behold, this is the conception of the world"). This is a figurative expression for the mystery of Christ's worldly conception, of the spirit taking on flesh. The previous phrase expresses the same idea in metaphorical terms: "Et intravit Et intrandes domum Seculorum." In the Middle Ages, figurative, abstract representations of Christ's conception could, in some situations, evoke facetiously eroticizing interpretations. Here the syllables *intra-vit* and *concipies* seem to have caught the monks' attention and suggested barbarously vernacular interpretations involving *con* and *vit*: "enter-prick" and "cunt-fetter," or something to this effect. Such verbal play is reflected in the analogous visual play involving the knight's sword hilt in the drawing of the secular players just described, who appear at the bottom of the page in the place of an illuminated capital, to the left of the rubric and "gloria" introducing the next tone. The juggler's balls enter the song text immediately above to redirect and enrich our interpretation of it. The additional meaning we now discover in the text, and in the figure of the knight, is erotic desire: *concupiens seculorum.*

The date of this tonary has been estimated as the mid-eleventh century, and its origin has been localized to the region around Toulouse.[43] Although the images of knight and juggler on fol. 107v precede by several decades the verse of the first known troubadour, Guillaume IX (ca. 1090–1126), this illumination represents quite accurately the spirit and intention of much early troubadour verse, which imitated religious song but mixed or subverted spiritual aspirations with sensual ones. I would like to believe that fol. 107v represents the early troubadours' method of juggling with the combination and meaning of syllables to suggest erotic senses in the context of religious-sounding songs. However, there is no way to prove this and much evidence to suggest a long tradition in the south and west of France of vernacularizing burlesques of religious song, ritual, and doctrine—in short, of what the troubadours called *foudatz*, the southern spirit of play, laughter, and "foolishness," which overturned the grave and serious and, on certain occasions, challenged the strictures imposed by the Church. Even before the first troubadours, jongleuresque song in the Midi may have been the "underside" of religious song, the playful secular reversal and subversion—but also, to the medieval mind, the necessary *complement*—of sacred gravity.[44]

In the same tonary, on the verso of fol. 111, there is another juggler, whose balls do not enter the text this time; beside him stands a double-flute player, both of them dressed in the multicolored clothing of jongleurs. (See fig. 33.) On the "right" side of the page, the religious text was taken in earnest; on the verso or "reverse" side, it might be taken in game. Many troubadour lyrics exhibit a similar doubleness or an even richer, polymorphous, equivocation, the mark of *gay saber*. It is time now to examine under a more intense light the earliest artifacts: the lyrics, or shards of lyrics, as they have come down to us, by Guillaume IX, along with his contemporaries' written judgments of him.

6

The "Young" Guillaume

Companho, farai un vers covinen,
et aura·i mais de foudatz no·i a de sen,
et er tot mesclatz d'amor e de joi e de joven.

Companions, I will compose a suitable lyric,
and there will be more foolishness in it than sense,
and it will be all mixed up with love and joy and youth.

—Guillaume IX, "Companho, farai un vers covinen"

In Latin charters, Guillaume IX is called "junior" into his early forties.[1] The epithet may have stuck so long after he came to power as Duke of Aquitaine and Count of Poitou (at the age of fifteen) because it fit his behavior. We know the "young" Guillaume mainly from his three lyrics addressed to his "companions" (nos. 1–3), his account of his adventures as a deaf-mute "En Alvernhe, part Lemozi" (no. 5, C ms. *incipit*), and his boasts of his mastery of verbal and physical games in "Ben vueill que sapchon li pluzor" (no. 6). All of these lyrics display the qualities Guillaume announces in "Companho, farai un vers covinen": they contain "more foolishness than sense" and mix "love and joy and youth." These lyrics—and others that we have generally considered to be more mature—are the products of a deliberate, willed adolescence. In the company of his fellow *jovenes*, throughout most of his adult life, Guillaume IX claimed the license of youth to engage in prankish or outrageous actions and words that contested authority on all levels: of husbands (over their wives), of the Church (over the behavior of laymen), of the rules of "proper" representation in language (over subjective, desirous intentions).

In spite of Guillaume's warning that his verse will be a foolish mixture, which might cue us to engage in equally foolish interpretation, most of us have persisted in trying to make good sense of Guillaume's verses. We do not take him at his word and try to give advice on which "horse" he should keep, but we do tend to read *through* his words to discover the true identity of the two "horses," either in contemporary historical reality (Guillaume's incompatible mistresses) or in the realm of ideas (such as incompatible kinds of love, spiritual and carnal, represented figuratively by the two lady-mounts).[2] These answers, which presume that Guillaume's words represent a reality beyond themselves, are not necessarily wrong, but what happens if we also listen to the lyric in a youthfully facetious frame of mind? What if we take it as a word game? Stephen Nichols has aptly punned on the term *canso* to label Guillaume's "companho" lyrics *con-so* due to the litany of *con-* (or *com-* or *co-*) prefixes that support, on a subjective level, the explicitly erotic themes of these lyrics.[3] In the spirit of *foudatz*, led by "foolish" desire, we might even go further to toy with the possible different senses of these sequences of syllables, especially those beginning with *con*.

In "Companho, farai un vers covinen," for example, we might understand the first syllables as two words, *con* + *panho* (from the verb *panar*, "to feed" or "to steal"), which suggests the senses "cunt-feeders" and "cunt-stealers." The rhyme word "covinen" ("suitable") we might understand as three separate words, *con vit nen* (cunt, prick, in). Charles Camproux has already explored several possible senses of the place and personal names in this lyric when these are understood "etymologically": "*Cofolen* . . . evokes at the same time 'folly' (*fol*) and 'arrogance' (*cofle*). Likewise, *gimel* evokes simultaneously *gem:gemissement* ('trembling') and *cimel* (pronounced with the first letter hushed, 'summit'); and *Niol* may be taken for *nivol* ('cloud') and for *ni olh* ('not eye,' 'no eye')." For the name of the first mount, Agnes, Camproux suggests associations with the Greek word *hagnos* meaning "chaste" or "pure," as well as with the Latin phrase *agnus-castus* and several Provençal phrases that involve decomposing *Agnes* into smaller meaningful words: *anc n'es* (never is), *anc necs* (never refuses), *anc nesci* (never foolish), and *anc nes* (never the same). The name Arsen he associates with *arsen* (burning) and with *ausen* (the Provençal word for "absinthe"), as well as the phrases *ar sen* ("now we are" or "now the sense") and *ara sen* (there will be sense).[4] Dietmar Rieger has proposed that in reading Guillaume's *vers* ("verses" or "reversed") we might sometimes reverse the direction in which we interpret syllable sequences[5] (which the *Leys d'amors* calls "reading backwards by syllables," vol. 2, p. 108). Such foolish misdirection would, for example, turn the place name Cofolen into *En-fol-co* (or *con*) meaning "Lord Foolish Cunt" and sounding like the name of the Count of Anjou, "Folcon" (son of the infamous

Bertrade de Montfort), whom Guillaume mentions in his lyric goodbye to the world.[6] There is virtually no end to the liberties that the playfully facetious interpreter might take with the language of this lyric demanding knightly counsel (*conselh*) on the subject of which *con* to saddle (*selhar*). One suspects, indeed, that the discovery of this ambiguity in the word *conselh* ("counsel" or "cunt-saddle") is what stimulated the riddling word game of the lyric, and not any real problem about choosing between two mistresses.

In all his "companho" lyrics and in "Ben vueill que sapchon li pluzor," Guillaume played in a schoolboyish way at discovering different "tropes" (that is, figurative expressions or metaphors) for the sex act. His discovery of new analogies often depended on etymologizing interpretation, that is, a kind of tinkering deconstruction and reassemblage using the syllabic building blocks of words. We call this play popular etymology—or free association. For example, both "Compaigno, non puosc mudar qu'eo no m'effrei" (no. 2) and "Companho, tant ai agutz d'avols conres" (no. 3) are about the "company" one keeps, but these lyrics addressed to Guillaume's companions are also about equivocally eroticizing ways of understanding words for "company": *con-res* (cunt thing), *con-rei* (cunt king), *con-res* (cunt saw). "Company" is one of Guillaume's favorite metaphors for sex. In "Compaigno, non puosc mudar qu'eo no m'effrei" (which has survived only in the N songbook), it is Guillaume, this time, who assumes an authoritative role to give "counsel" on the subject of husbands' setting guardians over their wives' chastity, and he gives this advice in the form of proverbial-sounding phrases that would make sense to a knightly audience: "Si non pot aver caval, compra palafrei" ("If she can't have a charger, she settles for a palfrey") and "Chascus beuri' ans de l'aiga que·s laises morir dessei" ("Everyone would sooner drink water than let himself die of thirst" (no. 2, p. 46). These proverbs suggest analogies with the situation of the guarded wife. If people would rather drink water than die of thirst, we may assume that a guarded woman would rather cheat with her guardians than do without sex (which may say little for her husband). The last two syllables of this proverb, which concludes the lyric, are equivocal, as I have earlier suggested and as the scribe of the N songbook himself pointed out by using two different spellings and word divisions in the repeated line: *de sei* and *dessei*. The first time we read the sentence, "de sei" seems to mean either "of thirst" or "all by oneself." The second time around, the grouping of the letters suggests the meaning "straightway." There are even further possibilities for play with the meaning of Guillaume's proverbial-sounding phrases. *Boire*, "to drink," is a metaphor for sexual intercourse in later French literature and may have been in Guillaume's day as well.[7] For lack of "strong wine," "vi fort" (which may sound exactly like *vit fort*, "sturdy penis"), rather than die of thirst (or all by herself), the wife will drink "water," "l'aiga" (which sounds almost like "the watchman," *l'agah* or *agach*). Guillaume repeats the line so that the audience may savor the erotic ambiguities of the language of his proverbial-sounding advice and the way he turns *sen* to *foudatz*.

We may also discover erotic innuendos in the two words beginning with the syllable *con-* (or *com-*) in an earlier strophe of the same lyric:

> si·l tenez acarcat lo bon conrei,
> adoba·s d'aquel que troba viron sei:
> si non pot aver caval, compra palafrei.[8]

One interpretation of Guillaume's counsel might go like this: "If you keep good company [or, equipment] at such a distance, / she arms [or, provides] herself with whatever she finds around her: / if she can't have a charger, she settles for a palfrey." Here is a revised version of the central metaphor of "Companho, farai un vers covinen" (no. 1), but this time it is the lady, not the man, who seeks a good mount. In such a context, "conrei" is a very suggestive rhyme word. We might understand it not only as (sexual) equipment, but also *per syllabas* as *con-rei* (king of cunt) . . . who other than Guillaume himself, the *vit fort* according to his own boasts in other "companion" lyrics. If the guarded ladies cannot have him, they will settle for a lesser man (a palfrey for lack of a charger). "Compra" ("settles for" or "buys") in this context might also be understood as two separate words: *con pra* (an abbreviation of the verb *proar*, "to test"): the cunt will test a palfrey if a charger is not available. The word "carcat" from the verb *carcar* or *cargar* (unnecessarily emended to a less ambiguous "acartat" by Pasero and other modern editors) supports the erotic *équivoque* and continues the poem's legal metaphors by suggesting the additional sense of "charged or inculpated." If Guillaume is held to blame for misconduct with the lady ("si·l tenez acarcat lo bon conrei") and she is thereafter kept under guard, she will make do with her watchmen. But better to have "lo bon con-rei" than to have "commerce" with hired watchmen.

The last surviving strophe of "Compano, tant ai agutz d'avols conres" (no. 3) reveals, through wordplay, a similarly teasing threat. In this lyric, Guillaume introduces the trope for the sex act in the first rhyme word, "conres" ("company" or "entertainment"), which might be understood *per syllabas* as *con res* ("cunt saw," from the verb *resar*). After comparing the guarded cunt to a pond without fish and to boasts without actions, Guillaume elaborates upon the central figure: the cunt (or married woman) as a woods that only "grows thicker" with frequent cutting of the trees:

> E quan lo bocx es taillatz, nais plus espes;
> e·l senher no·n pert son comte ni sos ses:
> a revers planh hom la tala, si·l dampn[atges no·i es ges.][9]

Modern readers generally interpret these lines something like this: "And when the woods is cut, it grows thicker / and the lord loses neither his account nor his revenues from it. / A man has it reversed to complain of the destruction [literally, the cutting; technically, imposed taxation] / if there is no damage at all." However, the strophe contains some clever ambiguities. We might understand "comte" not only as "account" (alternately spelled *compte*), but also as "count," with reference to Guillaume himself in his role as Count of Poitou. Likewise, we might take "hom" and "ces" (or the alternate spelling *ses*) in their feudal senses as "vassal" and "seat" or "seisein" (sometimes spelled *seyze*). Guillaume's advice to his vassals, voiced in the mock-authoritative voice of *con-rei*, weighs their possible losses against their possible gains. Guillaume argues that his *domneis* is no *dampnatges*; his fooling around with their wives is no damage or loss to them, but, rather, a gain if their wives produce more offspring. If they stop having their wives guarded, his vassals will lose neither their wives nor the offspring nor (the favor of) their count nor their feudal holdings.

Although it is not specifically addressed to his companions, Guillaume's "Ben vueill que sapchon li pluzor" (no. 6) is another lyric in the same vein, another *con-so* in which he delights in describing his sexual mastery in figurative language (troping love) and in punning on *con* in equivocal sequences of syllables. Because of its series of statements beginning "Eu conosc" ("I know"), this lyric has been understood as a companion piece to Guillaume's famous "vers de dreyt nien" (no. 4), with its sequence of statements beginning "no sai" ("I don't know").[10] Repetition is also a way of emphasizing equivocal wordplay. Repeated five times in two strophes, "eu conosc" might be understood as three words, *eu con osc* ("I cunt-notch," from the infinitive form *oscar*, "to break into," "to notch or cut"). In this lyric Guillaume also plays on the *con* in *conselh*. The kind of counsel that men ask of him, due to his mastery of the "juec doussa," probably has to do with his sexual techniques for pleasing the ladies, that is, his *con-selha* or *-sela* (saddling or sealing cunt):

> Dieus en lau e sanh Jolia:
> tant ai apres del juec doussa
> que sobre totz n'ay bona ma;
> e selh qui cosselh mi querra
> non l'er vedatz,
> ni un de mi no·n tornara
> descossellatz.[11]

Praise God and Saint Julian / that I have learned so much about the sweet game / that, "over" everyone, I have the good [or, upper] hand. / Never will the man [or, vassal] who seeks "counsel" of me / be turned away / nor will anyone turn away from me / "uncounseled" [or, unconsoled].

For his great learning in the arts of love, Guillaume claims the academic title of *maiestre certa* ("sure master"). He backs up this boast with the narrative, expressed through dicing metaphors, of a difficult test of his sexual mastery. The game, he announces, was a gross one and too good at its very beginning (with a possible pun on *cap* as "head"):

> Pero no m'auzetz tan guabier
> qu'ieu no·n fos rahuzatz l'autrier
> que jogav'a un joc grossier
> que·m fon trop bos el cap premier,
> tro fuy taulatz;
> que·m guardiey, no m'ac plus mestier,
> si·m fon camjatz.

But you don't hear me boasting much / because I was gnawed down to size the other day / while I was playing a vulgar game / that was quite good for me in the beginning, / until I was seated at the table; / when I looked at myself, I no longer had any need, / such a change had come over me.

But something goes wrong later, either when Guillaume sits down to the "gaming table" or perhaps because he has already seated himself too many times before (depending on how we understand the "tro," as "until" or "too"). When Guillaume looks at himself, he no longer has any need (or control), so much has he "changed." Just at this point, the lady becomes demanding and belittles Guillaume's "dice" (sexual organs):

> "Don, vostres datz son menudier
> et ieu revit vos a doblier."

> "Lord, your dice are on the small side, / and I challenge you to a second round [or, to redouble them]."

Guillaume, of course, rises to this challenge to his reputation:

> e leviey un pauc son taulier
> ab ams mos bratz.
>
> E quan l'aic levat lo taulier
> empys los datz;
> e·l duy foron cairavallier
> e·l terz plombatz.
>
> E fi·ls ben ferir al taulier
> e fon joguatz.

> And I lifted up a little her table / with both my arms.
>
> And when I had lifted the table, / I threw the dice, / and the two were flesh riders / and the third leaden.
>
> And I made them strike the table well, / and it was played out.

The different manuscripts' versions of the adjective that Guillaume uses to describe his testicles suggest that Guillaume either made up a word here or used a slang term of gaming that both later medieval and modern readers found ambiguous and modified according to their own interpretations, thus continuing Guillaume's game of invention. The C songbook reads "cairavallier"; E reads "caramaillier"; and N forms two words, "carat valer," as does D, "cairat nualler." The C interpretation suggests "flesh" (*caira*) as well as "knight" or "rider" (*cavalier*) and thus the bouncing of the testicles. The E songbook expresses the same idea with a beating metaphor, "cara-maillier" (flesh hammers). In the same sequence of letters, "carat" or "cairat," modern scholars have seen different meanings such as "squared off" or "precious." They have emended spellings and etymologized in the same ways that medieval interpreters did when faced with an ambiguous sequence of letters and sounds, continuing the process of *mouvance*, rewriting the lyric.[12]

Like his interpreters, then and now, Guillaume himself recomposed his own songs, using the same verbal "matter," making new out of old by changing a letter or a syllable to create a new word and a new trope to describe lovemaking—for example, *tala* (cutting) in "Companho, tant ai agutz d'avols conres" and *taula* (table) in "Ben vueill que sapchon li pluzor"—or by considering the same letters or syllables from different perspectives to evoke new meanings and metaphors, as when he toys with the syllable *con* in different combinations—*con-res*, *conselh*, *con-panho*. Guillaume turns the matter of words over and over in his lyrics as if the syllables were stones that take on different colors in different settings. He handles words as an imaginative child might play with a curious object, examining it from different points of view, seeing in it fanciful resemblances, making its meanings myriad.

To treat words in this way, making what one wants to out of them, is the essence of facetiousness according to a definition by the great grammatical authority for the Middle Ages, Donatus, in his gloss on Terence's *Eunuch*: "facetus est qui facit verbis quod vult."[13] Along with the adjectives *jocundus* (joyful or joking) and *lepidus* (witty or amusing), *facetos* is the term Odericus Vitalis repeatedly uses in his *Ecclesiastical History* to characterize Guillaume's verbal antics, which, in Odericus's judgment, surpass those of *histriones* (or jongleurs): "Hic audax fuit et probus, nimiumque jocundus, facetos etiam histriones facetiis superans multiplicibus" ("He was bold and worthy and very funny, outdoing even the witty professional entertainers with his many witticisms").[14] Even the melodies to which Guillaume sang songs of the "miseries of his captivity" after his return from Jerusalem were, in Odericus's view, clever or facetious:

> Pictavensis vero dux peractis in Jerusalem orationibus, cum quibusdam aliis consortibus suis est ad sua reversus, et miserias captivitatis suae ut erat jocundus et lepidus, postmodum prosperitate fultus coram regibus et magnatis atque Christianis cetibus, multotiens retulit rithmicis versibus cum facetis modulationibus.[15]

> The Duke of Poitou, having accomplished his prayers in Jerusalem, returned home with certain of his companions and, afterwards, because he was joyful and witty, encouraged by his prosperity, he frequently related the miseries of his captivity in accentual verses with clever modulations [or, melodies] in the presence of kings, magnates, and other Christians.

William of Malmesbury also singles out for criticism Guillaume's post-Crusade behavior, but he looks upon it with a slightly more jaundiced eye, seeing nothing but buffoonery and lasciviousness:

> Erat tunc Willelmus comes Pictavorum fatuus et lubricus; qui, postquam de Jerosolima . . . , rediit, ita omne vitiorum volutabrum premebat quasi crederet omnia fortuitu agi, non providentia regi.[16]

> At that time Guillaume, Count of Poitou, was foolish and lascivious, returning from Jerusalem just as he was before, . . . that is, he pressed himself down into the mire of all the vices as if he believed everything happened by chance, not ruled by Providence.

His contemporaries might have expected Guillaume to return somewhat chastened or downcast from his pilgrimage to the Holy Land, where he lost many companions in an ambush and accomplished no victories. On the contrary, Guillaume came back in an extremely playful mood—just as he had been before, just as facetious and full of pranks as ever.

Contemporary ecclesiastical commentaries on Guillaume's excessively "youthful" character throughout his life make it impossible to relegate to Guillaume's historical adolescence his three *companho* lyrics, the phallic bravado of "Ben vueill que sapchon li pluzor," his supremely facetious verses of "strictly nothing" ("Farai un vers de dreyt nien"), or his ribald account of his sexual adventures in the guise of a deaf-mute pilgrim "En Alvernhe, part Lemozi." When Guillaume returned from the Holy Land to regale audiences with facetious renditions of the "miseries of his captivity," he was already in his early thirties, twice married, with his succession secured by the birth of a son. Indeed, there is some evidence to suggest that at least one of the above lyrics Guillaume composed after he returned from the Holy Land. Because we know that he was never actually taken prisoner by the Saracens, at least not according to any surviving chronicle account, we have generally assumed that Guillaume made up these narratives of his captivity and that we have lost all of them. Nevertheless, we do have one lyric that nearly fits the description, although the miseries of the "captive" Guillaume occur much closer to home, "En Alvernhe, part Lemozi."

On the road, all alone in the guise of a pilgrim ("totz sols a tapi"), Guillaume encounters the wives of Lord Guari and Lord Bernart. The ladies greet him by the patron saint of prisoners, Saint Leonard, especially venerated in the Limousin. When Guillaume responds with a string of syllables that make no clear sense, the ladies Agnes and Ermessen are delighted to have "found just what [they] are seeking"—a sexual partner who will not talk—and they decide to show the pilgrim "hospitality." From Guillaume's point of view, this reception is both pleasurable and painful. In narrating what went on in the cookhouse hideaway where the ladies kept him for "more than eight days,"[17] he mixes the sadomasochistic vocabulary of Christian martyrdom, the saintly *agon* of enduring physical torture, with that of phallic bravado. Guillaume's adventure begins with an ambivalent image of protection tinged with eroticism: one of the ladies takes him "under her mantle." She leads him to their hearth or "furnace"—literally, to the outbuilding where the cooking is done. However, "fornelh" in this context takes on equivocal figurative meanings, evoking at the same time the female sexual organs, the iconography of hell, and saintly martyrdoms in fiery furnaces or cauldrons. To Guillaume, the "foc" ("fire") felt good, and he willingly warmed himself at the big coals. "Carbo," which puns on *car bo* ("good flesh," presumably that of the ladies), alludes as well to the grilling of martyrs such as St. Lawrence over hot coals:

La una·m pres sotz so mantelh
e a mi fon mout bon e belh;
meneron m'en a lur fornelh,
e·l foc fo·m bo,
et ieu calfei me voluntiers
al gros carbo.

One of them took me under her cloak / and this was just fine with me; / they led me to their "hearth," / and the "fire" felt good to me, / and I warmed myself willingly / at the big coals [or, "good flesh"].

Next follows a strophe on the pleasurable "company" of the feast; there is hot bread and good wine:

A manjar me deron capos,
e·l pan fon cautz, e·l vin fon bos,
et ieu dirney me volentos,
fort et espes;
et anc sol no y ac coguastro,
mas quan nos tres.

To eat they gave me capons, / and the bread was hot, and the wine was good, / and I dined eagerly, / strong and thick, / and there wasn't a single kitchen boy there, / but only us three.

To "put the bread in the oven" is a very old metaphor for sexual intercourse or impregnation in which the phallus or the foetus is represented by the "bread," the vagina or womb by the "furnace." Guillaume has played with the metaphor before in one of the facetious etymologies of his epithet for his fellow *jovenes*, "conpanho," those who engage in *con-panar*, feeding *con*. The adjectives "fort" and "espes" ("strong" and "thick") in the fourth line of the above strophe are syntactically ambiguous in a deliberate way. Do they modify "vin" (wine) two lines earlier, or do they describe the "I" ("ieu") of the immediately preceding line? In any case, this dinner was surely supposed to serve as an aphrodisiac. If we perceive in "vin" a pun on Old French *vit* or Provençal *vieg*, the distinction as to who or what is "strong and thick" hardly matters.[18]

After the pleasure comes the *"chât"iment*. The ladies test their pilgrim's inability to speak with a big red, diabolically ferocious "cat" (alternately spelled in Provençal *chat* or *gat*). The beast skins Guillaume from head to heels with its claws. Guillaume behaves like an exemplary early Christian martyr, unflinching through the whole ordeal. He is determined to die rather than give up his goal—of fucking the two ladies:

Quan aguem begut e manjat,
despulley·m a lur voluntat;
derreire m'aportero·l cat,
mal e fello;
et escorgeron me del cap
tro al talo.

Per la coa·l pres N'Ermessen,
e tira, e·l cat escoyssen;
plaguas me feyron mays de cen
aquella ves;
coc me, mas ieu per tot aquo
no·m mogui ges.

Ni o feyra qui m'aucizes,
entro que pro fotut agues
ambedos; qu'ayssi fon empres
a mon talen,
ans vuelc mais sufrir la dolor
e·l greu turmen.

When we had drunk and eaten, / I undressed myself according to their desire; / behind me they carried the cat, / bad-tempered and mean, / and they skinned me from head / to toe.

By the tail Lady Ermessen held it / and pulled, and the cat, scratching, / gave me more than a hundred wounds / this time. / Much as I wanted to, for all that / I didn't move a muscle.

Nor would I have, even if they killed me, / before I had fucked them both / good, because they were quite / to my liking. / Instead, I preferred to endure the suffering / and the grievous torment.

The real miseries of Guillaume's captivity begin after this initial, testing *"châť"iment*. The two ladies keep him in their cookhouse (more than eight days according to the N and V songbook versions), and during this time he fucks them 188 times, until he nearly breaks his "equipment" and tortures himself in the doing beyond description:

> Aitan fotey cum auziretz:
> .C. e quatre .XXVIII. vetz;
> ab pauc no·m rompei mos corretz
> e mos arnes;
> e venc m'en trop gran malaveg [*or*, mal a veg],
> tal mal me fes.

I fucked them such as you shall hear: / one hundred and eighty-eight times. / I almost broke my strap / and my harness, / and the pain of it [or, pain to my penis] was too much, / so badly did I hurt myself.

The C songbook's version of this lyric ends with an envoy to the two ladies—Agnes (the name of a female martyr) and Ermessen (a name that may recollect the lascivious she-wolf of the Renard legend)[19]—asking them to kill the cat and thus signaling the ladies' miscalculation and defeat. Their "deaf-mute" can write and send messages. What is worse, he can sing the story of his near-martyrdom. The N and V versions of the lyric end on a note of triumphant suffering, repeating the last two lines of the final strophe as if it were a refrain:

> e no·us puesc dir los malavegz,
> tan gran m'en pres.
> E·us no sai dir los malavegz,
> tan gran m'en pres!

And I can't tell you how much it hurt [or, punning, *mal a vechs*, "the penile pains"], / so great was my suffering.

And I don't know how to tell you how much it hurt ["the penile pains"] / so great was my suffering.

In the context of a story told by a "deaf-mute," Guillaume is playing facetiously here with the old "inexpressibility" topos.

Odericus Vitalis tells us that Guillaume performed his verses on the miseries of his captivity with "facetis modulationibus." The investigations of musicologists beginning with Hans Spanke strongly suggest that Guillaume borrowed and adapted the melodies, along with the rhyme schemes and metrical patterns, of contemporary religious songs. These religious songs are best exemplified today in the extensive surviving collections of the songbook-textbooks from St. Martial of Limoges and its dependent abbeys. The sacred connotations of such melodies, when performed to Guillaume's profane words, would only heighten the humor of Guillaume's burlesque martyrdom and his mockery of pious pilgrimage. A conductus for the feast of St. Leonard, for example, might make a fine melodic vehicle for Guillaume's account of his own captivity. Spanke, however, compares the meter of Guillaume's lyric to that of another St. Martial conductus, "In laudes Innocentium," for the Feast of the Innocents.[20] For Guillaume to narrate his own erotic martyrdom to the melody of a well-known song praising innocent infant martyrs is truly ludicrous. The facetiousness of Guillaume's melodies might also lie in more subtle ways of linking melody and words. In religious song, melodic pitch and phrasing were supposed to punctuate and clarify the meaning of the verbal text.[21] Melodic notation, as was already remarked, seems to have developed from earlier punctuation marks such as the *punctus* and *virga*. Presumably, melodic "pointing" of the verses could also be used facetiously, not to clarify but to equivocate, to bring out ambiguities and incongruities, to enrich the sense and make the audience laugh. But let me leave for later discussion the contextual issue of possible comic performance practices and techniques.

Medieval assessments of Guillaume IX are striking in their unanimity about Guillaume's "young" behavior, whereas our modern Guillaume is "bi-fronte" or "two-faced."[22] He is a paradoxical fellow who could jest in the most vulgar way about women and yet write tender "courtly love" lyrics to and about them, a man who defied excommunication to continue his liaison with the Viscountess of Châtellerault[23] (a seemingly romantic gesture) and yet made a joke of their lovemaking by putting an image of her on his shield and announcing that he wanted to carry her into battle exactly as she had carried him on the couch (thus exposing her image to other men's lances).[24] Some modern interpreters have been fascinated by the idea of the rose springing from the manure heap. Through his reading of Guillaume's "Molt jauzens mi prenc en amar," Reto Bezzola perceives a "profound transformation undergone by the count under the influence of the religious mysticism surrounding him." Bezzola judges that Guillaume, like a new Pygmalion, "before the mirage of 'My Lady' that he had just created . . . remains . . . filled with wonder."[25] Topsfield, Lawner, Bond,[26] and a number of other scholars argue against "sudden conversion" or "maturation" theories of Guillaume's personal and poetic development such as are implicitly enshrined in the order of Guillaume's lyrics in modern editions. Nevertheless, even Peter Dronke, who amply proves that Guillaume was by no means the first to express those fundamentally religious attitudes that we now label "courtly love,"[27] takes some of Guillaume's lyrics as jokes and others as serious praise, although not necessarily in the order of jokes first, seriousness later.

Almost universally, modern scholars have perceived a greater "sincerity" in four of Guillaume's love lyrics: "Ab la dolchor del temps novel" (no. 10), "Mout jauzens mi prenc en amar" (no. 9), "Pos vezem de novel florir" (no. 7), and "Farai chansoneta nueva" (no. 8). Nevertheless, the medieval interpreters of Guillaume's verse who composed his *vida* treated all his lyrics as if they were alike. His *vida* emphasizes that Guillaume was a great beguiler of ladies ("trichadors de dompnas") and that the main purpose of his travels was to seduce or trick ladies ("per enganar las domnas").[28] The *vida*'s coupling of the terms "majors cortes" and "majors trichadors de dompnas" does not necessarily represent the paradoxical duality modern readers find in Guillaume, the vulgar playboy and the sincere lover. "Cortes" may mean "good with words" (especially persuasive ones) and all the other social behaviors desirable in a man who spends much time in court. Included in these might be the mastery of the different friendly games ("juec d'amor") that Guillaume treats in "Ben vueill que sapchon li pluzor," from composing verses to pleasing his partner in bed.[29] Just as silent as the *vida* composer(s) about any change in Guillaume's excessively "young" behavior are the ecclesiastical chroniclers of his time. One called Guillaume, quite bluntly, the "enemy of everything proper and sacred."[30] William of Malmesbury and Odericus Vitalis were more specific in giving examples of just how Guillaume's actions fell short of the gravity they expected in a secular ruler of his rank. What comes through clearly from these accounts is Guillaume's penchant for burlesquing and mocking sacred institutions.

One wishes that William of Malmesbury had been more voluble in describing Guillaume's mock-monastery prank, especially the nature of the singing that went on in this "house of prostitution" organized by "Abbot" Guillaume as if it were a convent, with an abbess and other officiants and singing, presumably of the "offices":

> Denique apud castellum quoddam, Niort, habitacula quaedam, quasi monasteriola, construens, abbatiam pellicum ibi se positurum delirabat; nuncupatim illam et illam, quaecunque famosioris prostibuli esset, abbatissam vel priorem, ceterasve officiales institutorum cantitans.

> Then too at a certain castle called Niort he built some little houses, almost like monastic huts, and wildly proclaimed that he would found an Abbey of Whores. And he sang that he would establish this girl or that one, whom he named, all from famous brothels, as his abbess, his prioress, and his other officials.[31]

Bezzola has astutely pointed out that the reference to an abbess and prostitutes in this account make it very likely that Guillaume's "little monastery" was intended as a burlesque of the convent of Fontevrault, founded in Guillaume's territory by the ascetic preacher Robert d'Arbrissel and supported by the same bishop, Peter of Poitiers, who later excommunicated Guillaume. Peter went to Rome in 1105 to get papal confirmation of the new Order of Fontevrault. Churches of the order were dedicated to the Virgin and, as Bezzola remarks, Robert d'Arbrissel made the extraordinary decision to appoint a noble widow (still young and beautiful) as abbess over the entire order, including the men, who vowed to obey and serve the "handmaids of Christ" (the women) for the salvation of their own souls.[32] Bezzola also notes that Robert's exhortations to retreat from the world to a life of voluntary poverty and devotion seem to have appealed strongly to women of all classes: a house of prostitutes in Rouen, the Countess of Anjou (the infamous Bertrade de Montfort, who had so long defied papal excommunication for her liaison with the French King Philip I), Guillaume IX's own former wives and a daughter. To Guillaume, any sort of fanatical asceticism was a target for satire. Nothing was sacred. Although himself a pilgrim to the Holy Land, he mocked the piety of pilgrims. The vogue of sudden conversions and monastic retreats among noblewomen of Bertrade's sort—and of a whole house of prostitutes—was a subject ripe for Guillaume's plucking. His valorization of the *domna*, the "new" attitude of humble devotion he assumes in "Pos vezem de novel florir," "Mout jauzens mi prenc en amar," and in "Farai chansoneta nueva,"[33] may not be entirely sincere or serious. Guillaume's new attitude may have had its beginnings in facetious play, in burlesque imitation of the devotion to the *Domina* promoted by religious institutions, and in an especially concrete way at Fontevrault, where the Abbess held a supreme position.

The verb William of Malmesbury uses to describe Guillaume's behavior as mock abbot of his mock convent is "delirabat": "he went out of his mind." In the context of later Latin lyrics, Dronke notes that *deliramus* can have an almost mystical sense, "to be taken out of oneself, to be possessed by [divine] love."[34] *Deliro* might also describe the "madness" of festive occasions when youth joyfully "deviated" to overturn the regular order of things and to revel in its own power. Such madness usually involved deviant uses of ritual languages, a seizure of the old signs to make them mean new—and, generally, scandalous—things. In burlesque masses of the later Middle Ages, the choirboys roasted sausages on the altars and burned old shoe leather in the censers. Many of the exterior signs (words, gestures) were the same, but performing them with variations in a very different spirit radically changed their meaning. The choirboys and novices also troped the liturgy or the offices in facetious ways. We may find relics of these burlesques sandwiched between more serious tropes in songbooks such as Paris, B.N. lat. 3719 from St. Martial. In this collection, songs praising Mary's perpetual virginity nudge against the classical-sounding lament of a girl's guardian on the loss of her virginity before he himself had the chance to take it: "While I was diligently taking care of you till you grew up, oh Lyce! Lyce! secretly you sell that still so tender little, flighty and lascivious little body of yours—I am sad, sad, sad."[35] Tropes praising Mary, especially in the language and images of the Canticles, were easily reworked in a facetious way to produce "gay and provocative" songs (Dronke's words) such as the following one from the collection of Cambridge songs:

> Veni, dilectissime[36]
> et a et o,
> gratam me invisere,
> et a et o et a et o!
>
> In languore pereo.
> et a et o,
> Venerem desidero,
> et a et o et a et o! . . .
>
> Si cum clave veneris,[37]
> et a et o,
> mox intrare poteris
> et a et o et a et o![38]

Come, dearest, / and *a* and *o*, / to visit me welcoming, / and *a* and *o* and *a* and *o*!

> I perish of languor, / and *a* and *o*, / I long for love, / and *a* and *o* and *a* and *o*! . . .
>
> If you come with a key / and *a* and *o*, / soon you will be able to enter, / and *a* and *o* and *a* and *o*!

Here the onomatopoeic-erotic refrain of popular dance burlesques the refrainlike repetition of words such as *alleluia* in religious songs. The joyful performance of verses such as these would surely merit the term "delirabat."

The singing that went on in Guillaume's mock convent was probably of an equally foolish nature. Indeed, Guillaume would hardly need to change the "right" words of monastic song except, perhaps, to translate or write new versions of them in the vernacular. By casting himself in the role of monastic founder (that is, more precisely, in the role of Robert d'Arbrissel) and by casting prostitutes in the role of nuns (or, more likely, his fellow *jovenes* in female garments playing "converted" prostitutes), Guillaume radically changed the spirit in which the traditional words of conventual offices should be performed, and, consequently, their meaning. From the songbooks of St. Martial of Limoges, which collected songs widely, we may get some idea of the nature of the religious songs Guillaume might have burlesqued in his own "convent." The tenth- through twelfth-century St. Martial songbooks are rich in prose sequences and tropes in praise of the Virgin, and the offices of Fontevrault, we may presume, would have been at least as rich in praises of Mary.

The relationship between religious songs from the St. Martial collections and early troubadour verse has been explored by Spanke and Errante,[39] who have proven that the metrical and melodic forms of many troubadour lyrics are the same—indeed, derive from—those of contemporary religious song (although this may previously have incorporated aspects of secular song). We know from their *vidas* and from what they say about one another in their verse that a number of troubadours were educated as canons, and thus that they had been more extensively trained than the average medieval schoolboy in the forms of religious song. Three famous Peires (d'Auvernhe, Rogier, and Cardenal) were at one time canons.[40] Other troubadours, such as the Monk of Montaudon, wrote while retaining their religious status,[41] and quite a number of troubadours, according to their *vidas*, converted to monastic life in their later years and may have continued to write while in the monastery, composing vernacular songs when they were not singing the offices. Some monastic orders forbid monks to write verses, which may be taken as a sign that they were doing so.[42] Although he was reportedly chagrined by his earlier misuse of his education and skill in liturgical song to compose secular love lyrics, this did not stop Folquet de Marseille from becoming a bishop.

Their *vidas* note that many of the troubadours were lettered men (*savis de letras*), that is, educated in Latin letters, which they would have learned, at least initially, in monastic or cathedral schools from the texts of religious songs collected in psalters and other songbooks, such as those from St. Martial. The most basic instruction in reading at this period seems to have involved instruction in pious song.[43] Along with their Latin letters, the future troubadours learned religious songs; they learned to sing and read tropes for festive occasions, perhaps even, as a rhetorical exercise, to compose new versions of old tropes, varying the melodies and words. The cantor or singing master probably had to use the vernacular to explain the meaning of Latin songs to his young pupils. Several Provençal verses in a late-eleventh-century St. Martial songbook suggest that tropes and prose sequences and other amplifying embellishments of the liturgy and offices had more than an ornamental purpose; they were also explications or glosses of biblical texts. The leader or teacher of the songs reverts to the vernacular to terminate the "lecture" of the day, which he calls the *razos*. I transcribe this vernacular sequence (rhyming in "-os") as it appears in the manuscript (Paris, B.N. lat. 1139, fol. 44r), without the musical notation, but in the same lines, with raised periods representing the red dashes in the manuscript separating words and phonetic groups:

> Be deu·hoi mais·finir·nostra·razos·un pauc·soilas·que
> tropfo aut·losos·leven·doi·clerc que di ien·lo respos·tuau
> tem deus·q'est·paire·glorios·noste·preiam·quer remem
> bre·denos·quant·triaras·los mals·dantre·los bos.

> Now we must finish our explanation. I am a little tired because the tone was very high. The cleric must raise [his voice] to perform well the response. "Tu autem deus," God the Father all-glorious, we pray that you remember us when you separate the bad from the good.

In this same religious songbook, macaronic (Latin and Provençal) playlets involving several voices, such as the Nativity play beginning "In hoc anni circulo" (fols. 48r–49r), may have served to teach S/scripture to young boys, who might perform the different roles for the holiday, possibly before a lay audience.[44]

The importance of this primary education in reading and singing cannot be too strongly stressed, because it educated future troubadours not only in the melodic and metrical structures of religious songs, but also in Mariological themes and in role-playing. Such basic education in monastic or cathedral schools, which many noble boys destined for secular careers might never go beyond, created a common schoolish culture among the social elite of the eleventh and twelfth centuries. Songbooks rich in praise of the Virgin were probably the sort from which Guillaume IX learned to read and sing—whether in the cathedral school of Poitiers founded by a disciple of Fulbert of Chartres at the request of Guillaume's ancestor, Guillaume the Great, or in a monastic school such as St. Hilaire of Poitiers, or in the more "private" school of a court chancellor, chaplain, or other religious teacher.[45] With a group of other boys, the young Guillaume must have learned tropes and hymns to Mary couched in the language of divine love, songs that he would later parody facetiously in his mock-monastery prank and in vernacular lyrics praising secular ladies. What might these religious songs have been like?

7

O Gloriosa Domina

Ad te suspiro, domina.
Meas accepta lacrimas,
Signum misericordiae
Digneris mihi pandere.

I long for you, lady;
receive my tears;
deign to show me
a sign of mercy.

—Prayer to the Virgin,
possibly by St. Anselm

The development of Mariology in the Western Church merits at least a brief excursus here, because troubadour verse is much indebted to it, as are secular Latin love lyrics of the same period, and because scholars as authoritative as Marrou and Gilson have denied this debt.[1] The vogue of devotion to the Virgin long precedes St. Bernard's famous sermon cycle on the Canticles. Robert d'Arbrissel's elevation of a contemporary noble widow to a position of authority as head of the Order of Fontevrault was a sign of the great prestige of Mary as *domina* already in the late eleventh century in the West. The cult of the Virgin was first elaborated, however, in the Eastern Orthodox church, with its extensive literature of homilies and litanies refulgent with epithets for Mary and its icons of the Virgin and Christ child in which Mary is associated with divine wisdom, *sophia*.[2] She is depicted as *sedes sapientia*, the seat of wisdom, holding the infant Christ (in commanding miniature adult form) in front of her so that her rigid, chairlike body forms His throne. The fifth-century Archbishop of Ravenna, St. Peter Chrysologus, was the first to compose a treatise on the "names of the Virgin."[3] Over the centuries, Greek orants, often praying for themselves in the first person singular, wove an ever more elaborate tissue of names in Mary's praise. The Greek worshipper prayed from a position of weakness to a powerful lady patron who would serve as his intercessor vis-à-vis God.

Such, for example, is the stance of St. Germain of Constantinople in a seventh-century homily:

> O sovereign lady, my sole solace from God, / divine dew, tempering what burns in me, / raindrop from God that falls on my arid heart, / . . . remedy for my incurable wounds, / stop to my tears, / end to my trembling, / escape from my anguish, / comfort for my suffering, / forgetting of my bonds, / hope of my salvation, / hear my prayers.[4]

Many of the names for Mary in the Byzantine cult evoke her healing powers or the joy she brings man as a result of his redemption. The language of the Canticles echoes through some texts. For instance, at the turn of the ninth century, the monk and patriarch of Constantinople, St. Euthyme, described Mary as the "ointment blessed by God anointing us every day with mystical perfumes."[5] Eastern churches such as the famous Hagia Sophia were named after Mary. In the Eastern cult, earlier than in the West, the figure of Mary/Sophia represented the Church as the institution that controlled man's access to God. Western pilgrims would probably have been impressed by this symbolism.

By the eleventh century this authoritative image of Mary appears in many forms in the West as well. Fulbert of Chartres, St. Peter Damian, St. Anselm of Bec, all by birth Italians, promoted the cult of the Virgin as *domina*, queen of heaven and of the saints, man's powerful intercessor. They promoted this cult not only through their writings—in surviving prayers, homilies, verses, and such—but also through their direction of visual images—wall paintings, manuscript illuminations, sculpture, and church architecture—that magnified Mary/Ecclesia. Interpretations of the Canticles and amplifications thereof in tropes, litanies, and other religious texts seem to have provided a virtual program for medieval religious artists and architects, whose task it was to embody these interpretations in the structure and decor of Romanesque and early Gothic churches. If the female voice of the Canticles, the "bride," is Mary or the Church and the male voice is Christ, then the Canticles' description of the bride is a precious indication of what Christ loved in his Church and what the churches men constructed ought, ideally, to resemble. Statues of black virgins in the crypts of eleventh-century churches, especially in the south of France, in Auvergne and Catalonia,[6] seem to reify in a very literal way the opening lines of the Canticles, wherein the bride describes her blackness and her entry into her lover-king's chambers: "Introduxit me Rex in cellaria sua. . . . Nigra sum, sed formosa" (Canticles 1:3–4). Like the bride of the Canticles, the Romanesque church was dark but ornamented with colors, with precious jewels in reliquaries, and perfumed with rich odors on festive occasions. In a twelfth-century song celebrating the wedding of Christ and Ecclesia beginning "Epithalamia decantans dulcia," we may glimpse an interpretation of the Canticles that encourages or rationalizes the ever greater heights and more beautiful windows of late Romanesque and Gothic churches.[7] In this trope, Christ is the sun who visits and vivifies the bride-Church with his light. Ecclesia speaks:

> By day I take joy, by night I sigh; / I who am sad in the dark in the light become renowned.
>
> Look! he whom I'd been wanting so is bounding over mountains, / leaping over hills, longing to speak to me.
>
> He wanted to see me through windows, through railings; / my womb trembled at the touch of his hand.
>
> The voice of my lover rang out sweeter than honey; / his face was brighter than the bright sun itself:
>
> "My shining dove, my resplendent beloved, / arise! come, make haste! leave all that's old behind.
>
> . . . . / Come, my bride, come rise, come swiftly!
>
> I shall requite you—with me you shall touch heaven!"[8]

Mary's Assumption and the aspiring heights of medieval cathedrals may both be interpretations of the male lover's erotic exhortation in the Canticles: "Surge."[9]

In painted wooden or stone statues and also on the painted vaults of church apses in southern France in the eleventh and twelfth centuries, Mary is represented as *sedes sapientiae*. The same iconography appears in the north in the twelfth-century stained-glass windows of Chartres and in the right-hand tympanum of its west portal, completed before 1150.[10] Although she is seated on a thronelike bench, it is Mary's own rigid body that forms Christ's throne. Such austere and commanding Virgins are *dominae* indeed. At Chartres, where the church was dedicated to the Virgin, her statue on the tympanum over the doorway was decorated with gold: "Decoravit introitum hujus ecclesiae imagine beatae Mariae auro decenter ornata" ("He beautified the entrance to this church with a statue of the blessed Mary ornamented with gold in a comely way").[11] Mary's throne above the right portal is thus directly to the right of Christ on the judgment bench over the central portal. At Christ's right hand, surrounded by a ring of angels in the first voussoir, Mary is represented as queen of heaven and powerful intercessor. She is a figure for the Church, doorway to salvation, but also, in the iconographical program of Chartres, doorway to knowledge: she gives birth to the Word. In the outermost voussoir, figures of the seven liberal arts surround Mary, throne of wisdom. When this portal was carved in the mid-twelfth century, the Church was the doorway to education, and the schools of Chartres were at their peak. Fulbert and later Chartrians had good reason to promote the cult of Mary: in glorifying her, they glorified the Church in its educational and mediating roles.[12] Sometimes, especially in apsidal painting from Byzantine models, Mary is depicted ascending to heaven in a resplendent mandorla or glory flanked by angels. Manuscript illustrations treat the Assumption in similar terms. In a Gospel book from the monastery of Jumièges painted in the third quarter of the eleventh century, for instance, the crowned Virgin rises heavenward in a double glory surrounded by angels, and she holds a sphere and flowering scepter.[13]

Such exaltation of Mary as *domina*, queen of all the saints in heaven, was a more effective way of promoting the Church's universal dominion than the cults of individual saints, whose mortal remains were the property of various competing churches and monasteries. This "political" motive for the cult of the Virgin is perhaps most evident in versified prayers to Mary such as the one from which I have quoted several lines as this chapter's epigraph. The prayer ends with a consideration of Mary's merits as a patron compared to those of other saintly or angelic intercessors:

Cum mente tracto angelos,
Prophetas et apostolos,
Victoriosos martyres
Et praepudicos virgines;

Nullus mihi potentior,
Nullus misericordior,
Illorum pace dixerim,
Videtur matre Domini.

Quapropter hanc praecipue
Patronam meam facere
Nihil religiosius,
Nihil puto salubrius.

Ergo, mater melliflua
Et virgo pudicissima,
Nunc in praesenti sentiam,
Quam de te do, sententiam.[14]

> In my mind, I consider the angels, / the prophets and apostles, / the victorious martyrs, / and the most virtuous virgins.
>
> None of them is more powerful, / none more merciful, / with all due respect, / than is, evidently, the mother of the Lord.
>
> That is why I anticipate / that nothing is more pious, / nothing, I believe, more salutary, / than to make her my patron.
>
> Therefore, mother of the honeyed word, / O most virtuous virgin, / may I now experience the effect / of the [laudatory] message I have given concerning you.

The author of these verses, rather like the troubadours, expects his patron lady (Mary, but also the Church) to reward him for his praise of her.

A great deal of early verbal exaltation of Mary in the West was communally rather than individually expressed. In St. Martial songbooks from the eleventh and twelfth centuries, the Annunciation and Nativity, as well as the Assumption of the Virgin, were frequently troped or elaborated in prose sequences and other forms that harmonized words and music. Some of these religious lyrics were for more private communal, others for more public and festive celebration. Many of the St. Martial tropes are of a truly hermetic (*clus*) nature, because they are couched in pedantic—nearly Hisperic—Latin that would be "Greek" even to the most literate listeners. Nevertheless, such pedantic praise is appropriate to Mary's role as *sedes sapientia*, as the being through whom the incarnate Word was born into the world. Many of these songs, such as the immensely popular and often parodied sequence on the Virgin beginning "Verbum bonum et suave," are veritable celebrations of the W/word, of Christ's birth and of man's delight in language. Some are tissues of exotic words, "precious" names for Mary with which to bejewel her. Léon Gautier, who knew the St. Martial songbooks so well, divulged some of the worst—"Baroque" Latin—offenses against his classical taste. In Paris, B.N. lat. 1338, fol. 70r, for example, one of the epithets for Mary, referring to the Incarnation, is "velata [veiled] choica [earthen] trabaea [purple-striped toga of state]."[15]

In these tropes, it is not only Mary who receives such elaborately euphemistic treatment: every aspect of earlier texts is refurbished and decorated anew in an effort to produce ever more ornate patterns of melodic verbal sounds (which make less and less sense in themselves). Many of the words, as Gautier complains, are sheer inventions to produce the desired assonance (or outright rhyme): "they sought, they adored the use of invented words: man is *terrigena* [born of earth], Christ is *verbigena* [born of the Word], the saints are *paradisicolae* [inhabitants of Paradise]." From time to time, Gautier allows, the modern reader would have the patience to tolerate such pedantic constructions, but "this is the general pattern of the style, and there are hundreds of pages written in this manner: 'Castorum proles dedicativa jam epithalamia reciprocata recolat solempnia; dulcorata recinat orthodoxorum soboles euphonia.' "[16] The reasoned sense (*razo*) of such texts is probably far less important than the aesthetic, intuitive sense we make of their sound patterns. Their sheer irrationality is exalting. To render incomprehensible, to mystify, is to magnify. Nevertheless, to the extent that these hermetic pieces are "new" songs, retroped tropes, refinements of earlier, less incomprehensible lyrics, their intellectual comprehension might have been easier for medieval monastic performers than for us. They had the contextual keys to unlock the meaning of such mystifying language.[17]

There were other pedantic ways of elaborating praise of Mary with more emotional, sensual appeal—at least to modern readers. One of these was to weave words and images from the Canticles into texts in praise of the Virgin. Peter Dronke cites the relatively early Western example of a song beginning "Audite cuncti canticum almificum," written in a ninth-century hand in an even earlier manuscript (Paris, B.N. lat. 17655). Its litany of names for Mary includes Solomonic description that we can visualize; the words might describe a gilt statue or other image of the Virgin to which the medieval worshipper attributed miraculous powers:

O speciosa inter mulieribus,
. . . .
Similis auro erit tua facies,
Argento vero cum distinctionibus:
Miraculorum sancti vernant opera
Gratiarumque tui replent oculi,
Anima digna deoque coniungitur.

You who are lovely among all women, / . . . your face will be like gold, / like true silver preciously carved, / your blessed eyes thrive in working wonders / and make every grace abound, / your peerless soul is joined to God.[18]

The St. Martial songbooks contain similar elaborations. For example, in a late-tenth-century section of Paris, B.N. lat. 1338, fol. 24r–v, strands of the Canticles are worked into the familiar phrases of acclamation of a prose sequence celebrating the Incarnation (which I reproduce approximately as it appears on the manuscript page):

> Aureola dilecta que venit Maria est intacta sportula
> Inquid sofia Et ce puer pera genuit hemanuel
> regem in secula.

> And the dear glory comes. Mary is a spotless little basket wherein, still Virgin, Wisdom engenders Emmanuel, king of the world.

The "new" song begins "Aevia Epithalmia" and narrates Christ's choice of Mary, purest and most beautiful of women, for his mother and bride. As above, I transcribe selected passages from the St. Martial sequence in the spellings and letter groupings of the manuscript. A number of the differences between the medieval sequence's grammar and syntax and those of the Vulgate Latin text produce more melodic sound patterns (assonance in "a" and more regular rhythms) or richer senses (as by combining words to make new ones such as "iherasolomonia," which seems to be a conflation of Jerusalem-Solomon-harmonia):

> Pulcra hamicha estumea suavis atque decorata
> Ceu iherasolomonia ornata
> (fol. 24v)

> (Canticles 6:3) Pulchra es, amica mea, suavis et decora sicut Jerusalem (You are beautiful, my friend, sweet and comely as Jerusalem).

Elaboration of Mary's praise in the language of the Canticles not only encourages a more personal, sensual conception of Mary, but also encourages role-playing. In order to perform such praise, the singers must, in effect, assume the role of the bridegroom, imitate Christ. The relationship between religious tropes and the beginnings of "true" drama (as we know it) has long been a subject of investigation,[19] although scholars have not often considered the more subtle effects of what we might call semi-dramatic choral role-playing, imitation with intent not to deceive, but, rather, to teach and internalize piety. The meditative prayers addressed to the Virgin by St. Anselm are particularly interesting in this light for their alternation of moods or attitudes of the lover, that is, of Anselm or anyone else who would perform his *orationes*. This alternation of moods imitates the alternation of the female lover's moods in the Canticles, but it probably also reflects the variation of attitudes of the singer/servant toward his patron—God—in the Psalms, the singing of which formed the core of monastic worship.

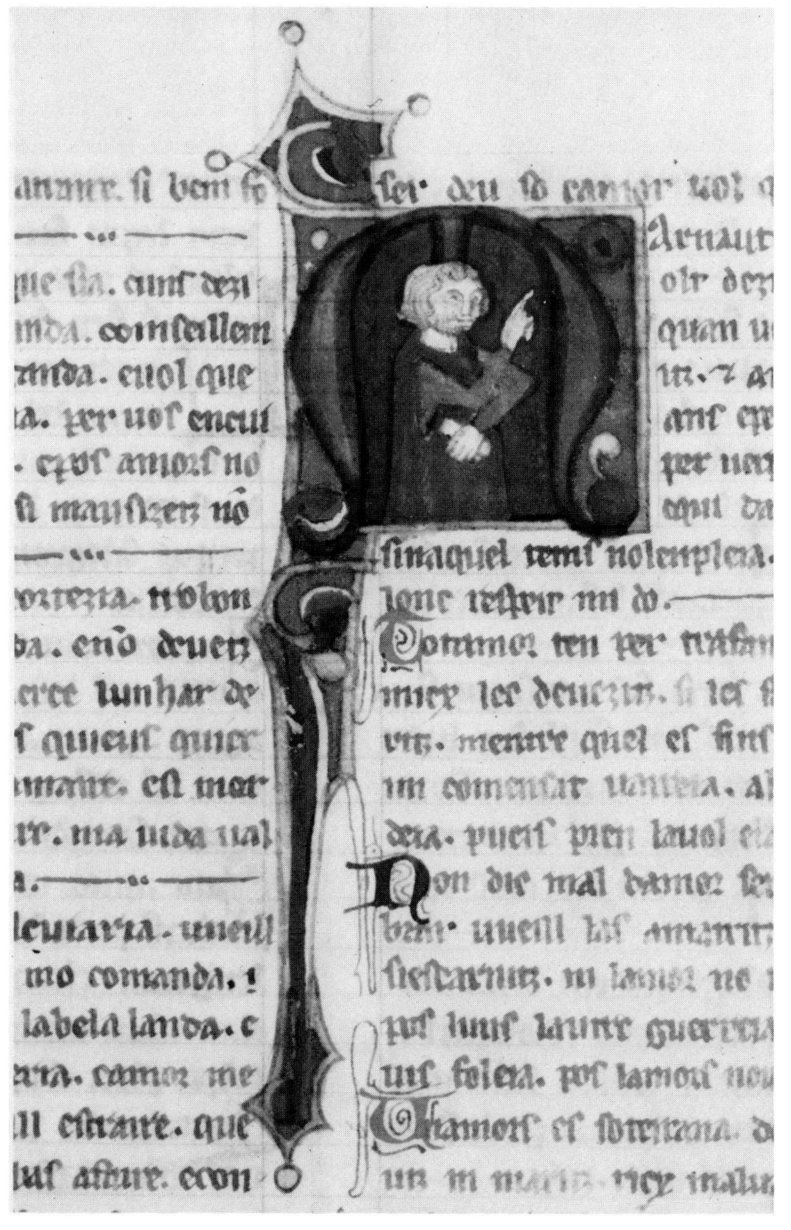

1. Arnaut Tintinac and roll. Paris, B.N. fr. 1749, fol. 69r (E songbook) (phot. Bibl. nat. Paris).

2. Gaubertz de Poicibot displaying a roll. Rome, Vat. lat. 5232, fol. 115r (A songbook) (foto Biblioteca Vaticana).

3. The devil leading the dance of lovers, from Matfre Ermengaud's *Breviari d'amor*. Paris, B.N. fr. 857, fol. 196v (phot. Bibl. nat. Paris).

GENERATIONIS IHU XPI .
Filii dauid . filii abraham . Abraham genuit
isaac . isaac autem genuit iacob . Iacob autem .
genuit iudam et frs eius . Judas autem genuit
phares . et zara dethamar . Phares autē . genuit

4. The word *Liber* from an eleventh-century Bible from St. Martial of Limoges. Paris, B.N. lat. 8[2], fol. 173r (phot. Bibl. nat. Paris).

5. "In principio" from an eleventh-century Bible from St. Martial of Limoges. Paris, B.N. lat. 8[1], fol. 5v (phot. Bibl. nat. Paris).

6. Giraut de Bornelh with his singers. Paris, B.N. fr. 12473, fol. 4r (K songbook) (phot. Bibl. nat. Paris).

7, 8. Marcabru (above) and Bernart de Ventadorn (below). Paris, B.N. fr. 12473, fol. 102r (Marcabru) and fol. 15v (Bernart) (phots. Bibl. nat. Paris).

9. Two needles. New York, Pierpont Morgan 819, fol. 187v (photo Pierpont Morgan Library).

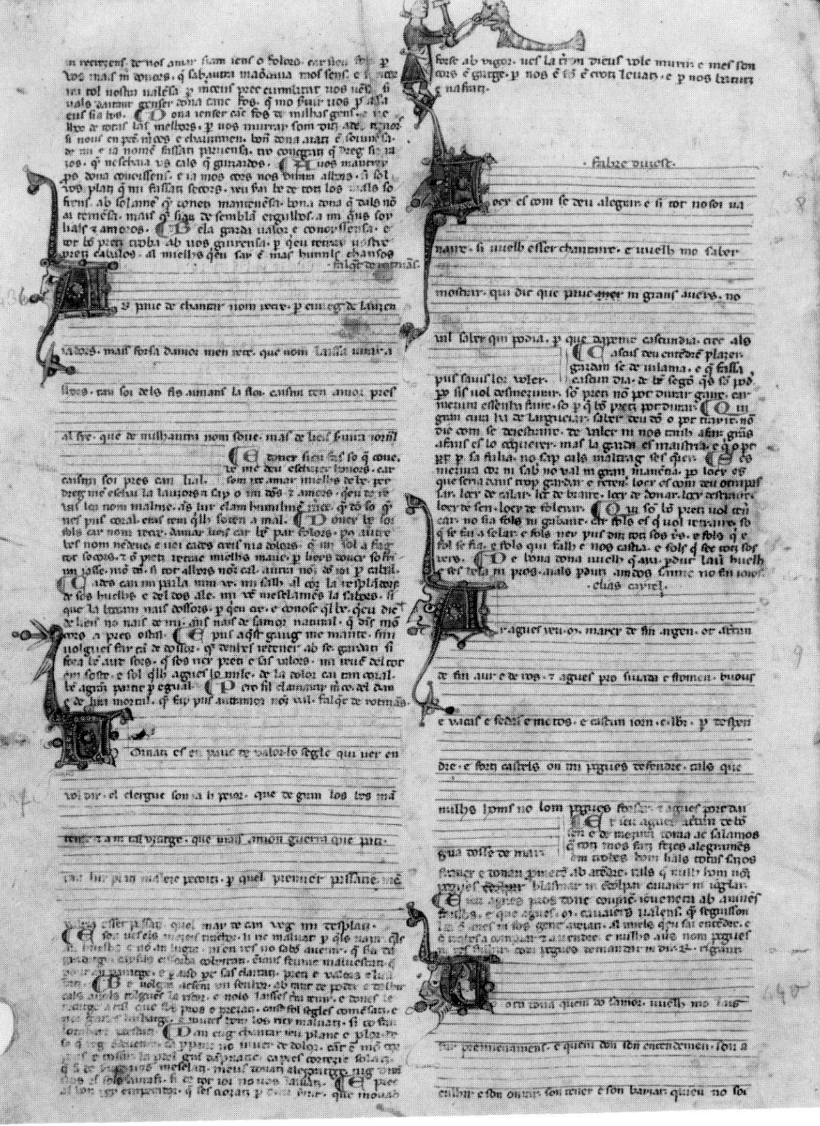

10. Blacksmith pinching the nose of a chimera (top of col. 2). Paris, B.N. fr. 22543, fol. 52v (R songbook) (phot. Bibl. nat. Paris).

11. Peire Cardenal's nose (col. 1, top initial). Paris, B.N. fr. 22543, fol. 69r (R songbook) (phot. Bibl. nat. Paris).

12. Bernart de Ventadorn's noses (col. 1 initials); Bertran de Born's head (col. 2, bottom initial). Paris, B.N. fr. 22543, fol. 57v (R songbook) (phot. Bibl. nat. Paris).

13, 14. Hat in an initial letter and textile initial *I*. Paris, B.N. fr. 856 (C songbook), fol. 366r, col. 2 (hat) and fol. 326v, col. 2 (*I*) (phots. Bibl. nat. Paris).

15, 16. Arnaut Daniel in an initial *L* and fork-tailed lion in an initial *Q*. Paris, B.N. fr. 856 (C songbook), fol. 202v, col. 2 (Arnaut) and fol. 214r, col. 1 (lion) (phots. Bibl. nat. Paris).

17, 18. Chimeras in initial letters. B.N. fr. 856 (C songbook), fol. 212v, col. 1 (lone chimera) and fol. 210r, col. 2 (chimerical couple) (phots. Bibl. nat. Paris).

19. Chimeras. Paris, B.N. fr. 856, fol. 344v (C songbook) (phot. Bibl. nat. Paris).

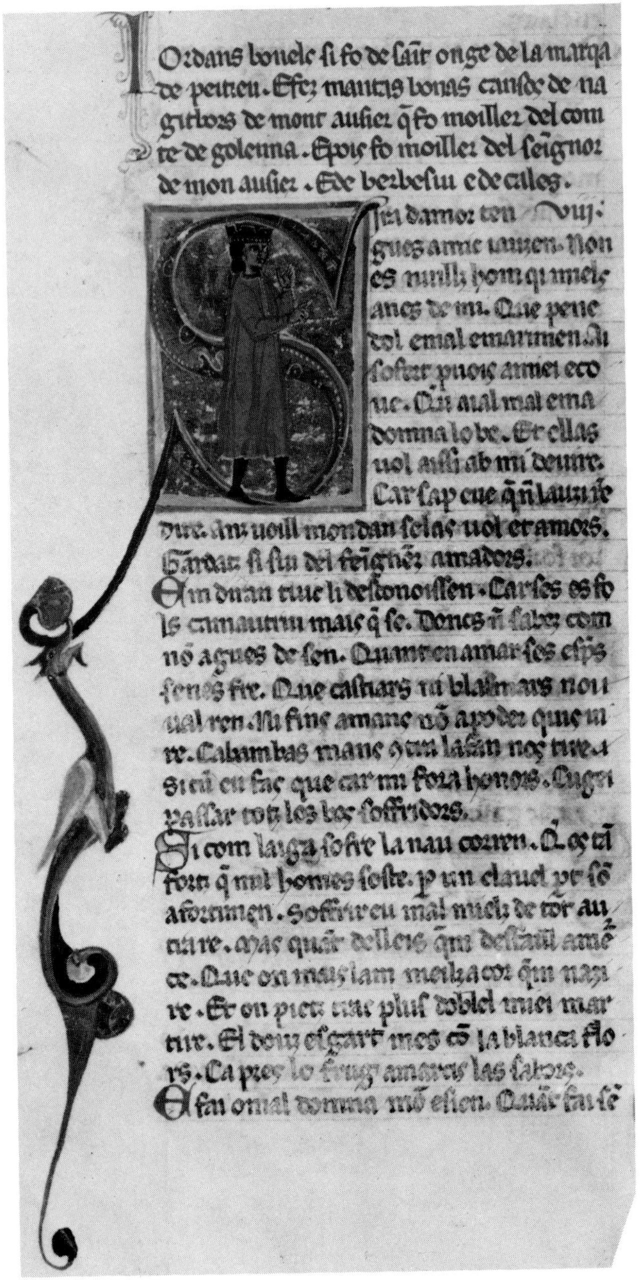

20. Chimerical extension of a letter (left margin). Paris, B.N. fr. 854, fol. 121v, col. 1 (I songbook) (phot. Bibl. nat. Paris).

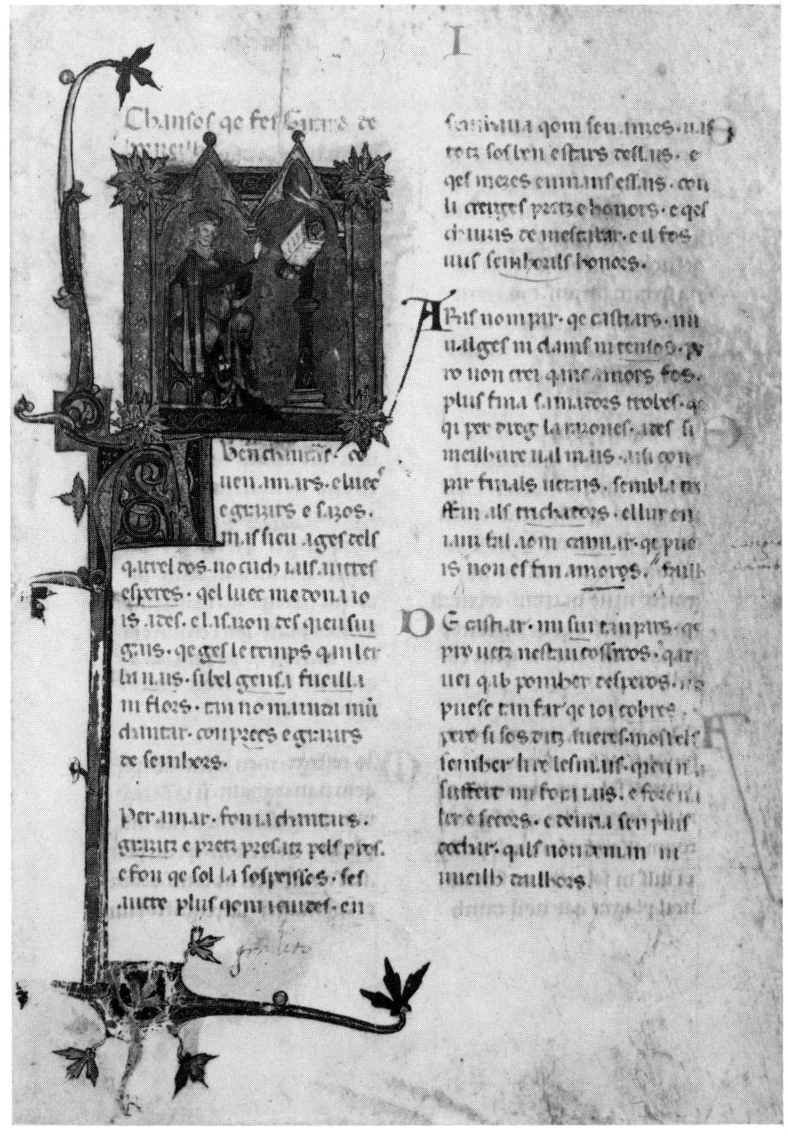

21. Giraut de Bornelh as master. Paris, B.N. fr. 12474, fol. 1r (M songbook) (phot. Bibl. nat. Paris).

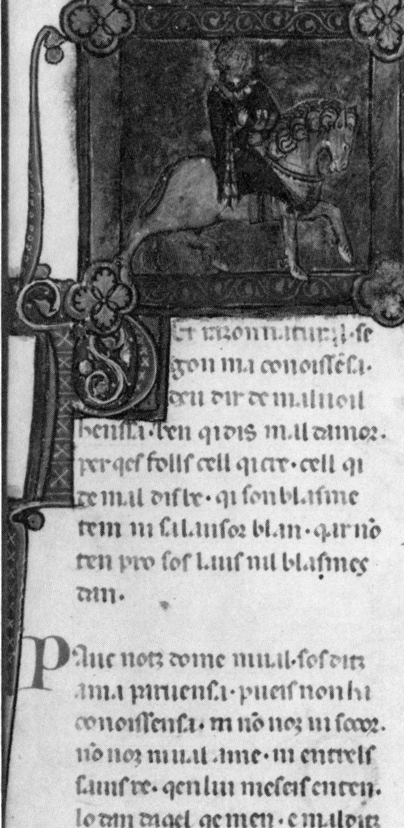

22. Aimeric de Peguilhan and *bas-de-page* grotesque. Paris, B.N. fr. 12474, fol. 89r (M songbook) (phot. Bibl. nat. Paris).

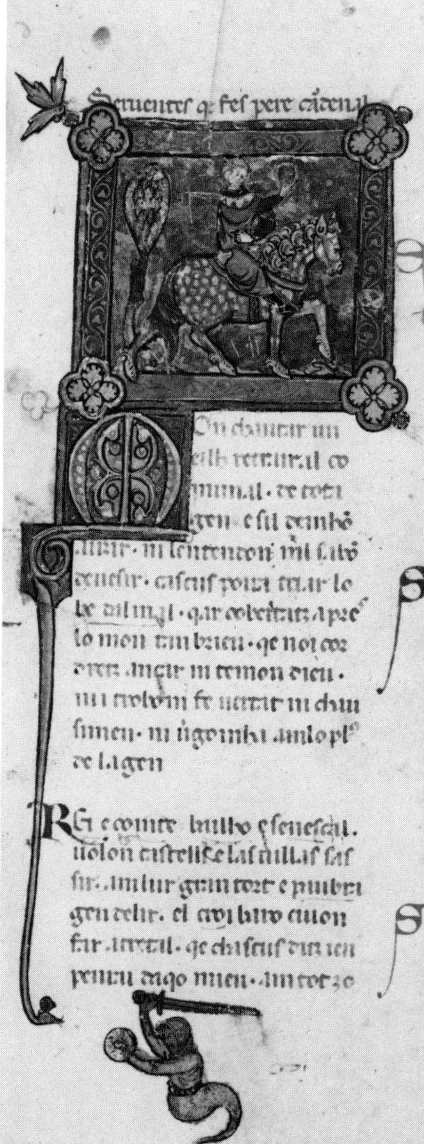

23. Peire Cardenal and *bas-de-page* grotesque. Paris, B.N. fr. 12474, fol. 207r (M songbook) (phot. Bibl. nat. Paris).

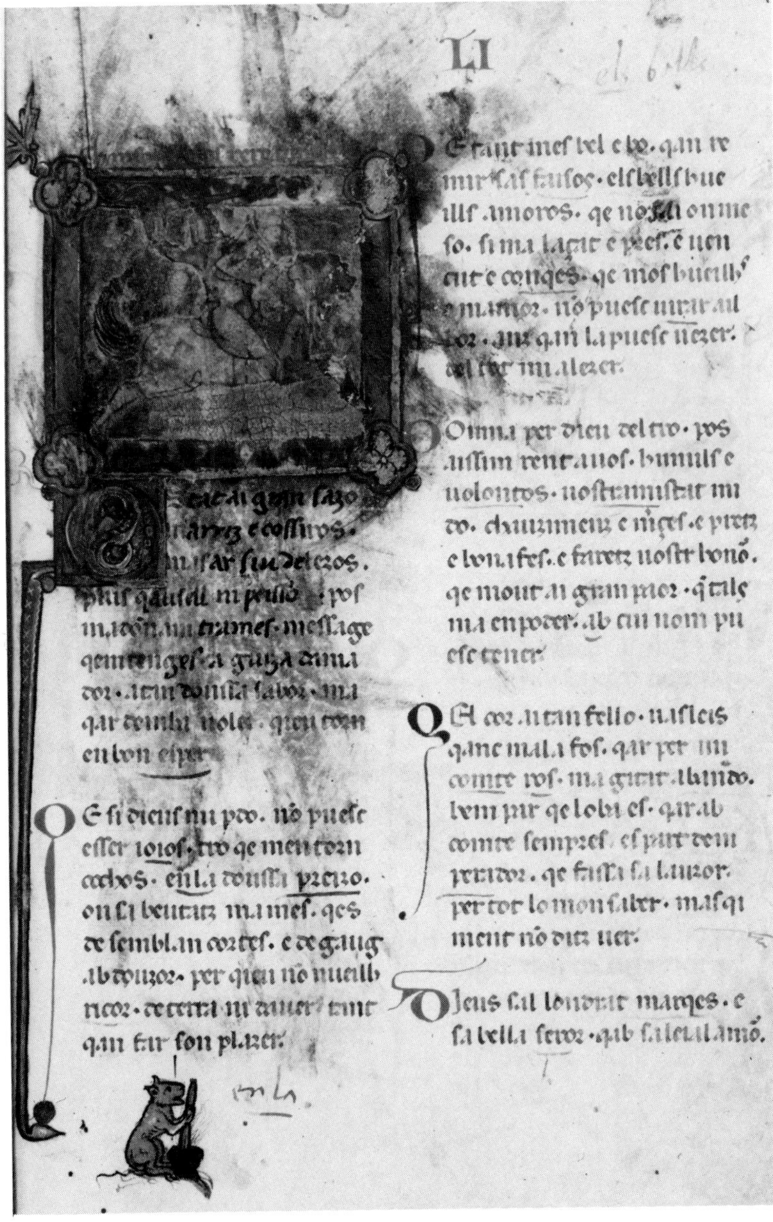

24. Peire Vidal and *bas-de-page* grotesque. Paris, B.N. fr. 12474, fol. 51r (M songbook) (phot. Bibl. nat. Paris).

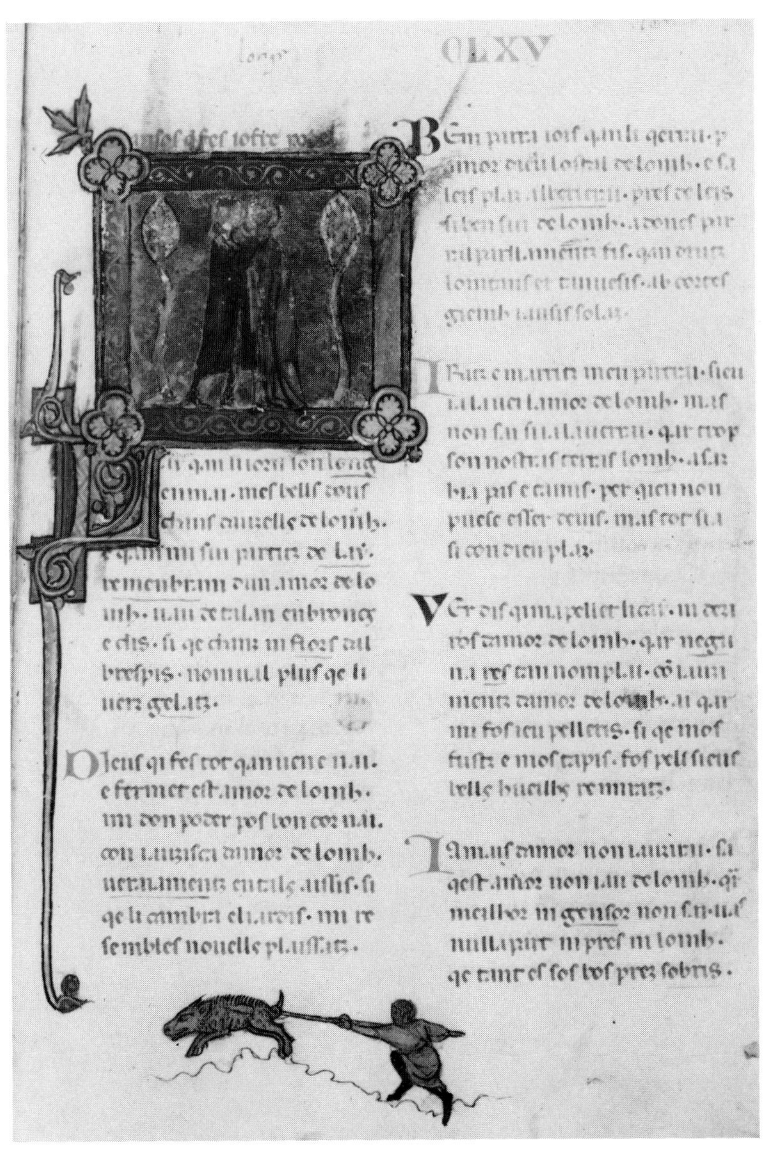

25. Jaufre Rudel and *bas-de-page* grotesque. Paris, B.N. fr. 12474, fol. 165r (M songbook) (phot. Bibl. nat. Paris).

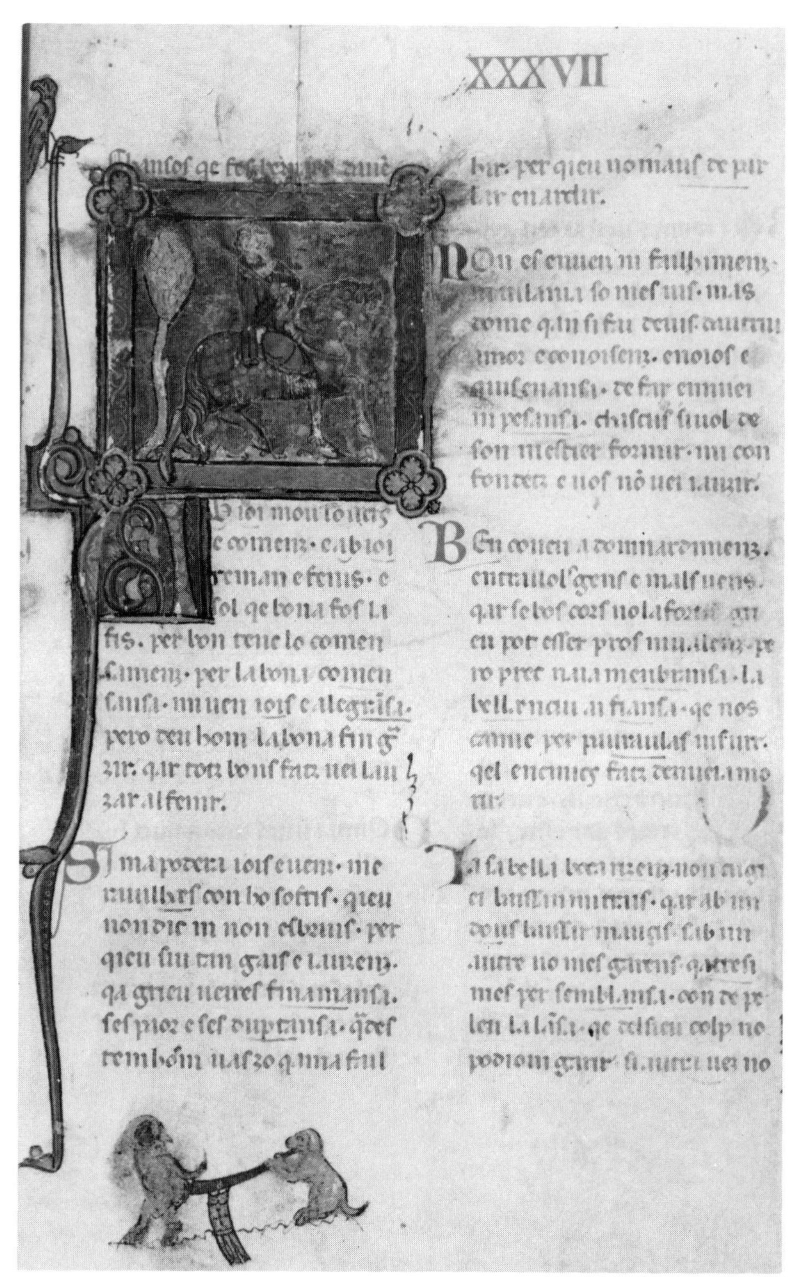

26. Bernart de Ventadorn and *bas-de-page* grotesque. Paris, B.N. fr. 12474, fol. 37r (M songbook) (phot. Bibl. nat. Paris).

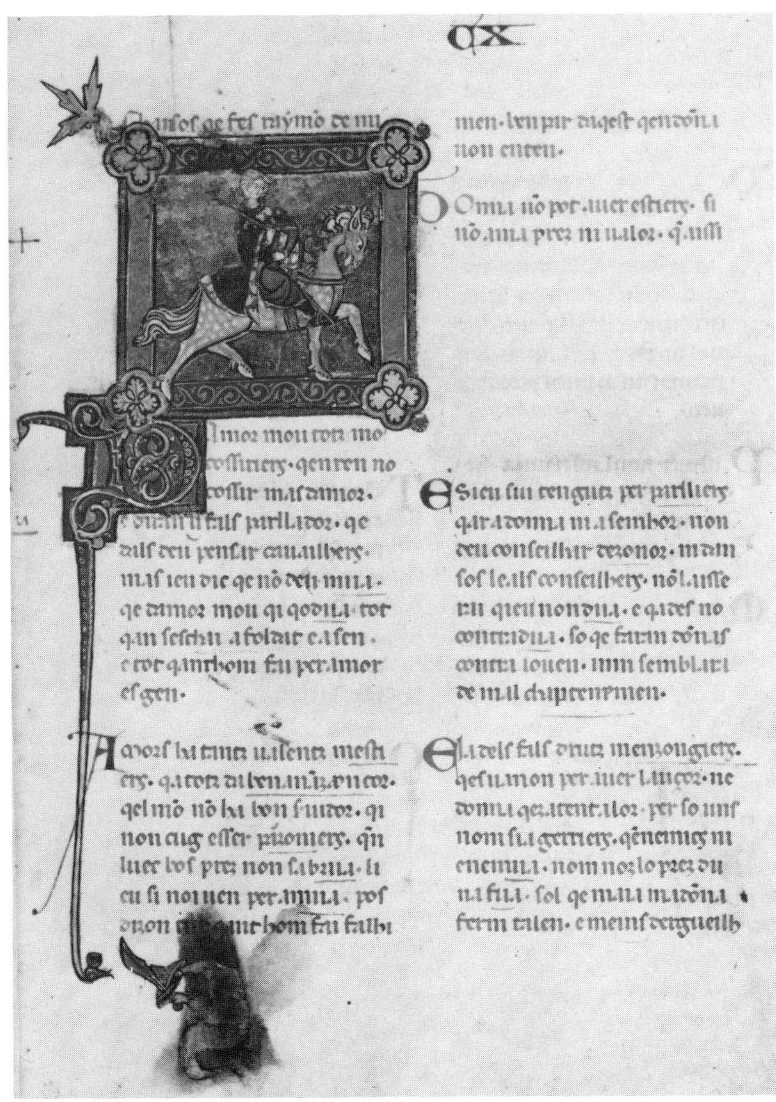

27. Raimon de Miraval and *bas-de-page* grotesque. Paris, B.N. fr. 12474, vol. 110r (M songbook) (phot. Bibl. nat. Paris).

28. Provençal catechism with an erotic initial. Paris, B.N. fr. 2427, fol. 45v (phot. Bibl. nat. Paris).

29. Column of letters as a tree trunk branching into right margin. Paris, B.N. fr. 22543, fol. 21r (R songbook) (phot. Bibl. nat. Paris).

30. Manuscript page as a leaf sprouting from the branch at bottom right. Paris, B.N. fr. 22543, fol. 30v (R songbook) (phot. Bibl. nat. Paris).

31. Human *Q* from an eleventh-century St. Martial trope collection. Paris, B.N. lat. 1119, fol. 69r (phot. Bibl. nat. Paris).

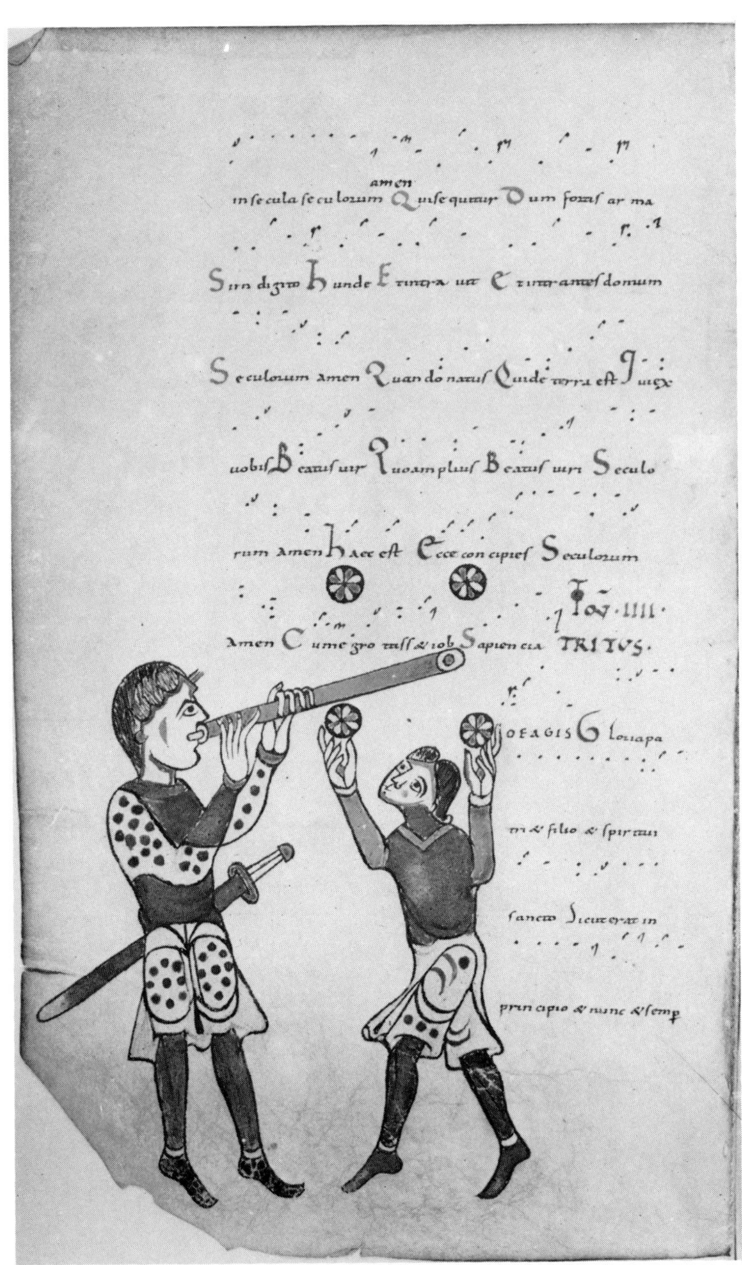

32. Knight and jongleur from an eleventh-century St. Martial tonary. Paris, B.N. lat. 1118, fol. 107v (phot. Bibl. nat. Paris).

33. Two jongleurs from an eleventh-century St. Martial tonary. Paris, B.N. lat. 1118, fol. 111v (phot. Bibl. nat. Paris).

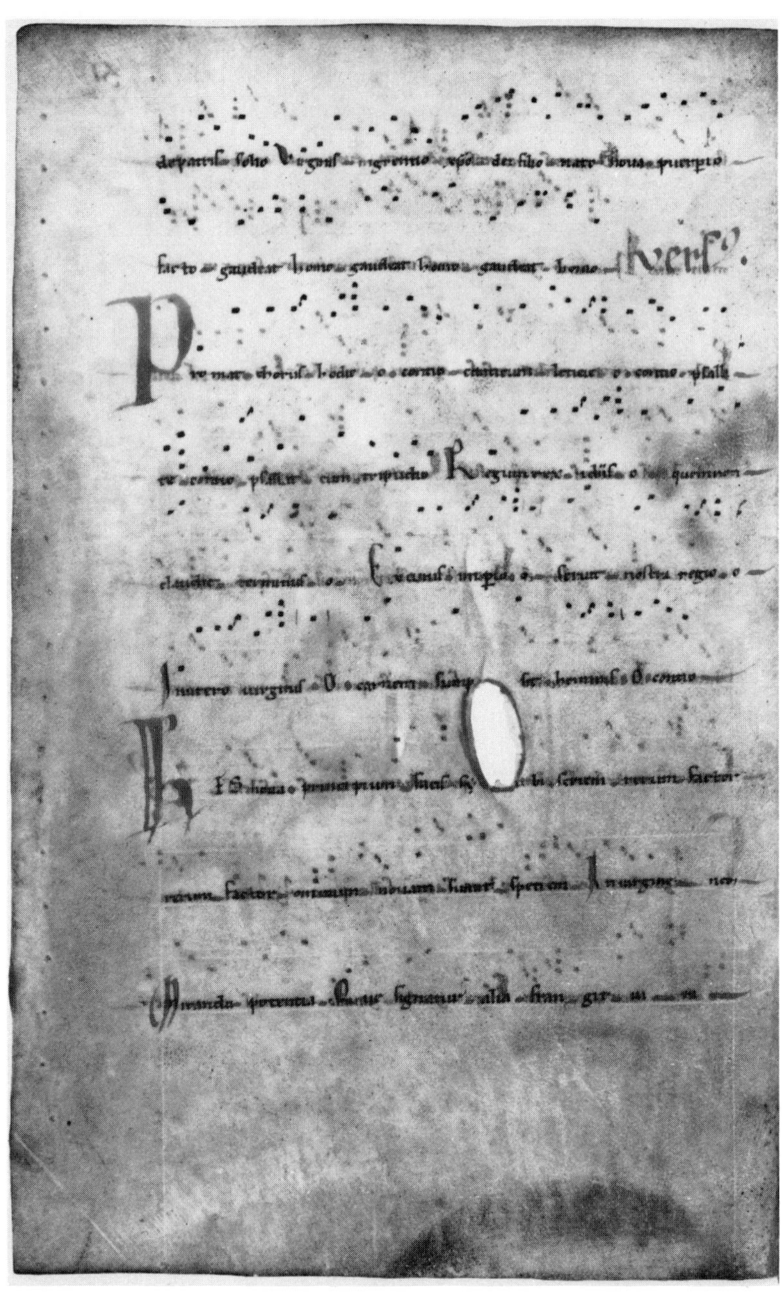

34. Rubricated hole. Paris, B.N. lat. 1139, fol. 51v (phot. Bibl. nat. Paris).

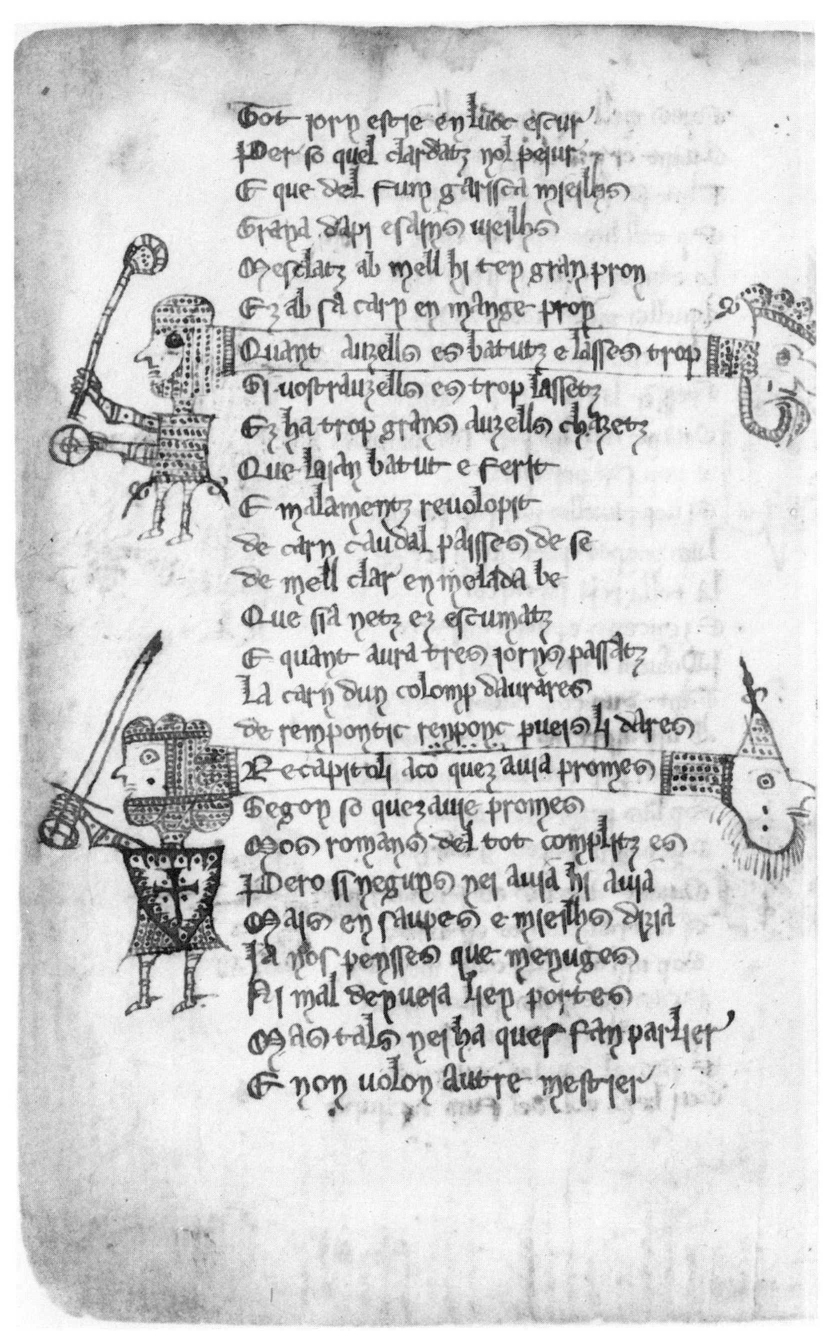

35. Warriors and jongleuresque masks from Daude de Pradas's *Dels Auzels cassadors*. Paris, B.N. nouv. acq. fr. 4506, fol. 70v (phot. Bibl. nat. Paris).

36, 37. "Helias Cairels . . . a jongleur with a viola" (above) and "Marcabruns . . . a male jongleur without an instrument" (below). Rome, Vat. lat. 5232 (A songbook), fol. 50v (Helias) and fol. 27r (Marcabruns) (fotos Biblioteca Vaticana).

From Anselm's cover letter to his friend Gondolphus, who had requested "a great prayer on St. Mary," we know that sometime in the 1070s (the decade of Guillaume IX's birth) Anselm completed three Marian *orationes*.[20] Anselm apologizes to Gondulphus for the length of his missive, explaining that the first two versions of his "oratio ad sanctam virginem mariam" did not satisfy another friend. The third, satisfactory but long, version makes the most extensive use of the erotic love language of the Canticles. All of Anselm's prose prayers are highly rhetorical, ornate in vocabulary, full of alliteration, assonance, and grammatical rhyme. All are divided by Anselm himself into paragraphs that correspond roughly to different names or attributes of Mary which, in turn, elicit different attitudes or roles of the speaker. This continual alternation of attitudes of the first-person speaker in his prayer to Mary as *domina* is similar to the alternating moods from strophe to strophe in many later troubadour *cansos*.

Anselm opens his long, third Marian *oratio* by announcing his desire to praise Mary, whom he names "domina magna":

> Maria, tu illa magna Maria, tu illa maior beatarum Mariarum, tu illa maxima feminarum: te, domina magna et valde magna, te vult cor meum amare, te cupit os meum laudare, te desiderat venerari mens mea, te affectat exorare anima mea, quia tuitioni tuae se commendat tota substantia mea.
>
> (p. 18)

> Mary, you that great Mary, you the greater of the blessed Marys, you the greatest of women: you, great lady, truly great, my heart wants to love you, my mouth yearns to sing your praises, my mind desires to venerate you, my soul aspires to entreat you, my whole being commends itself to your protection.

Not only does Anselm adapt the affective language of the Canticles to his own praise of Mary, but he also humbles the role of the masculine lover. He celebrates Mary's uniqueness in the opening lines, for example, in terms of her greatness above all women, using the word "domina," rather than giving Solomonic descriptions of the beloved's surpassing beauty. From addressing Mary, Anselm turns to address his own heart, which he urges to make every effort "to praise her merits, love her blessed condition, admire her celestial hauteur, and implore the grace of her whose patronage his heart needs every day, and needing desires, and desiring implores, and imploring obtains, if not according to its desires, nevertheless, far beyond its merits" (p. 18).

In a later passage, Anselm engages in some conventional and serious etymologizing wordplay on *mundus* as "world" or "clean" in order to contrast his lady's purity with his own impurity:

> Regina angelorum, domina mundi, mater eius qui mundat mundum, confiteor quia cor meum nimis est immundum, ut merito erubescat in tam mundam intendere, nec digne possit tam mundam intendendo contingere.
>
> (p. 18)

> Queen of the angels, sovereign mistress of the world, mother of Him who purifies the world, I confess that my heart is too impure for me not to blush, deservedly, in striving for one so pure, nor am I able, worthily, stretching toward [you], to touch such purity.

Anselm puts distance between himself and the object of his desire by considering himself too sinful even to touch the purity of his *domina*. Nevertheless, it is in her power to "purify, enlighten, . . . awaken, save" him.

The next paragraph of Anselm's prayer begins in a jubilant mood. He thanks Mary for his salvation, naming her now "genitrix vitae animae meae" ("bearer of the life of my soul"), "altrix reparatoris carnis meae" ("foster mother of the redeemer of my flesh"). But his tongue and mind fail to find words sufficient to praise such benevolence: "Sed quid dicam? Lingua mihi deficit, quia mens non sufficit. Domina, domina, omnia intima mea sollicita sunt, ut tantorum beneficiorum tibi gratias exsolvant" (p. 19). It is Mary who resuscitates, renews, brings back to life, not only the speaker, but "terra, flumina, dies, nox," all of creation. Nevertheless, Anselm's desire is not satisfied. In his own weakness, he fears that he will never attain her. Like the *sponsa* of the Canticles, he seeks and languishes:

> O nimis exaltata, quam sequi conatur affectus animae meae, quo aufugis aciem mentis meae? O pulchra ad intuendum, amabilis ad contemplandum, delectabilis ad amandum, quo evadis capacitatem cordis mei? Praestolare, domina, infirmam animam te sequentem. Ne abscondas te, domina, parum videnti, animae te quaerenti. Miserare, domina, animam post te anhelando languentem.
>
> (p. 21)

> O none-more-exalted, whom the ardor of my soul tries to follow, where do you flee from the sharp regard of my mind? O beautiful to perceive, lovely to contemplate, delightful to love, how do you evade the capacity of my heart? Await, lady, my feeble soul following you. Do not hide, lady, from this weak-spirited soul following you. Have pity, O lady, on the languishing soul sighing for you.

The language Anselm uses to describe his desire for Mary is often highly erotic, Solomonic, full of sensuous physical images and sound patterns:

> Bone tu et bona tu, dulcis tu et dulcis tu, dicite et date animae meae, quo affectu vos memorando de vobis delectetur, delectando iucundetur, iucundando impinguetur. Impinguate et succendite eam vestra dilectione. Vestro continuo amore langueat cor meum, liquefiat anima mea, deficiat caro mea. . . . Utinam sic intima spiritus mei dulcedine vestri affectus impinguentur, ut medullae corporis mei exsiccentur!
>
> (p. 24)

> So good you, you so good; so sweet you, you so sweet, speak to enable my soul, with what emotion remembering you, to desire you, desiring to rejoice, rejoicing to feed. Nourish it, set it afire with your desire. May my heart languish continuously for your love, may my soul melt, may my flesh fail. . . . Oh that the innards of my flesh may burn up! Oh that my intimate spirit may feed on the sweetness of your love, that the marrow of my body may dry up!

Although not worthy of it, Anselm asks for the gift of Mary's love. Only her goodness gives him the temerity to speak:

> Date itaque, piissimi, date obsecro, supplicanti animae meae, non propter meritum meum sed propter meritum vestrum, date illi quanto digni estis amorem vestrum. . . . Forsan praesumendo loquar, sed utique bonitas vestra facit me audacem.
>
> (p. 24)

> Give, therefore, most holy one, give, I beseech you, with my soul imploring you, not according to my merit, but according to your merit, give your love according to however much you are worthy. . . . Perhaps I speak presumptuously, but only your goodness makes me bold.

Anselm closes his prayer with a series of parallel phrases that echo those of the opening lines listing his desires: to venerate Mary with his mind ("mens"), to love her with his heart ("cor"), to desire her with his spirit ("animum"), to serve her with his flesh ("caro"), and to spend his life in this in order to enjoy heaven.

The language of divine love, as Anselm uses it in veneration of Mary and as it is used in hundreds of anonymous Mariological tropes and sequences, was a model for parody by secular poets long before Guillaume IX, with his mock monastery prank, placed it in the mouths of truly "unworthy" lovers. In the tenth century or even earlier, an anonymous composer seems to have had the idea of parodying the Annunciation in a light vein by performing Gabriel's salutation of Mary to a melody with an equivocal refrain, "Deus amet puellam" ("May God love the girl"). Peter Dronke reads this lyric as praise of a living girl and consequently finds it "astonishing." Indeed, he singles it out as the "first lyric in medieval Europe which is wholly courtois" in its praise of a human lady.[21] The lyric appears, as Dronke remarks, in an otherwise highly serious collection of theological texts from a monastery in Erfurt. Although they were not necessarily right in this interpretation, I suspect that its original collectors understood "Deus amet puellam" as a seriously didactic lyric that attempted to bring the Annunciation to life by dramatizing and humanizing it. More fully dramatized verse treatments of the Annunciation, with Mary replying to Gabriel, are not uncommon, even in the tenth century.[22] "Deus amet puellam," however, has only one Latin voice, that of Gabriel, or rather, of the singer who would perform Gabriel's role. As we shall see, the way this lyric was performed could point its meaning in different directions.

The bare text of "Deus amet puellam," without the missing signs of performance, will support either idealizing or materializing, serious or playful interpretations. To us it may seem improperly cute or demeaning to call Mary a "puella," but she is very commonly called such in early texts, as, for example, by Hrothswitha of Gandersheim ("Hinc, quia virgines portasti ventre puella / Inclusum, cuncta qui regit imperio" ["And also because, young girl, you carried in your virginal womb / enclosed, Him whose supremacy rules"]), or by Peter Damian ("Quem mundus ferre nequit, / Totum virgo concepit, / Quo circuitur aether, / Puellae claudit venter" ["He whom the heavens could not bear, / the Virgin conceived entirely; / He who encompasses the skies, / the womb of a young girl enclosed"]).[23] The purpose of this sort of humbling or diminishing praise of Mary is to point the paradox, the mystery of the little girl's bearing the king of heaven. Dronke himself cites from a ninth-century Latin translation of the Greek "Hymnos Akathistos" which begins, "Dulcis et preciosa puella / Relatu angelico habens / Ultra omnes homines dona decoris." Dronke, in turn, translates these lines as "Sweet and precious girl / who through the angel's message / had gifts of beauty beyond all mankind."[24] It is thus not at all unthinkable—at least not to the medieval mind—that God may love a "girl."

In a serious, spiritualizing interpretation of "Deus amet puellam," the singer is Gabriel announcing God's love of Mary and praising her virtue and beauty in the language of the Canticles and of conventional litanies of Mary's names:

Deus amet puellam,
claram et benivolam,
   Deus amet puellam!

Quae sit mente nobilis
ac amico fidelis,
   Deus amet puellam!

Constans gemmis similis
atque claris metallis,
   Deus amet puellam!

. . . .

Cedunt illi rosae
simul atque liliae,
   Deus amet puellam![25]

May God love the girl, / radiant and gracious; / may God love the girl!
How noble of mind / and faithful to her friend; / may God love the girl!
Unchanging as jewels / and bright metals; / may God love the girl! . . .
Roses give way to her / and also lilies; / may God love the girl!

That the saints love the girl ("amant illam sancti") is to be expected if she is Mary. The adoration of saints and angels is part of the iconography of Mary's Assumption. Exclamations such as "Quae fit illi dignitas / cui manet caritas" may be understood both as praise of Mary and as an announcement of her motherhood: "How worthy she is / in whom *caritas* [Christ] dwells." The next lines carry this imaginative replaying of the Annunciation to its figurative "fulfillment." The singer urges Mary to accept her divine lover. In the language of the Canticles, he calls God Mary's "ami" and holds out the promise of the "kiss of his mouth":

Stringe tuum animum,
iunge tuum amicum,
   Deux amet puellam!

Qui tibi noctu dulcia
dare poscit oscula,
   Deus amet puellam!

Clasp your soul, / join your lover. / May God love the girl!
He who by night may give you / the sweet kiss. / May God love the girl!

Strange as they may seem to us, exhortations to Mary to love and embrace Christ appear in other religious verses as well. Peter Damian, in the eleventh-century hymn "O genetrix aeterni," naturalizes the situation by stressing the mother-child relationship in urging Mary to "caress and cherish" the baby who is her own creator, to "cover him with pleasing kisses" ("Oscula grata fige"), and, finally, to "swaddle his members."[26]

The singer of "Deus amet puellam" takes his leave of the girl with a valediction that is perfectly appropriate to a dramatization of the Annunciation:

Vale iam per evum,
Christus sit et tecum.
  Deus amet puellam!

Farewell now and always. / May Christ be with you. / May God love the girl!

Like another dramatizing Annunciation lyric that addresses "brothers" at the end,[27] the final words of "Deus amet puellam" are addressed to everyone:

Omnes dicant Amen
Qui in caelo poscunt requiem!
  Deus amet puellam!

The singer asks all who seek peace in heaven—through Mary's intercession, enabled by God's love of her and hers of Him—to say "Amen." If understood in this way, the lyric is not unfit for inclusion in a collection of religious writings.

Dronke's interpretation of "Deus amet puellam" as a secular poem that applies religious language to a living girl is also a serious, albeit secularizing, interpretation. He reads the refrain as a prayer that God should love (or bless) the speaker's beloved. The central strophes on love's fulfillment, in Dronke's interpretation, urge the girl to take the speaker himself as her lover, to accept his kisses. When it comes to the strophes of farewell and benediction, Dronke's secular reading seems somewhat strained. Nevertheless, he demonstrates many later instances of the serious application of the language of divine love to living female patrons and lovers, such as Peter Damian's use of the phrase from Canticles 6:12, "Revertere, revertere, Sunamitis, revertere ut intueamur te" ("Return, return, O Sulamite, return, return, that we may look at you"), as a refrain in a letter to the Empress Agnes, Guillaume IX's aunt;[28] and the imitation of the Canticles in the twelfth-century secular Latin love lyric "Hebet sydus leti visus," which Abélard (Guillaume IX's contemporary), speaking the language of the *sponsa* of the Canticles, may have written to Héloïse:

Tempus queror tam diurne
  solitudinis,
qui furabar, vi nocturne
  aptitudinis,
  oris basia
a quo stillat cynamomum—
et rimatur cordis domum
  dulcis cassia!

I lament my day-to-day / loneliness, / I who with the strength of night's / compliantness / stole many a kiss / from lips dewy with cinnamon— / and still her scent of cassia pierces / my heart's home![29]

Both Peter Damian and Abélard were proceeding along well-worn paths. Medieval language instruction, following classical methods, encouraged the imitation of model texts, and this involved role-playing, assuming the voice and style of earlier speakers (with varying degrees of faithfulness and seriousness). The Bible was the model text for Christians, and the ideal language of love was inscribed in the Canticles. In his own praise of a living girl, the composer of "Deus amet puellam" might have been inspired by the model of Gabriel's salutation to Mary and the liturgical tropes and figures with which the Annunciation was elaborated. Dronke's secularizing interpretation is just as plausible as the spiritualizing interpretation of the medieval monastic compilers. Neither interpretation is definitive—and many medieval readers would have recognized this.

As Dronke himself suggests, a verse parody of the Canticles such as the famous "Iam dulcis amica" was probably "sung as a sacred conductus at Saint-Martial or Saint-Martin in the same decades as it was performed as a sophisticated love-song for the entertainment of an ecclesiastical court or cathedral school."[30] In the "sacred" version of the St. Martial songbook (Paris, B.N. lat. 1118), the echoes are chiefly Solomonic, whereas in the "secular" version of the Vienna manuscript (CV 116), Dronke notes that the last strophes contain more Ovidian and Virgilian echoes, which would help to signal that the subject of this version is secular love. Even in the St. Martial manuscript, "Iam dulcis amica" has an ambiguous status with respect to the rest of the collection of religious songs. Although it might be performed, with the proper intonations, as a sacred conductus, its position—written on the back of the penultimate leaf of the collection in a different hand from preceding folios—suggests that the late-eleventh-century collector(s) may have been aware of its possible use as a secular love song. The object of desire in "Iam dulcis amica" would depend chiefly on the manner and setting of its performance. The "props" of the religious procession would color its meaning one way; those of the bishop's private quarters could color it another. We might take its description of the lover's splendidly decorated chamber as a description of heaven, figured on earth by the splendid ornamentation of the interior of the Church—or we might take the same description somewhat more literally with reference to the bishop's bedroom:

Iam dulcis amica venito,
Quam sicut cor meum diligo,
Intra in cubiculum meum
Ornamentis cunctis ornatum.

Ibi sunt sedilia strata
Atque velis domus ornata,
Floresque in domo sparguntur,
Herbaeque flagrantes miscentur.

Est ibi mensa apposita,
Universis cibis ornata,
Ibi clarum vinum abundat
Et quidquid te, cara, delectat.

Ibi sonant dulces harmoniae,
Inflantur et altius tibiae,
Ibi puer et docta puella
Cantant tibi cantica pulchra.

Hic cum plectro citharum tangit,
Illa melos cum lyra pangit,
Portantque ministri pateras
Universis [dapibus] plenas.

Ego fui sola in silva
Et dilexi loca secreta,
Frequenter effugi tumultum
De vita in populum multum.

Iam nix glaciesque liquescit,
Folium et herba virescit,
Philomela jam cantat in alto,
Ardet amor cordis in antro.[31]

Now, come, sweet friend, / whom I love as my own heart, / enter into my chamber / ornamented with every ornament.

There are seats arranged / and the house adorned with tapestries, / flowers spread throughout the house, / mixed with fragrant grasses.

> There is a table set / laden with every food; / there clear wine abounds / and whatever you, dear, enjoy.
>
> There resound sweet melodies, / and high-toned flutes are played; / there clever boys and girls / sing for you beautiful songs.
>
> This one touches the zither with the plectrum, / that one composes her melodies with the lyre, / while servants bear bowls / full of every drink.
>
> "I was alone in the wood / and enjoyed its secret places / and I frequently fled the tumult / of life among a multitude of people.
>
> Now the snow and ice melt / and the leaves and grasses grow green. / Now the nightingale sings on high, / the heart's love burns in the hollow of the breast."

In his edition of this lyric from the St. Martial songbook, which he supplies with the title "To the Blessed Virgin Mary," G. M. Dreves notes echoes of the Canticles and interprets the song as Christ's call to Mary, probably at the moment of the Assumption, inviting her to join him in heaven. The problem with this spiritualizing interpretation, in the view of other scholars, is what to do with the voice of the last two strophes, especially the last on the renewal of nature and desire in springtime. If this is the voice of Mary, in response to Christ's call, what is she doing in the woods? The secularizing interpreters see this as the response of a worldly female lover. But one might make the same objections about the *sponsa* and the nature imagery of the Canticles. There is no solid reason why we might not understand the "I" as Mary or the Christian soul. Perhaps we might even think of a choir of monks responding antiphonally to the call of Christ voiced by the first choir. In this interpretation, we might take the "woods" metaphorically—as the woods of the secular world—and the "secret places" as the *hortus conclusus* of the monastery set apart from the tumult of the cities. Or perhaps we might think, more literally, of the contrast in the daily life of a monk between outside and inside—the woods, where he went to meditate or work, and the church's interior, where he went to pray. Only the situation and manner of performance of "Iam dulcis amica" could clear up the ambiguities of the written text.

Scribes, illustrators, and compilers of medieval songbooks occasionally give us evidence of contemporary interpretation, sometimes even of playfully facetious interpretation, of medieval minds toying with signs to produce worldly or erotic meanings in the texts of sacred songs. For example, in one St. Martial songbook (Paris, B.N. lat. 1139), the scribes, rubricators, and compilers seem to have collaborated to play, quite literally, with nothing (although "nothing" of a different sort from Guillaume's "dreyt nien"). They played with a hole in the leather of the page. Instead of stitching the hole together or trying to situate it in an unobtrusive spot or simply ignoring it and writing around it, the compilers placed a large hole directly in the middle of fol. 51, outlined it in red on the verso, and divided a word with it. (See fig. 34.) The reason for such unusual highlighting of this hole becomes more evident upon reading the text in which it intervenes.[32] The song is a joyful one with repeated exclamations of "o," sometimes coupled with "contio" ("O reunion"). It begins, "Promat chorus hodie, o contio, canticum leticie, o contio, psallite contio, psallat cum tripudio" ("Let the chorus sing today—O reunion—a joyful song—O reunion—let the assembly sing to musical accompaniment, let it sing to religious dancing"). This festive conductus, evidently to be accompanied by rhythmic, dancing movements ("cum tripudio"),[33] presents a litany of *cons*. The large hole outlined in red appears in a line that describes the Incarnation:

. . . In utero virginis·o·
carnem sum (   )sit hominis·o·contio.

Hans Spanke has singled out this Limoges Nativity conductus as the metrical and melodic model for Guillaume's "Companho, farai un vers covinen,"[34] the erotic wordplay of which we have already discussed. Full of high spirits, no matter what his age, Guillaume IX seems to have deliberately, facetiously misunderstood the words of the sacred song: "In the womb of a virgin, O, He took on the flesh of a man. O reunion!" The "young" Guillaume may have thought that one good *con-so* deserved another.

8

Jonglerie and the Missing Signs

Facetus, qui jocos et lusus gestis et factis conmendat.

[He is] facetious who accompanies pleasantries with playful gestures and actions.

—Isidore of Seville, *Etymologiae*

The reason for feast days, pagan or Christian, was to remake or renew a connection between man and God. Their purpose was "reunion." The love—or desire—of God for mortals and vice versa was the theme, in one version or another, of most holidays. Earlier unions between God and man would be replayed or mimed in various ways during the course of the celebrations, sometimes in high seriousness (as in the taking of the Eucharist), sometimes in great levity, even in lewdness. The Christian fathers had especially censured the immorality of the theatrical games of the Roman spring holidays or *Floralia*, when Jupiter's love affairs with mortal women (a union of divine and mortal) were a favorite subject for burlesque imitation.[1] Mimes, sometimes barely clothed, played Jupiter's metamorphoses, his ploys for copulating with enticing human ladies. (One of these divine tricks, insemination by shower of gold, puts one in mind of medieval pictorial representations of the divine insemination of Mary by golden rays.) God's love for a "puella" was just the sort of subject that choirboys might take up on festive occasions in facetious burlesque of the language of divine love. The meaning of "Deus amet puellam," of "Iam dulcis amica," and of a host of other love songs using the language of the Canticles depended entirely on who performed them, in what context, and how.[2] Such sensuous imagery was easy to tilt back to the world of the flesh, reversing the direction of Christian exegesis.

The context of Guillaume IX's mock convent of "prostitutes" (probably fellow *jovenes* in female disguise)[3] would surely have brought the meaning of the language of divine love—as expressed in tropes of the offices and other liturgical songs—down to earth. Instead of, or in addition to, foolish misinterpretation of well-known Latin songs, such as the previously discussed conductus as *con-so*, Guillaume and his companions may have invented new tropes of praise in the vernacular. One famous lyric attributed to Guillaume, "Mout jauzens me prenc en amar" (no. 9), may not have been as seriously intended as we have supposed. Its program for the "courtly lover" might be performed as a burlesque of religious, especially monastic, devotion, perhaps more specifically of devotion at Fontevrault to the Virgin and of obedience and service to the first abbess of the order, the beautiful widow Petronille de Craon, and to all the religious sisters.[4] But let me consider Guillaume's lyric first as if he intended it as serious praise of the Virgin. This will require a willing suspension of disbelief.

The opening strophe announces a joyful mood. Many religious tropes begin likewise, although usually in the first person plural, with words such as *congaudeamus*. The singer announces the joy he experiences in love, which he wants to experience again even more intensely. Already, even before straining to do better, Guillaume claims that he loves (or honors or ornaments) better than others are capable of perceiving:

> Mout jauzens me prenc en amar
> un joy don plus mi vuelh aizir,
> e pus en joy vuelh revertir,
> ben dey, si puesc, al mielhs anar,
> quar mielhs or n'am [*or*, ornam], estiers cujar,
> qu'om puesca vezer ni auzir.
> (Paris, B.N. fr. 856, fol. 230r)

Full of high spirits, I get out of loving / a joy that I want to enjoy again, / and because I want to return to joy, / I ought, if I can, to do better, / because already I love ["or n'am"] better, all foolish belief aside, / than one can see or hear.

The next strophe presents images of flowering and illumination that may have religious connotations. It is almost as though Guillaume were troping his joy in terms of a tree of Jesse worked in stained glass that culminates in images of the Virgin and Christ, her chief "joy":

> Ieu, so sabetz, no·m dey gabar
> ni de grans laus no·m say formir,
> mas si anc nulhs joys poc florir,
> aquest deu sobre totz granar
> e part los autres esmerar
> si cum sol brus jorns esclarzir.

I, as you know, should not boast, / nor do I know how to profit from high praise, / but if ever any joy was capable of flowering, / this [joy] ought to bear seed above all / and shine beyond all others, / just as an overcast day usually grows brighter.

The next strophe is formulated around the topos of inexpressibility. It is impossible to imagine such joy or to express it through *trobar*, lyric composition or the "art" of *tropes* (*trop-ar*):

Anc mais no poc hom faissonar
con en voler ni en dezir
ni en pensar ni en cossir;
aitals joys no pot par trobar,
e qui be·l volria lauzar
d'un an no y poiri' avenir.

Never could one imagine / how [it was] by wanting or desiring / or thinking or considering; / such joy cannot find its peer [is not possible through poetic invention], / and whoever would want to praise it well / would not be able to accomplish this in a year.

The next two strophes introduce several themes concerning the effect of a lady on her worshippers that would not, at first glance, seem applicable to the Virgin: the gracious reception and regard of "midons" elicit humble obedience; the man who is able to "seize the joy of her love" should last over a hundred years:

Totz joys li deu humiliar
e tota ricors obezir
midons, per son belh aculhir
e per son belh plazent esguar,
e deu hom mais cent ans durar
qui·l joy de s'amor pot sazir.

Every joy ought to bow to her / and every wealth obey / milady, because of her gracious reception / and her beautiful, pleasing regard, / and the man ought to live more than a hundred years / who is able to seize the joy of her love.

Through her "joy" she can transform men from sickness to health, but also the reverse, if she is ill-tempered:

Per son joy pot malautz sanar,
e per sa ira sas morir,
e savis hom enfolezir,
e belhs hom sa beutat mudar,
e·l plus cortes vilanejar,
e·l totz vilas encortezir.

> Through her joy the sick can get well, / and through her displeasure the healthy can die, / and the wise man can behave foolishly, / and the handsome man can lose his beauty, / and the most courteous can behave rudely, / and the utterly rude can behave courteously.

"Ira" is not one of the traits we usually think of attributing to Mary. Nevertheless, according to popular notions, saints were to be feared for the harm they could do if not worshipped according to their liking, and as chief of the saints, Mary could be a fickle patron like the rest of them.[5] The speaker's desire to use his lady to refresh his heart and renew his flesh so that it would never age may express his belief in saintly charisma or even in the Virgin's redemption of "the flesh" through Christ (albeit this interpretation of salvation is overly literal):

> Pus hom genser no·n pot trobar,
> ni huelhs vezer, ni boca dir,
> a mos obs la·n vuelh retenir,
> per lo cor dedins refrescar
> e per la carn renovellar,
> que no puesca envellezir.

> Because one cannot find a more noble [lady], / nor the eyes see, nor the mouth proclaim, / I want to keep her for my own needs / in order to refresh my heart within / and to renew the flesh / so that it will not be able to grow old.

It is almost as though the speaker were talking about an image or statue of the Virgin, the most beautiful he has ever seen, a private idol or fetish. His request for his lady's love and his promise to keep their relationship secret and to praise her may also apply to the Virgin:

> Si·m vol midons s'amor donar,
> pres suy del penr' e del grazir
> e del celar e del blandir
> e de sos plazers dir e far
> e de son pretz tenir en car
> e de son laus enavantir.

> If my lady wants to give me her love, / I am ready to accept it and appreciate it / and hide it and cherish it / and to say and do her pleasure / and to hold her reputation dear / and to publish her praise.

St. Anselm in his Marian *oratio* requested the Virgin's love, although professing himself to be unworthy of it, and he promised to give Mary what she merited in return, presumably his praise and love. Promises of secrecy in private love relationships with the Virgin were not uncommon in religious lyrics. Dronke has pointed out that "the secrecy of *amour courtois* springs rather from the universal notion of love as a mystery not to be profaned by the outside world, not to be shared by any lover but the beloved."[6] Even the final strophe of "Mout jauzens" is not impervious to pious interpretation. Guillaume does not dare to use a mediator for fear of offending his lady, nor does he dare to express his love too openly. But she can bring out the best in him, "cure" him:

> Ren per autruy non l'aus mandar,
> tal paor ay qu'ades s'azir [*or*, sazir];
> ni ieu mezeys, tan tem falhir,
> no l'aus m'amor fort assemblar.
> Mas elha·m deu mon mielhs triar,
> pus sap c'ab lieys ai a guerir.

I do not dare to send anything by another, / such fear I have that she will suddenly become angry [or, of its being seized on the spot], / nor do I myself, fearing failure so much, / dare to make a strong showing of my love, / but she ought to choose the best for me [or, bring out the best in me], / because she knows that I have to be healed [or, saved] by her.

In some respects, individual worship of Mary privatized religion and encouraged the development of moral conscience. Mary was the intercessor; the sinner-lover did not solicit her "per autrui" (through someone else).

A serious Mariological interpretation of "Mout jauzens" has never been suggested and is almost certainly wrong if the lyric is indeed Guillaume's. Such a pious intention seems incompatible with what we know from other sources about his character. We may assume, then, that the object of Guillaume's desire in "Mout jauzens" is a less exalted lady and that he is using some of the language of contemporary Mariology to praise a living lady—either in earnest or in game. The object of his desire may even be feigned. What if the context of this lyric were the mock-monastery prank? What if the lady were Petronille or, rather, one of Guillaume's fellow *jovenes* got up in a nun's robes to imitate her? Although we do not have any melodic notation for "Mout jauzens," it was probably sung, like others of Guillaume's lyrics, to the melody of a contemporary religious song. A straightforwardly religious performance style would emphasize the poem's Mariological themes and suggest pious adoration of a lady. On the other hand, by vocal or gestural pointing, Guillaume might perform the religious melody and link it with the words of the text facetiously in order to create ambiguities or comic discord. He might, in performance, break up the words and phrases (as we see them fixed on the printed page) in order to evoke equivocal senses and to turn "Mout jauzens" into another *con-so*.

Let me run through the same lyric again, this time imagining a foolish performance context rather than a serious one. If we imagine Abbot Guillaume singing the song in his burlesque convent surrounded by companions playing the roles of prostitutes turned religious, many words take on the lowest, most physical or sensual, of their possible meanings. In the first strophe, love is carnal; "joy" suggests physical excitement or ejaculation; "doing his best" refers to sexual performance, surpassing his own former feats, for Guillaume already loves "better than anyone can see or hear" (that is, "in secret" or "inexpressibly well"). In this eroticizing reading, the second strophe continues the phallic bravado. His own "joy" (or sexual pleasure) is more likely than any other to flourish and produce seed ("granar"), and it deserves admiration over all the rest. Gesture would be all the punctuation necessary to bring out these erotic innuendos. The third strophe might be voiced in such a way as to suggest a lewd sense:

> Never could a man make cunt resound ["fais-sonar con"][7] / by wanting or desiring / or thinking or imagining; / such "joy" cannot be equaled [or, achieved by composing verses, "trobar"], / and whoever would want to praise it [such sexual ecstasy] / would not be able to accomplish this in a year.

The next two strophes might be about love service of a sexual nature or the rules of good masculine performance (a topic dear to Guillaume in his "companho" lyrics). The man must put his every pleasure and "rigor" ("ricors," which sounds like *rigors*) at the humble service of his lady: "Totz joys li deu humiliar / tota ricors obezir / midons." The man must last more than a hundred years who is able to capture the "joy" of her love. In the context of physical lovemaking, this is a richly equivocal statement. The fifth strophe in the C songbook (missing in E) expresses the lady's power over men with emphasis on the damaging effects of her ill-humor. In the sixth strophe, we might take "cor" as "body" or possibly as "horn," which Guillaume wants to refresh "dedins," "within" (the lady?). The fleshly renewal she stimulates may be the lover's erection:

> For my needs I want to "keep" ["retenir"] her, / to refresh the body "within" / and to renew the "flesh" / so that it cannot grow old.

In the next strophe, where Guillaume promises to say and do "the lady's pleasure" as well as praise her, the verbs describing his love service may be tinged with erotic innuendo: "penr'" (take), "grazir" (appreciate), "celar" (conceal or, punning on *selar*, "seal"), "blandir" (caress). In his final prayer, we might even understand "mon mielhs" (my best) as "my honey" (*melhs*), a metaphor for his seminal fluid, which the lady will "draw out" to "cure" him. Other interpreters then and now might discover other pious or profane meanings in the text of "Mout jauzens me prenc en amar." My point in elaborating these two extreme interpretations is to demonstrate how relative the meaning of this sequence of letters or sounds may be, how much their signification depended on the manner and context of their performance.

The modern setting of Guillaume's lyric is an authoritative printed edition surrounded by glosses: introduction, translation, notes. Such an authorizing context compels serious—although not necessarily religious—interpretation. We do not generally read vernacular lyrics praising anonymous ladies as hymns to the Virgin, because we tend to assume (sometimes incorrectly) that religious love poetry at this time would be written in Latin. Thus the standard modern interpretation of "Mout jauzens" treats it as a lyric of serious praise of a living lady, as a "courtly love" lyric, perhaps the very first.[8] Nevertheless, Guillaume IX's original audiences did not interpret his lyrics in such authorizing contexts. Even if the original setting for "Mout jauzens" was not the mock-monastery prank, we know from chroniclers something about Guillaume's performance style and his intention: to entertain. Odericus Vitalis writes that Guillaume performed his lyrics in such a way as to "surpass by far the facetiousness of the jongleurs": "facetos etiam histriones facetiis superans multiplicibus."[9] In classical Latin, *facetus* had a more positive range of meanings than among later medieval Christian authors, who tended to associate facetiousness less with eloquence, refinement, cultivation, or courtesy, and more with inappropriate levity, with using language too lightly, falsely. The ability to "make what one wants of words," as Donatus defined *facetus*, was not necessarily good. In the sentence before he relates the mock-monastery episode, William of Malmesbury, who sums up Guillaume's character as that of a lascivious buffoon ("fatuus et lubricus"), describes his performance style and its effect on audiences: "Composing his trivial amusements with false embellishment, he sang them facetiously to elicit the gaping laughter of his audience" ("Nugas porro suas, falsa quadam venustate condiens, ad facetias revocabat, audientium rictus cachinno distendens").[10]

William of Malmesbury's use of the phrase "ad facetias revocabat" is particularly evocative in this context. *Revoco* could mean "to celebrate" religiously, especially the mass.[11] Hence the phrase might mean "he celebrated in a witty way." But *revoco* could also mean "invite"; thus the phrase might also suggest that he invited wit (or facetious interpretations). The "false ornamentation" with which Guillaume composed his trivial songs may refer to their verbal virtuosities, such as figurative language, which Guillaume himself, boasting in "Ben vuelh que sapchon li pluzor," called the fine coloration ("bona color") of his lyric. "False ornamentation" may also refer to rhyme. Some contemporary religious writers objected to heavily rhymed, leonine verse, which they considered trivializing and hollow, a kind of false embellishment. William of Malmesbury might also be referring to a false melodic ornamentation, the singing of Guillaume's songs in the manner of liturgical ones. Such melodic embellishment would be false, in William's view, because inappropriate to the trivial and vulgar nature and entertaining purpose of Guillaume's lyrics.

The way Guillaume "celebrated" his songs "facetiously" may have been by singing them to the melodies of tropes and other religious songs. Spanke's comparisons of the metrical patterns of St. Martial songs with Guillaume's support this interpretation of William of Malmesbury's complaint: Guillaume was falsely embellishing his profane lyrics by singing them to the melodies of well-known religious songs. Guillaume may also have invited foolish interpretation by the ways he combined religious melodies and singing styles with his own words to bring out equivocal senses. He might occasionally, for example, have performed elaborate melismas on the *con* syllables to emphasize them. He could have divided words—mispunctuated them—with his melodic phrasing, playing the melodic syntax against the proper grammatical syntax. Musicologists would no doubt be able to suggest other ways of linking melodies to words facetiously to bring out multiple senses.[12] The way Guillaume surpassed the cleverness of the jongleurs may have been by using exaggerated refinement in incongruous combination with exaggerated vulgarity, by combining religious performance styles with jongleuresque ones, or by using the "wrong" performance style for the words, mixing registers to comically equi-vocal—double- or multi-voiced—effect.

In performing his own lyrics, Guillaume, the very authoritative and powerful count, was playing the role of the jongleur, which was often a clownish, self-mocking, and completely unauthoritative one.[13] From chronicle accounts such as the story of his mock convent, we infer that Guillaume loved to play roles and that these could be very complex, multilayered roles that set one of Guillaume's personas off against another. In order to perform a lyric such as "En Alvernhe, part Lemozi," the great lord behaved like a jongleur, and in so doing lived up to his own name of "Guillaume" (or Guillem, "trickster"). His performance of this lyric probably involved at least partial impersonation of the deaf-mute pilgrim and gestural emphasis of the pilgrim's grueling experiences making love with the wives of two local lords (Guillaume's vassals). Such role-playing was not intended to persuade or fool the audience into believing the narrative in the same way that a modern actor assumes a role to "realize" a story. On the contrary, the effect of Guillaume's jongleuresque role-playing was to destabilize and call into question the meaning of all signs—musical, gestural, and verbal—by employing incongruous juxtapositions. However much he fooled it up, it would have been difficult for Guillaume's audiences to forget that he was the count when he performed a *con-so* such as "Companho, tant ai agutz d'avols conres." The count's voice under the voice and role of the jongleur would help to point the pun on "comte" as "Count" and bring out the threatening joke, previously discussed, concerning his vassals' properties. One simple gesture of performance—pointing to himself—might unveil the pun that writing disguises for us. When William of Malmesbury uses the phrase "ad facetias revocabat," he may also be referring to the facetious gestures of Guillaume's performances, to "pronunciation" involving his whole body as well as his voice.[14] In his *Etymologies*, in the definition with which I headed this chapter, Isidore of Seville explains *facetus* in terms of games that are gestured or acted out. He seems to be thinking of mime: "facetus, qui jocos et lusus gestis et factis conmendat" ("[He is] facetious who accompanies pleasantries with playful gestures and actions").[15]

From the early Christian fathers on, the comments of censorious ecclesiastics suggest that the art of Roman mimes, *histriones*, and medieval jongleurs involved role-playing, often burlesque in intention, and that the occasion for such performance was the license of the feast. The immoral image of jongleurs that arises from these castigations—which depict jongleurs performing lewd words with lewd gestures, dancing in a lascivious manner, wearing masks and other disguises, and playing and singing erotic songs[16]—contrasts very sharply with the image we have formed of the jongleuresque performance of troubadour love lyrics. Rather than an impersonating performance, possibly burlesque in intention, with music, song, gestures, and distinctive costume, we tend to imagine a staid modern poetry-reading session, and this greatly narrows the range of meanings we discover in troubadour lyric texts.

The troubadours, as I have argued, were for the most part lettered men who composed in writing or with the aid of it and whose compositions might sometimes be displayed in writing and explained competitively in a courtly parody of schoolish exegesis. Nevertheless, the thirteenth-century *vidas* of the Italian AIK songbooks tell us that many troubadours were also performers or jongleurs, that is, secular entertainers who earned a living by singing their own lyrics, and probably also other men's. There were, of course, exceptions. Guillaume IX, Raimbaut d'Orange, and a few other nobles performed their own lyrics—played the jongleur—mainly for the fun of it, not for the profit. To be a "professional" jongleur required a distinctive outfit or *arnes* of bright or multicolored clothing such as is depicted in the eleventh-century St. Martial tonary previously discussed (Paris, B.N. lat. 1118, fols. 107v, 111v; see figs. 32, 33).[17] Often the jongleur assumed a clownish or self-mocking name and a matching persona, such as Papiol (one of Bertran de Born's jongleurs) or Guillem Mita ("Tricky Big-nose"),[18] or a name that characterized the actions of a jongleur in some way, such as the peripatetic title Cerca-mon (World-circler). According to their *vidas*, certain troubadour-jongleurs did not go "in arnes" because they were too poor or spent all they earned in taverns, such as Cadenet and Gillems Magretz. Others, such as Aimeric de Peguilhan, were given a horse and jongleur's garments by a patron lord.[19] The jongleur played a special role and assumed a kind of disguise, rather as a nobleman did when he donned the *arnes* of full knightly armor. In a marginal drawing in Daude de Pradas's *Dels auzels cassadors* (see fig. 35), these two roles, and the games of war and peace, seem to be suggested by the jongleuresque mask in the right margin attached by double lines to the head of the warrior in full armor in the left margin. The phrase the Provençal *vidas* use to describe the assumption of the role of jongleur is usually "fetz se joglars." Arnaut Daniel, for instance, "abandonet las letras, et fetz se joglars."[20] He abandoned a clerical profession and used his literacy, his ability to "juggle letters" in an entertaining way, in the secular role of jongleur.

When a troubadour such as Arnaut performed his own verses, he probably did not speak in his own voice. He played the jongleur, who, in turn, impersonated the lover character of Arnaut's lyrics. This duplicity—or, sometimes, multiplicity—of voices or personas tended to bring out potential ambiguities in the verbal text and to point the erotic innuendos of a lyric such as Arnaut's tour de force, the song "of nail and uncle," in which Arnaut dazzles us with his linguistic dexterity by juggling the same rhyme words in ever different combinations. A medieval audience would not react to Arnaut's performance of this lyric—or of Guillaume IX's of his experiences "En Alvernhe"—as if they were listening to authoritative personal testimony. Instead, licensed by the traditional jocular implications of mime or jongleuresque performance in a secular context, they would become players as well, taking the meaning of the lyrics in game and relishing fleeting equivocations.[21] Guillaume IX's "extraordinary insolence" (to use Rita Lejeune's term)[22] was just that. It was "outside the rules" of everyday social discourse, licensed by Guillaume's creation of a play world within the enclosure of his mock convent or, more often, within the *loc aizi* of the secular court. Inside these bounds, no one, neither the foolish performer-interpreter nor the foolish listener-interpreter, could be held responsible for the meanings he discovered in the combinations of verbal, melodic, and gestural signs that together made up the text of the lyric's performance.

Unfortunately, our means of knowing about the technical methods of medieval jongleuresque performance or about medieval audiences' reactions to these are extremely limited. Most verbal descriptions of jongleurs performing are terse and negative. They occur in ecclesiastical documents that condemn jongleurs for their immorality or attempt to reform them and promote a better kind of jonglerie.[23] Their purpose is not to explain the jongleur's art, but to stop it—or to stop Christians from enjoying it. Although there are many pictorial representations of jongleurs performing, they are not videotapes; they do not capture the movement or syntax of the language of bodily gesture. Furthermore, these static images of jongleurs vary greatly in the degree of seriousness they seem to attribute to the jongleur's art. The grotesque faces on the backs of initials in the Provençal R songbook, with their outstretched tongues releasing or balancing gold balls, seem to represent a very playful kind of jonglerie with the mouth or voice ("de bouche" or "de voz," as it was called in the fourteenth century).[24] Likewise, the playful metamorphosis of meaning involved in jongleuresque interpretive games may be depicted in an initial *S* from a twelfth-century Cistercian manuscript of the *Moralia in Job*.[25] Out of the ends of the *S*, shaped as horns (with a phallic allusion perhaps intended), emerge the naked torsos of four jongleurs: one blowing a horn; one doing a sword trick; one fiddling; one juggling knives. At the center of the *S*, two exactly similar jongleur heads meet, nose to nose, mouth to mouth, so that their features in profile combine into the image of one larger, front-facing head, a jongleuresque trick involving changing perspectives—now we see two heads, now one.

Compared to such images, the depictions of certain troubadours performing as jongleurs in the "textbooks" of the Italian songbooks are highly didactic, and intentionally so. These illustrations have encouraged an overly narrow view of how troubadour lyrics were performed. Within the space of the initial letter of the lyric in these songbooks executed in Italy, we usually see a figure dressed in regular medieval clothes standing in profile or in a frontal pose and gesticulating with outstretched arms. This is a pose of serious communication, not of mime. There is no important difference between the A songbook's depiction of Marcabru's hand gestures and the I and K songbooks' depiction of Giraut de Bornelh's. Nevertheless, we know from the marginal gloss meant for the illustrator of the A songbook, which calls for a jongleur without a musical instrument (".I. homo iugular senca strume[n]ta," fol. 27r; see fig. 37),[26] that Marcabru is supposed to be depicted in the act of jongleuresque performance, whereas Giraut, in accordance with his *vida*, is supposed to be explicating his songs after their performance by his singers (who stand behind him in the picture). Giraut's *vida* specifically remarks how "worthy, understanding" men and women in Giraut's audiences honored him for his masterful explications of his songs: "Fort fo honratz per los valenz homes e per lo entendenz e per las dompnas qu'entendian los sieus maestrals ditz de las soas chansos" ("He was greatly honored by the worthy men and by the intelligent and by the ladies who paid attention to his masterful explanations of his songs").[27] To prevent facetious interpretation of his lyrics, to improve the quality of singing, and probably also to preserve his own dignity and authority, a didactic troubadour such as Giraut traveled with his own singers (Giraut's are called "cantadors" rather than jongleurs) who performed his lyrics under his own supervision (see also Peire Cardenal's *vida*).[28] Yet there is no difference in the Italian illustrations between Giraut's expository hand gestures and Marcabru's, which are, according to the illuminator's instructions, those of a jongleur.

In general, the Italian songbooks, IKN as well as A, represent jongleuresque performance as a dignified rhetorical recitation that involves, to use Geoffrey of Vinsauf's formula, three "tongues" or languages, those of the mouth, face, and hands: "In recitante sonent tres linguae: prima sit oris, altera rhetorici vultus, et tertia gestus."[29] In his *Institutiones* Quintilian gives a very detailed description of various hand gestures that the orator may use to emphasize what he is saying and thus persuade his audience. Quintilian considers the language of gesture to be universally understood: "ut in tanta per omnis gentes nationesque linguae diversitate hic mihi omnium hominum communis sermo videatur" ("And, certainly, in such a great diversity of languages spoken by all peoples and nations, this [of hand gestures] seems to me a speech common to all men").[30] The oversized hands and emphatic gestures of Byzantine and early medieval religious iconography in Western Europe—as, for example, the religious celebrants depicted in a St. Martial tonary such as Paris, B.N. lat. 1118—represent serious, persuasive communication. These silent figures "speak" with their hands in the sign language of lettered men, in an iconography based on classical teachings such as Quintilian's.[31] The same sort of gestures may be used to represent teaching or persuasion in more secular contexts. Preachers in outdoor pulpits in later medieval illuminations display these emphatic gestures—and so do the majority of the troubadours performing as jongleurs in the Italian songbooks. Encouraged by such images of "serious" jonglerie in these didactic songbooks, we have tended to believe that jongleurs delivered troubadour lyrics as ascetic churchmen would have liked; we imagine them reciting or singing in a dignified manner, sometimes to musical accompaniment, but with little or no attempt at impersonation, with none of the "feminine" gestures or the theatrical ones that medieval ecclesiastics, following classical rhetoricians,[32] objected to in mime.

Although there is general scholarly agreement that medieval jongleurs were "descendants" of the Roman mimes, we have generally not imagined the medieval jongleur to be an impersonator in the way Roman mimes were.[33] Nevertheless, the warnings against the use of mimic techniques in Latin writings nearly contemporary with the early troubadours suggest that mime was still thriving in the Middle Ages. For example, Alain de Lille and Matthew de Vendôme both criticized leonine—internal or heavily rhymed—verse (such as that of Guillaume IX or of many religious tropes). In his twelfth-century *De Arte praedicatoria*, Alain considered leonine verse to be theatrical, suited to actors and mimes, hence to be avoided in preaching: "For preaching ought not to have in it scurrilous words or childish ones or the melodies of rhythms or the harmonies of meters, which are made more to soothe the ears than to instruct the mind; such preaching is theatrical and typical of mimes and therefore in every way contemptible."[34] According to Matthew de Vendôme in his early-thirteenth-century *Ars versificatoria*, the empty formalism of leonine verse was the province of jongleurs and "gesticulatrices" (mimes); he might well have been alluding to the jongleuresque, impersonating performance of troubadour verse: "the present teaching . . . excludes deficient verses . . . , that is to say, leonine verses, of which the charm as well as the reason for the name are unknown, and on which certain pipers and the untutored . . . pride themselves."[35] That Matthew substituted "elegy, which sings of winged loves," for the classical genre of mime in his grammar may be due to the medieval practice of dramatizing, impersonating performance of love lyrics.[36]

The first modern scholar to argue that we should read much troubadour verse as dramatized monologue was D. R. Sutherland in an article that has received little attention, "L'Elément théâtrale dans *la canso* chez les troubadours de l'époque classique."[37] In a more recent dissertation, Roy Rosenstein has made a similar suggestion: "when we add . . . that the troubadours called . . . themselves *joglars* (from *joculatores*), the performative, theatrical meaning of *joc d'amor* and of troubadour love lyric leaves little doubt."[38] Sutherland argues that each troubadour tried to create a lover persona with a peculiar temperament that became his "trademark": for Bernart de Ventadorn, the timid, humble lover; for Peire Vidal, the boastful but naive conquerer; for Arnaut Daniel, an eccentric character, love's fool; for Jaufre Rudel, the nostalgic lover-from-afar. She speculates that the kind of persona a troubadour invented, if he also intended to perform his verse, had to do with his own social status, talents for mime and singing, and the quality of his voice and physique. In some cases, she suggests, the persona accurately reflected the "real character" of the troubadour: "the casualness of the great lord had to come naturally to Guillaume of Poitiers or Raimbaut d'Orange, but it was very cleverly exploited in their works."[39] In its larger outlines, Sutherland's view of troubadour lyric as dramatic monologue, as opposed to romantic self-confession, seems right, although her conception of dramatic monologue is insufficient to describe the complexity of medieval jongleuresque performance, which seems to have involved impersonation, that is, obvious, and often multilayered, role-playing that was *not* intended to delude the audience.

In the Middle Ages, impersonation in a secular context signaled game and challenged the audience to play with the possible meanings of the text in ways that recitation, even enlivened by the moderate gestures of rhetorical persuasion, did not. The reciter witnessed to the veracity of the text with the authority of his own person. The jongleur, on the other hand, played one role on top of another. He did not face the audience in his own personality, but, rather, in the entertaining role of jongleur, which, as I have already suggested, could be a "foolish" or vulgar one. Even if a troubadour performed his own compositions, he might behave like a jongleur ("fetz se joglar") when he did so. To debase himself in this way was one of Guillaume IX's sins in the eyes of religious chroniclers.

When a troubadour sent another man to courts to perform his lyrics, this man, too, would play the jongleur playing the lover. Professional jongleurs sometimes developed as trademarks scurrilous or foolish personas. Incongruities between the vulgar jongleuresque persona and the more refined lover persona implicit in the lyric might encourage playful interpretations of a facetious or burlesque nature. It would be difficult to take the lover or his language seriously if played by a clownish jongleur. Primed by expectations of facetiousness aroused by the jongleuresque persona, medieval audiences would be prepared to discover equivocations and innuendos in the language of the lover voiced through the "mask" of the jongleur.[40] The grotesque jongleur faces, with tongues outstretched in song, on the backs of the initials of the southern French R songbook suggest just such a playful dynamic, as opposed to the images of serious delivery within the initial letters in the Italian illuminations.

Bernart de Ventadorn's verse seems to have been especially open to this sort of entertaining burlesque "misinterpretation" that made a joke of the sufferings for love ("pena d'amor") of Bernart's "timid, humble" lover persona, whom he sometimes describes by the *senhal*—or the adjective—"tristans" ("sorrowing" or "the sorrowing one").[41] With a scatological horn- (*cor-* or *corn-*) blowing in a *bas-de-page* grotesque (see fig. 24), the illuminator of the M songbook mocked Bernart's idealism and possibly, more specifically, his testimony to his own purity and refinement ("fin cor"). Other medieval interpreters debased the opening imagery of Bernart's "lauzeta" lyric by understanding it as an autobiographical allegory, with Bernart in the unflattering role of voyeur watching his lady make love with another man.[42] Yet others burlesqued Bernart's refined *cor* by playing on the syllable "venta" in the name "Ventadorn," understanding it as "windy" or "gaseous."[43] Even Peire d'Auvernhe, in his critical portraits of contemporary troubadours in "Cantarai d'aqestz trobadors," demeaned Bernart and ridiculed his "timid, humble" lover persona by dwelling on Bernart's vulgar birth: according to Peire, Bernart's mother was a lowly kitchen servant and vineyard laborer.[44]

One begins to suspect that Bernart did something to encourage such debasing misinterpretation of his lyrics. Sometimes Bernart himself suggests a mocking response to his verse. For instance, at the end of "Amors, e que·us es vejayre," he tells us that he expects his lady to laugh at this lyric on his unrequited love of her. Why, we modern readers wonder, imagining Bernart's poignantly sincere accents, would the lady make fun of a lover who admits his foolish incapacity to do anything but love her, in spite of the social disparity between them? Why should she laugh when Bernart, here or elsewhere, describes his suffering for her in the language of martyrdom?[45] Why should she make fun of his requests? I quote and translate the lyric from the C songbook's version:

Amors, e que·us es veiayre?
Trobatz pus folh mas quan me?
Cujatz vos qu'ieu si'amaire
e que ia no·i trop merce?
Que que·m comandetz a faire,
farai, qu'en aissi·s cove;
mas vos non o faitz ges be
que·m fassatz tot iorn mal traire.

Qu'ieu am la plus de bon aire
del mon mai que nula re;
et elha no m'ama guaire;
no sai per que s'esdeve!
Ans quant ieu m'en cug estraire,
no pues ges, qu'amors mi te;
traitz sui per bona fe,
amors, be·us o puesc retraire!

Ab amor m'er a contendre,
qu' eu no m'en puesc mai tener,
qu'en tal luec m'a fag entendre

don ia nulh ioy non esper;
ans per pauc en feira pendre
quar anc n'aic cor ni voler;
mas ieu non ai ges poder
que·m puesca d'amor defendre.

Pero amors sol dissendre
lai on li ven a plazer,
que·m pot leu guizardon rendre
delh maltrag e del doler,
tan no pot comprar ni vendre
que mais no·m puesca valer,
sol ma dona·m deng voler
e sa paraula atendre.

Qu'ieu sai ben razon e cauza
que puesc a midons mostrar,
que ges longamen no·m auza
la su'amor contrastar
qu'amors que vens tota cauza
que·m venquet de lieys amar,
atretal si pot lieys far
en una petita pauza.

Mout es enveitz e gran nauza
de tostemps merce clamar,
mas amors que ses enclauza
no puesc obrir ni serrar;
las, mos cors no dorm ni pauza
ni pot en un loc estar
ni ges non o puesc durar
si·l dolors no m'asuauza.

Dona, nulhs hom no pot dire
lo bon cor ni·l bon talan
q'eu ai quan de vos cossire,
quar anc re non amei tan;
be m'agron mort li sospire,
dona, passat a un an,
si no fos so·l [*or*, fos sol] bel semblan
per que·m doblon li dezire.

No faitz mais gabar e rire,
dona, quan vos sui denan,
mas si vos m'amessetz tan,
d'alre vos o vengra dire.

Ma chanso apren a dire,
alegret; an dalferan,
porta la na mon tristan
que sap ben gabar e rire.

(Paris, B.N. fr. 856, fol. 58v)

Love, what is your opinion? / Have you ever found a bigger fool than me? / Do you believe I should be a lover / without ever finding favor? / Whatever

> you order me to do, / I will do, as agreed. / But you are not doing the right thing / when you treat me so badly every day.
>
> For I love the noblest woman / in the world more than anything else, / and she does not love me at all. / I don't know why it's that way! / Yet when I think about extricating myself, / I can't, because Love holds me. / I am betrayed by [my] good faith; / Love, I can certainly blame you for that!
>
> I will have to fight with Love, / because I cannot contain myself any longer, / for he makes me aspire / to such a place, where I have no hope of joy. / It almost makes me repent / that I ever had heart or desire. / But I don't have the power / to be able to defend myself against love.
>
> However, Love knows how to strike / wherever he wants to, / and he can easily reward me / for my suffering and grief. / He cannot weigh and sell enough / to be of any value to me, / if only my lady deigned to want me / and to carry out her word.
>
> Well I know reasons and arguments / that I can demonstrate to my lady; / however, I do not dare for long / to dispute her love. / For love, which conquers every argument, / forced me to love her; / and it may do the same to her / in a short space.
>
> It is very bothersome and terribly disruptive / to plead for grace all the time, / but love, which has shut itself in, / I cannot let out or seal up. / Alas, I neither sleep nor rest / nor can I stay in one place, / nor can I endure it / if the suffering does not let up.
>
> Lady, no man can express / the good heart or the good desire / that I have when I think of you, / because I have never loved anything as much; / the sighs would have killed me, / lady, over a year ago, / if the beautiful appearance were not such that / my desires double [or, if it were not for the beautiful appearance alone, / which makes my desires double].
>
> You do nothing but mock and laugh, / lady, whenever I am before you, / but if you loved me much, / you would come to say other things.
>
> Learn to sing my song, / Alegret [or, lightly]; Andalferan [or, Sir Simpleton], / carry it to my Lady Tristan [or, my Sadness] / who knows so well how to mock and laugh.

We might wonder why Bernart would choose, to perform his love-complaint, someone called Alegret, which sounds like the trade name of a jongleur with a "light-spirited" or "joyful" persona. Is Bernart being ironic in naming the performer Alegret? Or is he using the word *alegret* as an adjective to describe his "chanso" and thus to instruct a performer in how the lyric should be performed, that is, lightly, quickly? In the latter case, the performer's name is Andalferan or, dividing the letters of this group and reading "an" as "en," and "dalferan" as a name derived from the root *dauf* meaning "naive or foolish," we might understand the performer's title to be "Sir Simpleton" (*en Dalferan*). Has Bernart deliberately chosen a jongleur with a light-spirited persona—

or instructed a performer with a simpleminded persona to perform his song joyfully—in order to create incongruities between style and content and thereby amuse and elicit the laughter and mockery of his lady, whom he calls "mon Tristan" (my Sadness)? Modern readers of authoritative printed editions of Bernart's lyric take him at his word, believe in his plight, and refrain (according to modern notions of propriety) from laughing at suffering. But what would it do to the meaning of this lyric to interpose between Bernart-as-suffering-lover and his audience a joyful, joking persona, Alegret or Sir Simpleton, dressed foolishly in a jongleur's costume?

Consider the lover's opening interrogation; consider Bernart-Tristans impersonated—ever so imperfectly—by Alegret: "Love, . . . have you ever found a greater fool than me?" The meaning of musical and verbal texts was almost infinitely malleable in performance, and the twisting of their sense was a game sometimes encouraged by the troubadour-composer himself. By having Alegret play Tristans, Bernart may have wanted to make light of the lover's misery and thereby to amuse his lady and others who would hear and see the lyric performed. The game might have gone even further if Alegret intermittently punctuated Bernart's lyric with his voice or gestures in a foolishly erotic or scatological fashion worthy of farce or of even older ithyphallic mime. Alegret might seesaw in his impersonation of the lover's tribulations between spiritualizing and eroticizing interpretations. Gesture might ludicrously reify, for example, in the sixth and seventh strophes above, the lover's complaints about not being able to hide his love or to keep his "cors" in one place, or his statement about the fine quality of his "cor" (heart, body, horn). If Bernart's lyrics were often burlesqued, I suspect that this was because Bernart himself sometimes—although not always—encouraged the game of facetiously debasing interpretation of his lyrics; he may willingly have set up the *lauzengiers*' feast.[46]

Preexisting jongleuresque practices of role-playing and mime encouraged equivocation and were fundamental to the way the early troubadours, from Guillaume IX on, conceived their verse, as fundamental as the ambiguities of writing in the vernacular and the lack of authority of the vernacular script. The medieval audiovisual media both of writing/reading and of mimed song distanced the audience from the composer's directly spoken, authoritative word and thereby helped to license re-creative, playful interpretation. Didactic troubadours who wanted to maintain authority over their "own" texts, such as Giraut de

Bornelh, had every reason to try to avoid interposing an irresponsible jongleuresque persona between themselves and their audiences, every reason to try to replace role-playing, with all of its licentious implications, by recitation and *razo*. This is the serious image of the troubadours given us by the illustrations of the Italian songbooks—and by Dante of himself in his *Vita nuova*. For Guillaume IX and his at least intermittently facetious followers, the grotesque faces and chimeras of the southern French R and C songbooks are far more appropriate representations.

Different medieval performance contexts and techniques could radically change the meaning of the troubadour lyric text just as, today, even a tiny change in tone of voice can reverse the meaning of a statement. The malleability of the meaning of troubadour verse can perhaps best be illustrated by counterpoising pious and burlesque interpretations and imagined, albeit possible, medieval performance contexts for the same lyric text, Guillaume IX's "Pus vezem de novelh florir," which modern scholars have generally considered to be among Guillaume's most refined lyrics. I quote first the C manuscript's version (Paris, B.N. fr. 856, fol. 231r–v) and offer a middle-of-the-road translation that may subsequently be pointed in more extreme directions:

Pus vezem de novelh florir
pratz e vergiers reverdezir,
rius e fontanas esclarzir,
  auras e vens,
ben deu quascus lo ioy iauzir
  don es iauzens.

D'amor non dey dire mas be—
quar no n'ai ni petit ni re?
Quar ben leu plus no m'en cove;
  pero leumens
dona gran ioy qui be mante
  los aizimens.

A totz iorns m'es pres enaissi
qu'anc d'aquo qu'amiey non iauzi,
ni o faray ni anc no fi,
  qu'az esciens
fas mantas res que·l cor me ditz:
  "Tot niens."

Per tal n'ai meyns de bon saber
quar vuelh so que no puesc aver,
e·l reprovier ditz ver
  certanamens:

"A bon coratge bon boder,
  qui·s ben sufrens."

Obediensa deu portar
a motas gens qui vol amar,
e coven li que sapcha far
  faigz avinens,
e que·s guart en cort de parlar
  vilanamens.

Del vers vos dic que mais en vau
qui ben l'enten e n'a plus lau,
que·ls motz son fag tug per egau
  cominalmens,
e·l son et [*or*, sonet], qu'ieu mezeis lo·m lau,
  bos e valens.

Mon Esteve, mas ieu no·i vau,
  sia·l prezens
mos vers e vuelh que d'aquest lau
  sia guirens.

Because we see the meadows flowering again / and the orchards turning green, / the streams and springs running clear, / breezes and winds, / each person ought to delight in the joy / that makes him happy.

Of love I should say nothing but good—/ Why do I have little or none of it? / Simply because more is not suitable for me, / yet easily / he who maintains well the boundaries / gives great joy.

Always I have been caught like this, / for never have I enjoyed what I loved, / nor will I, nor ever have I, / for consciously / I do many things while my heart tells me, / "Everything [is (or) for] nothing."

For this I am the less wise, / because I want what I cannot have, / and the proverb tells the truth, / surely: / "To good courage good power / if one is patient."

He who wants to love / must be obedient to many people, / and he ought to know how to do / gracious deeds / and restrain himself in court from speaking / rudely.

Of the verse I tell you that it is worth more / to the one who understands it well, and has more praise / because the words are all made equal / in common [or, in the vernacular], / and the sound [or, melody] is, even if I praise it myself, / good and worthy.

To my Steven, although I don't go there, / let my verse be a gift, / and I want him [or, it] to be the witness for me / of this praise.

"Pus vezem de novelh florir" rather resembles a catechism for the refined lover, a lesson in which Guillaume internalizes the *tenso* and takes both the side of the teacher who lays down the rules and of the student who questions the benefit of following them. In his internal debate, the lover persona considers alternately what should be and what is: in springtime he ought to celebrate the joy in which he rejoices; he ought to say nothing but good of love—but why is he unfulfilled? Why is his share so small? Why does he feel that everything is for nothing? Why does he want what he cannot have? In an idealizing interpretation of this lyric, the love in question does not necessarily have to be for a living woman; it might as well be love for God or the Virgin or *caritas*. The lover aspires to something that seems unattainable and often feels that he is getting nowhere (str. 3), yet he tells himself to keep on trying (str. 4). Loving requires "obedience" to many people, good deeds, and good speech in court or assembly (str. 5). There is really nothing about the language of this lyric that might not apply to a monk or a canon as well as to a secular lover. Medieval religious buildings, as well as secular ones, had enclosed spaces, "courts" or *loc aizi*. The speaker's statement that his words are made for everyone equally, in common ("que·ls motz son fag tug per egau / cominalmens"), might describe the communal life of convent or court or both. The same value words, such as *fis* (faithful), expressed both feudal and monastic, secular and religious, obedience.

It is conceivable that Guillaume intended "Pus vezem" seriously, either as a statement of religious obedience (capitulation?) or of adherence to a preexisting set of rules of refined worldly love. If so, contemporary chroniclers have not given him his due for piety or refined manners. On the other hand, it is also possible to imagine various ways of setting up the interpretive context of this lyric so as to reverse and profane its message. What if, for example, Guillaume performed the lyric as a kind of catechism during the course of his mock-monastery prank? What if he intoned it with exaggerated religious solemnity and a mixture of pious and profane gestures? The nature of the "joy that everyone rejoices in" would then suggest the springtime orgy. All of the abstract, religious-sounding language would immediately be rerooted in the material world. The proverbial-sounding expression "pero leumens / dona gran joy qui be mante / los aizimens" may mean "but he [Love] who maintains the boundaries well easily gives great joy."[47] However, the sentence could also suggest carnal pleasure, especially if accompanied by lewd gestures: "But he [the man] easily gives great 'joy' who keeps up the 'accommodation'" (or "easement," from the verb *aizir*). As in "En Alvernhe, part Lemozi," where he describes his sexual adventures as a kind of martyrdom, Guillaume might turn ascetic expressions around by describing the ascesis of the sexual athlete or the prostitute who keeps on performing even when not for love and when the heart is not in it, as in the fourth strophe above: "I have the less pleasure / because I want what I cannot have, / and the proverb tells the truth, / certainly: / 'To good courage good power / if one is patient.'" In an eroticized context, emphasized by gestures, the proverbial "where there's a will there's a way" ("A bon coratge bon boder, / qui·s ben sufrens") might also refer to a secular sexual ascesis that is the reverse of religious abstinence—a test involving too much (the theme of several of Guillaume's "companho" lyrics) rather than too little.

We need only imagine "Abbot" Guillaume's mock convent of converted prostitutes as the context for performance of the following strophe (in the a[1] manuscript version, missing in C) for impiously erotic innuendos to surface above its seemingly pious didacticism:

> Ja no sera nuils hom ben fis
> contr'amor, si non l'es aclis,
> et al estranhs et als vezis
> non es consens,
> et a totz sels d'aicels aizis
> obediens.[48]

No man can ever be entirely faithful / to love without humbling [or, bending] himself to it, / being agreeable / [or, "con-sens," "cunt-senting"] to strangers and neighbors alike, / and to everyone in this place / being "obedient."

The next strophe repeats the necessity of obedience as well as of "good deeds" (deeds of what nature? good in what way?) and refined speech in court (euphemism? figurative expressions that barely conceal erotic suggestions?).

The final strophe and envoy Guillaume devotes to authorization of the lyric. First he himself praises its, and implicitly his own, quality or craftsmanship: his verse is worth more if it is understood well, and its sound is good too. If we find the lyric lacking, the fault is in us, for we are not understanding it well. Guillaume is covered. In his envoy he sends this *vers* of praise ("aquest lau"), presumably in writing, to someone he calls "Mon Esteve," whom he asks to "guarantee" ("sia guirens") or witness to it. Rather as a man might witness an act drawn up in a charter, "Esteve" is supposed to vouch for Guillaume's merit and probably also for his authorship of the verses in which Guillaume has inscribed his own worth. However, if preserving authorship required a live witness or guarantor in the new interpretive situation, this suggests that the written text was merely an aid to living memory. Once the signs of its original oral performance were missing, once it had been abbreviated into writing, to maintain control for long over the meaning of the inscribed lyric text or *breu* was virtually impossible. This would require controlling all of the new interpretive contexts—and the minds of auditors—as Giraut de Bornelh apparently tried to do by traveling with his lyric, having his singers perform it, and explicating its meaning himself. Guillaume IX, in contrast, seems to have wanted credit for the technical virtuosities of his compositions, for posing the evocative riddle of his lyrics, but not so much for conveying any single message in them.

All of Guillaume IX's songs are really about "dreyt nien," the nothing of words. Like other secular lords of his time, Guillaume IX was suspicious of the written word and of claims to authoritative interpretation of written texts. Such abstract inscription was not to be trusted, because it left out *actio*; too many signs were missing, especially the important gestural ones. Furthermore, words—more than actions—were the instruments of ecclesiastical control and, increasingly, of the French and English monarchies. Distrust of the written word did not spring from ignorance, but, rather, from knowledge of how words could be used to manipulate those who accepted the meaning other men found in them.[49] There was perhaps even more *mouvance* in the legal charters and documents of ecclesiastical institutions of the time than in the texts of troubadour love lyrics. And if the words of a written text, such as the Bible or a charter, did not change, their meaning might, through interpretation.

Guillaume's linguistic facetiousness was a challenge to the Church on its own battleground. The pope and his representatives might use words to mobilize great numbers of nobles to fight for their feudal overlord, God, in the Holy Land, or to wash away their sins via pious pilgrimage and perhaps martyrdom on the way. Guillaume mocked the language of authority by singing the "miseries of his captivity." Robert d'Arbrissel and other ascetic preachers might use their tongues to persuade Guillaume's fellow noblemen and their wives to give up the material concerns of this world (leaving them to the monasteries and churches). Guillaume countered with his own "abbey" and "liturgy." The bishops of his domain might try to curb Guillaume's libido and control his actions with binding words of excommunication. Guillaume's response was to joke and mock, to overturn an authoritarian sense with foolishness, to play love's martyr and use religious language facetiously, framing it in his *vers* in such a way as to topple its spiritual meaning with physical, erotic innuendoes.

If, in any of his lyrics, Guillaume's tongue was not in his cheek, this was in the final strophe of "Ab la dolchor del temps novel" (in the N manuscript, not collected in C):

> Qu'eu non ai soing de lor lati
> que·m parta de mon Bon Vezi;
> qu'eu sai de paraulas com van,
> ab un breu sermon que s'espel:
> que tal se van d'amor gaban,
> nos n'avem la pessa e·l coutel.[50]

> For I am not worried about their language, / that it should separate me from my Good Neighbor, / because I know how it goes with words, / how they disperse with a brief speech [or, with a brief speech that signifies] / how such people go around bragging about love. / We have the piece and the knife.

As Rita Lejeune remarks, this strophe seems to defy those who would try to part Guillaume from his mistress, whom he calls by the playfully "charitable" *senhal* of "Good Neighbor."[51] The last word of the last line rings out, Lejeune says, like a threat; it recollects Guillaume's very dramatic threat to end the excommunicating bishop's life on the spot with his sword. The "piece and the knife" ("la pessa e·l coutel") are also old symbols of investiture, of possession,[52] symbols that meant more to a secular lord such as Guillaume than did the written words on the legal documents. Guillaume's lyric is an affirmation of old ways and of symbolic gestures that took their meaning from actions—giving and receiving the ring of "drudaria" before putting his hands under his lady's cloak, passing the "piece and the knife" from former to future owner. This secular language of symbolic action Guillaume trusts far more than the new one involving mere words on paper or in the air or the ear in "their language" (or "their Latin"). Guillaume knows "how it goes with words": "ab un breu sermon que s'espel." This line is particularly evocative. In the very passage where he tells us he knows all about words, Guillaume equivocates with words and encourages us to do so. "Breu" might allude to a written parchment "brief" or the abbreviation of speech in writing and also to the short length of an enunciated speech. "S'espel" thus suggests both the letters that signify or "spell themselves out" on the page and the dispersal of voiced speech, its evanescence. With a "brief speech," the words of Guillaume's excommunication disperse and vanish into thin air. Others may go around bragging about love (thinking they may possess it through words), but Guillaume and his lady know otherwise. They have acted, have taken *real* possession of love: to witness, the "piece and the knife."

Conclusion
The Game of Love as "Deep Play"

Societies, like lives, contain their own interpretations.
—Clifford Geertz, *The Interpretation of Cultures*

Guillaume IX's gut reaction may have been to distrust words without actions and to wish for a more macho, bygone era when it was not so important for secular rulers to be skilled in the forms of verbal persuasion. Nevertheless, Guillaume seldom gave up words for actions, seldom acted the deaf-mute for long. He announced his "wordless conquests" in words. He wanted to be good with words, to demonstrate his prowess at appropriating other men's words and making them mean what he wanted by the way he reframed and performed or enacted them. In his contest with the Church, Guillaume appropriated the forms of religious language and filled them with his own content: he farced his new monastery with "prostitutes" and sang religious songs to profane words, turning them into blatant *con-so* or into praise of secular women. His most religious-sounding lyrics concealed phallic bravado and erotic innuendos that could be brought out with the slightest vocal or physical pointing. Guillaume's game of misusing and misinterpreting religious language to make it mean what he wanted was analogous to, a vernacular version of, goliardic or student festive verbal games. Guillaume's game, however, had a cutting political edge to it, for it was the Count of Poitou and Duke of Aquitaine who, using the excuse of youthful high spirits, was turning religious sense into foolishness. Nor was he alone. Guillaume's game quickly caught on—at the *scola neblo* of his vassal, Eble of Ventadorn, called the "cantor," and in other courts of the region as well.

For Guillaume IX and his facetious troubadour followers, the stakes in the game of love were not the sexual favors of living ladies; Guillaume IX did not have to write poetry to get what he wanted from women, nor did other noblemen and courtiers. The object of the twelfth-century game of love was to win with words, just as the object of medieval war games was to win with weapons. The player's goal was not to win the lady, but to win the game, to conquer the masculine opponent(s).[1] The secular *domna* presided as a figurehead (abstract, distant, absent) over the troubadours' vernacular language games in secular courts—much as her religious counterpart, the *domina* of Mary/Ecclesia, presided over the scholarly Latin language games of ecclesiastical schools and courts. To win the lady's favor, to rise in her esteem, to be desired by her: these were the nominal objects of most of the troubadours' verbal contests in the arenas of secular courts. With nearly all games, however, the "material" prize of winning the game is, of itself, not worth the players' effort; it is merely a symbol of a more intangible prize or *pretz*. Everyone knows that the prize of the Olympics is not the gold—or the stamped gold medals. The real object of the troubadours' game of love was to assert personal prowess by wielding words to attack and destroy opponents' words, reversing or modifying their meaning by dismembering or "cutting them up" or by reframing and reinterpreting them in one's own new context.

Sometimes the verbal contest of the game of love took the form of an open debate or *tenso* between two opponents who chose sides in the "joc d'amor" to argue different views of love, one generally more ascetic, one more sensual, as in the debate between Cercamon and a troubadour called Guillaume ("Guilhalmi").[2] More often the "debate" or contest was implicit and involved the "equivocation" of two voices, one superimposed on the other, within the written or the performed text of a single lyric. In such an implicit contest, the composer took both sides of the argument in order to favor one. For example, a facetious troubadour might load the dice by imitating the refined, religious love language of his opponent, only to subvert ascetic views by means of erotic innuendos of a familiar kind easy for audiences to recognize and easy to point in burlesque performance. The ascetic Marcabru used much the same method to burlesque the language of Guillaume IX and his followers in the dialogues of his famous "starling" lyrics and his pastorelles, where the "ladies" (either prostitutes or peasant girls) have the last word.[3] In Marcabru's monologues of castigation, too, he imitated the language of troubadour love lyrics to mock it. For example, he burlesqued troubadour *senhals* by exaggerating and demasking the troubadours' more vaguely suggestive images with his own unequivocally vulgar ones in *senhals* such as "Bon-al-fo" ("Good-to-Fuck") and "Na Cropa fort" ("Lady Strong Crupper").[4]

Marcabru played the facetious troubadours' debasing game on their terms, going them one "down," which only heightened the contest. Other ascetics—some of them monks, canons, and clergy—took a different, and ultimately more promising, tactic; they cleaned up the facetious troubadours' lyrics by interpreting them in a deliberately "good" way; they found sincere adoration of a lady or of the Virgin to be the "true" object of the lyrics, however ambiguously expressed, and wove the facetious troubadours' phrases into the new contexts of their own "sincere" love lyrics. It is not at all inconceivable that Cercamon's lady in "Assatz es or' oimai qu'eu chan" was, as Jeanroy once suggested, the Virgin.[5] In all these cases, however, a contest is implicit in the language of the lyric, a debate between points of view that we sense, if at all, as ambiguity or equivocation.

The jongleuresque performance of a lyric could point its meaning in either ascetic or sensual directions, in accordance with the composer's original intentions or in opposition to them. The ensuing contest of interpretation of the lyric by members of a medieval audience might reinforce or change the emphatic pointing of the jongleuresque performance. Indeed, one of the greatest proofs of medieval intellectual, interpretive prowess seems to have been to twist the meaning of the most challenging phrases or whole texts, either from a sacred meaning to a profane one—as did goliards, Guillaume IX, and other facetious troubadours—or the reverse, from profane to sacred, as did the participants in the Toulouse Consistory's annual spring poetry contests or the anonymous preacher who argued that the dance song of "Bel Aelis" should really be understood as praise of the Virgin,[6] or as did the many medieval monks who invented slightly different spiritualizing glosses for the erotic love songs of the Canticles.[7] Once a written text had traveled beyond its original performance situation, there was no controlling its interpretation. Almost any counterkey—even if it did not match the composer's—would work to unlock the treasure of textual meaning. Marcabru complained that there were too many "counterkeys," with the pernicious result that not a *con*—and not a text—remained wholly one man's; someone else was always breaking into it.[8]

The early troubadours' language of desire was, in many respects, really a desire of language. What they actually accomplished through their verbal contests—besides personal and partisan assertions of interpretive prowess, proving the powers of their "counterkeys"—was the invention and mastery of a written vernacular, of a highly expressive, "literary" language that rivaled Latin. Through their verbal game of love they forged the weapons of peace, that is, the language skills that had become necessary for contemporary secular rulers and courtiers. In "pleading" their causes before their "ladies," they elaborated and refined rhetorical models of persuasion and practiced role-playing; they also polished their interpretive skills on other men's lyrics, finding ever more sophisticated ways to make vernacular words mean what they wanted. The game of love became the vernacular language school of courtiers. Love was, so to speak, the *magister ludi litterarii.*

The game of love undoubtedly had other useful social functions that may also help to account for its survival—with many modifications—over several centuries. As game and play have always done, the largely verbal game of love enabled the dramatization of social tensions and their resolution through symbolic action or dissipation through laughter. According to Erich Köhler's analysis, the game of love may have given a compensatory chance at distinguishing themselves to young nobles and courtiers whose ambition to establish themselves as heads of households was frustrated by peace and by the increasing emphasis on primogeniture.[9] Serious adoration of an unattainable, socially superior *domna* in twelfth-century troubadour love lyrics was, in Köhler's view, a socially sanctioned expression of this otherwise frustrated ambition for material betterment. But what of the facetious troubadours' burlesque interpretations of such thwarted ambition? What would be the effect of pointing the near-pun on *ric* ("wealthy, powerful")/*rege* ("rigid") either in the context of a debate on the relative merits of the poor versus the rich lover or during the poor lover's attempt to redefine *pretz* by claiming that his lady's favor alone makes him *ric*?[10] What of the diligently aspiring, long-suffering lover performed by the foolish jongleur? What of the "windy" version of Bernart de Ventadorn? Such incongruous performances might serve to dissipate social tensions in laughter.

The game of love surely was, to use Clifford Geertz's term, "deep play," in which "much more is at stake than material gain: namely, esteem, honor, dignity, respect—in a word . . . status."[11] In all its various versions, the game of love was highly significant, "artful" play that mirrored and dramatized the key values and conflicts of the various medieval societies that played it. What was at stake was not only the status of individuals or small groups in specific contests and contexts, but, in the broadest sense, as I argued in Chapter 1, the status of an older culture: the voice-, action-, and reality- (rather than representation-) oriented culture of prefeudal southern and western France. In effect, the verbal game of love both eased and helped to accomplish the transition to literacy and to a centered, hierarchized social structure based on authoritative written representations. Even the most radically relativizing or "enriching" troubadour interpretations and the most facetious jongleuresque oral performances of written texts, even those seemingly intent on deauthorizing vernacular inscription, were contestatory or rebellious *in game*, that is, in a *representative* contest, a symbolic opposition, a protest profoundly accommodating.

Notes

CHAPTER 1

1. Juan Ruiz, *Libro de buen amor*, trans. Raymond Willis (Princeton, 1971), pp. 22–26. The chapter epigraph is cited from the critical edition of the *Libro de buen amor* by Manuel Criado de Val and Eric W. Naylor, 2d ed. (Madrid, 1972), S manuscript version, p. 7.

2. Augustine, *On Christian Doctrine*, trans. D. W. Robertson, Jr. (Indianapolis, 1958), I.x–xi, p. 13: "Therefore, since that truth is to be enjoyed which lives immutably, and since God the Trinity, the Author and Founder of the universe, cares for his creatures through that truth, the mind should be cleansed so that it is able to see that light and to cling to it once it is seen. Let us consider this cleansing to be as a journey or voyage home. . . . Although He is our native country, He made Himself also the Way to that country." In a later passage, Augustine states his rule on how to reduce ambiguous scriptural texts to a single, true meaning (III.xv, p. 93): "what is read should be subjected to diligent scrutiny until an interpretation contributing to the reign of charity is produced. If this result appears literally in the text, the expression being considered is not figurative."

3. R. Howard Bloch, *Etymologies and Genealogies: A Literary Anthropology of the French Middle Ages* (Chicago, 1983), p. 44.

4. *T. Lucreti Cari. De rerum natura. Libri sex*, ed. Joseph Martin, 5th ed. (Leipzig, 1963), bk. 2, vv. 251–93, pp. 52–54.

5. Lucretius, *"De Rerum Natura": The Poem on Nature*, trans. C. H. Sisson (Manchester, 1976), bk. 1, vv. 820–29, p. 36.

6. Varro, *De lingua latina: On the Latin Language*, trans. Roland G. Kent, 2 vols. (London, 1938). See also Daniel Taylor, *Declinatio: A Study of the Linguistic Theory of Marcus Terentius Varro* (Amsterdam, 1974).

7. Frederick Ahl, *Metaformations: Soundplay and Wordplay in Ovid and Other Classical Poets* (Ithaca, 1985), pp. 54, 53. Other studies of this nature are Rosamund Deutsch's 1939 doctoral dissertation, *The Pattern of Sound in Lucretius* (rpt. New York, 1978), and Jane Snyder, *Puns and Poetry in Lucretius' "De rerum natura"* (Amsterdam, 1980).

8. Isidori Hispalensis Episcopi, *Etymologiarum sive originum*, ed. W. M. Lindsay, 2 vols. (Oxford, 1911). For example, Isidore's tenth book, "De vocabulis," although it follows immediately on his orderly illustrations of genealogical tables, creates an impression, due to partial repetitions and resemblances of sound that Isidore ignores in his paradigms, of the inextricably complex relationships of words, of an extremely complicated horizontal configuration (rather than an orderly vertical paradigm or a ring of concentric circles leading back to a single original word or letter). Isidore's drive to include everything

(albeit within the bounds of one text) resulted in his becoming, along with the Epicureans' adversary, Lactantius, the chief disseminator of Lucretian atomistic theory in the schools of the high Middle Ages. See Jacques Fontaine, *Isidore de Seville et la culture classique dans l'Espagne wisigothique*, 2 vols. (Paris, 1959), vol. 2, p. 723.

9. Augustine, *The City of God*, trans. Marcus Dods (New York, 1950), IV.8, pp. 116–17.

10. For an outline, based on the best recent historical studies, of the "horizontal" socioeconomic structure of regions of France up to the eleventh century, see Bloch, *Etymologies*, pp. 64–70. To Bloch's list of sources one might add, for the southwest, Archibald R. Lewis, *The Development of Southern French and Catalan Society, 718–1050* (Austin, 1965), and the collection of articles in *Les Structures sociales de l'Aquitaine, du Languedoc et de l'Espagne au premier âge féodale*, Colloques internationaux du Centre National de Recherche Scientifique, Sciences Humaines, Toulouse, 28–31 March 1968 (Paris, 1969).

11. Some of these divergent religious beliefs were labeled and pursued periodically as heresies. On Catharism see Christine Thouzellier, *Catharism et Valdéisme en Languedoc à la fin du XIIe et au début du XIIIe siècle*, 2d ed. (Paris, 1969). On the cult of the saints, see Pierre-André Sigal, *L'Homme et le miracle dans la France médiévale (XIe–XIIe siècle)* (Paris, 1985).

12. M.T. Clanchy, *From Memory to Written Record: England, 1066–1307* (Cambridge, Mass., 1979), p. 233:

> without documents, the establishment of what passed for truth was simple and personal, since it depended on the good word of one's fellows. Remembered truth was also flexible and up to date, because no ancient custom could be proved to be older than the memory of the oldest living wise man. There was no conflict between past and present, between ancient precedents and present practice. Customary law "quietly passes over obsolete laws, which sink into oblivion, and die peacefully, but the law itself remains young, always in the belief that it is old." Written records, on the other hand, do not die peacefully, as they retain a half life in archives and can be resurrected to inform, impress or mystify future generations.

13. Stephen G. Nichols, Jr., *Romanesque Signs: Early Medieval Narrative and Iconography* (New Haven, 1983). Further, for a reproduction and discussion of the tympanum of Vézelay, see Emile Mâle, *Religious Art in France: The Twelfth Century—A Study of the Origins of Medieval Iconography*, trans. M. Mathews (Princeton, 1978), fig. 231, pp. 327ff. For the tympanum of Autun see fig. 292, and pp. 413–14, 417–18 on the iconography of the weighing of souls in southern and western French art.

14. See Mâle, *Religious Art*, fig. 149, and Bloch, *Etymologies*, pp. 87–91.

15. This is what I have done, to some extent, in reading the accounts in Sigal's *L'Homme et le miracle*. Many medieval writers of saints' lives and more general histories, and even some poets, had polemical intentions that led them to record "what ought to have been" as if it were "what was." Marcabru, for example, laments the decline of "old" ways, but he projects onto the past a feudal order. The old order he laments is really the new order he is promoting, a more rigorously hierarchized order from emperors, kings, dukes, and *rics* on down. Thus he ends his crusade exhortation, "Emperaire, per mi mezeis" (J. M. L. Dejeanne, *Poésies complètes du troubadour Marcabru* [Toulouse, 1909], no. 22, pp. 107–10), with a call for princes to serve God, the ultimate suzerain,

for their "fiefs." Marcabru's biblical metaphors of lineage ("Dead are the good old trees," no. 3, p. 9) may seem old to us, but they are a relatively new imposition on the social structure of southwestern France. Likewise, his repeated castigations of "exchange" and barter in social relations may sound like resistance to newly mercantile behavior on the part of the *rics*, but what Marcabru is really opposing is the old acentric order of constantly shifting loyalties, of change and exchange. For a keen analysis of how Marcabru's ideal of poetic language is linked to his ideal of social order, see Bloch, *Etymologies*, pp. 109–113. Quotations from Marcabru are from the Dejeanne edition.

16. Sigal, *L'Homme et le miracle*, p. 41 n. 165.

17. Ibid., pp. 91–92.

18. Ibid., p. 65.

19. Clovis Brunel, *Les Plus Anciennes Chartes en langue provençale* (Paris, 1926).

20. Brunel, *Anciennes Chartes*, no. 4, pp. 6–7.

21. See Clanchy, *Memory to Written Record*, pp. 248–57, on the forgery of documents in the eleventh and twelfth centuries; he suggests that "in England in the century after the Norman Conquest forgery of charters was the rule rather than the exception" (p. 248).

22. From all the charters he has edited, Clovis Brunel lists two charters cut through a design and over fifty cut through a series of letters (by ABC) (*Les Plus Anciennes Chartes en langue provençale. Supplement* [Paris, 1952], p. x n. 7). Clanchy, *Memory to Written Record*, pp. 65–67, defines *charters* more narrowly than does Brunel. Whereas Brunel follows liberal medieval vernacular usage of the word *carta*, Clanchy distinguishes charters from documents called, in medieval Latin, *chirographs* (*chirographi*), which were copied twice or more on the same sheet and then authenticated by cutting through letters or images common to all copies.

23. Bloch, *Etymologies*, p. 13.

24. Ibid., p. 14. On the shift to literacy, see also Brian Stock, *The Implications of Literacy* (Princeton, 1983); Walter Ong, *Orality and Literacy: The Technologizing of the Word* (London, 1982), and "Orality, Literacy, and Medieval Textualization," *New Literary History* 16 (1984): 1–12; Jack Goody, *La Logique de l'écriture* (Paris, 1986).

25. William of Malmesbury, *Gesta regum anglorum*, ed. William Stubbs, 2 vols. (London, 1881, 1889), vol. 2, p. 510. For a useful collection of the texts and translations of historical documents concerning Guillaume IX, see Appendix A in Gerald Bond's *The Poetry of William VII, Count of Poitiers, IX Duke of Aquitaine* (New York, 1982).

26. William of Malmesbury, *Gesta*, vol. 2, p. 510.

27. Odericus Vitalis, *Historia Ecclesiastica*, ed. and trans. Marjorie Chibnall, 6 vols. (Oxford, 1969–1981), vol. 5, 324–25; cited by Bond, pp. 116–17.

28. William D. Paden, Jr., Tilde Sankovitch, Patricia H. Stäblein, *The Poems of the Troubadour Bertran de Born* (Berkeley and Los Angeles, 1986), no. 14, p. 211.

29. The quotation is from Daude de Pradas's lament over the death of a noble patron, "Ben deu esser solatz marritz," ed. A. H. Schutz, *Poésies de Daude de Pradas* (Toulouse, 1933), no. 17, p. 83.

30. Dejeanne, "Lo vers comens quan vei del fau," no. 33, pp. 159–60.

31. The Christian sense of Marcabru's "fin amors" is evident, for instance, in his "Pus mos coratges s'es clarzitz" (no. 40, p. 198), where he calls "fin amors"

the "fountain of goodness that has enlightened the whole world": "Ai! fin' Amors, fons de bontat, / C'a[s] tot lo mon illuminat." Those who blame "fin' Amors" (who behave disloyally and uncharitably) will, according to Marcabru, go to hell.

32. Carl Appel, *Provenzalische Chrestomatie*, 6th ed. (Leipzig, 1932), no. 42, pp. 82–83.

33. Nicolò Pasero, *Guglielmo IX d'Aquitanía: Poesie* (Modena, 1973), no. 4, p. 92, C manuscript variants. Quotations of Guillaume's verse are from this edition, unless otherwise noted.

34. Charles Camproux, "Remarque sur la langue de Guilhem de Peitieus," *Mélanges . . . Rita Lejeune*, 2 vols. (Gembloux, 1969), vol. 1, p. 83.

35. L. T. Topsfield, "Three Levels of Love in the Poetry of the Early Troubadours: Guilhem IX, Marcabru, and Jaufre Rudel," *Mélanges . . . Jean Boutière*, 2 vols. (Liège, 1971), vol. 1, p. 578. In Pasero's notes, the résumé of interpretations of the phrase "Norman ni Franses" takes two pages, 105–7.

36. Barthes uses the phrase in an interpretive preface to Pierre Guyotat's *Eden, Eden, Eden* (Paris, 1970), p. 9.

37. Coming sometime later, the counterpoems of Marcabru's interpretations of Guillaume's verse are grossly demeaning. For example, the figurative and literal "counterkeys" Marcabru discovers are those that enable the servants of a lord to cuckold him (no. 41, pp. 202–3):

> Tans n'i vei dels contraclaviers,
> Greu sai remanra conz entiers
> A crebar ni a meich partir.

I see so many counterkeys / that here a cunt will with difficulty remain whole / to penetrate or divide in half.

38. Marcabru reverses the name *trobador* to give "torbador" (perturber), in imitation of the troubadours' mixing or reversal of good and bad (no. 36, p. 175):

> Lonc temps auran cossentida
> Els maritz lor desonor,
> Als acropitz lenguas planas
> Torbadors d'amistat fina.

For a long time husbands have consented / in their own dishonor / by the vulgar smooth tongues, / disrupters of true friendship.

39. Alberto del Monte, *Peire d'Alvernha: Liriche* (Turin, 1955), no. 16, pp. 159–60:

> Cui bon vers agrad' a auzir,
> de me lo cosselh qu'el escout
> aquest c'ara comens a dir;
> que pus li er sos cors assis
> en ben entendre·ls sos e·ls motz,
> ia non dira qu'el anc auzis
> melhors ditz trobatz lujnh nj prop.

Whoever delights in listening to good verse, / I counsel him to listen / to this one that I have just begun to speak; / for once his heart is set / on understanding well the sounds and the words, / he won't say that he's ever heard / better instruction invented far or near.

The instruction of this verse, which Peire says he "reads" ("legir," C variant "legit," p. 163) terminates with an exegesis of a Last Judgment scene with Christ in majesty displaying signs of the crucifixion, which Peire asks his listeners to gaze at above an arch (a painted roof vault or, more likely, a sculpted tympanum): "Ben deuria pensar morir / qui dreitz huils garda sus lo vout" ("He ought to think of dying / who looks straight above the arch").

40. Pasero, "Pus vezem de novelh florir," no. 7, p. 198, C ms. variants: "Del vers vos dic que mais en vau / qui be l'enten, e n'a plus lau" ("Of this verse I say that it is worth more / when understood well and [it] has more praise").

41. Carl Appel, *Bernart von Ventadorn: Seine Lieder* (Halle, 1915), no. 15, p. 87. (Citations are from this edition, unless otherwise identified.)

42. Robert Lafont, "Travail et retravail textuel: Le Poème à structure répétitive et sa tradition manuscrite," *Revue des Langues Romanes* 87 (1983): 56: "we are attempting . . . not an establishment of the archetypal text, but an evaluation of the thickness of scriptural interventions."

43. Charles Camproux, "'Seigneur Dieu qui es du monde tête et roi,' canso III de Guilhem de Peitieus," *Mélanges . . . Pierre Le Gentil* (Paris, 1973), p. 172.

44. Roger Dragonetti, "*Aizi* et *aizimen* chez les plus anciens troubadours," *Mélanges . . . Maurice Delbouille*, 2 vols. (Gembloux, 1964), vol. 2, p. 152.

45. Roger Dragonetti, *La Vie de la lettre au moyen âge* (Paris, 1980), p. 216.

46. See Nathaniel Smith, *Figures of Repetition in the Old Provençal Lyric* (Chapel Hill, 1976), esp. chapter five, "Sound Effects"; Linda Paterson, *Troubadours and Eloquence* (Oxford, 1975), pp. 182–84; Paul Zumthor, *Langue, texte, énigme* (Paris, 1975), pp. 59–67; and, for a similar study of sound textures in Old French lyrics, see Roger Dragonetti, *La Technique poétique des trouvères dans la chanson courtoise* (Paris, 1957), pp. 422–31.

47. See Michel Meylakh, "Troubadours et anagrammes (structures anagrammatiques dans la chanson X d'Arnaut Daniel)," *Mélanges . . . Charles Camproux* (Montpellier, 1978), pp. 149–58; and F. R. P. Akehurst, "The Paragram *Amor* in the Troubadours," *Romanic Review* 69 (1978): 15–21.

48. Charles Camproux, "'Faray un vers tot covinen,'" *Mélanges . . . Jean Frappier*, 2 vols. (Geneva, 1970), vol. 1, esp. pp. 164–66, and "'Seigneur Dieu qui es du monde tête et roi,'" p. 165; Dragonetti, *La Vie de la lettre*, pp. 22–40, and *Le Gai Savoir dans la rhétorique courtoise* (Paris, 1982), pp. 17–18; Dietmar Rieger, "Guillaume IX d'Aquitaine et l'idéologie troubadouresque: Remarques sur l'emploi des noms propres chez le 'premier' troubadour," *Romania* 101 (1980): 433–49.

49. See, for instance, Stephen G. Nichols, Jr., "*Canso→Conso*: Structures of Parodic Humor in Three Songs of Guilhem IX," *L'Esprit Créateur* 16 (1976): 16–29.

50. On Jaufre Rudel's famous lyric concerning "love from afar" see John A. Rea, "The Pilgrim Figure in Jaufre Rudel," *Neophilologus* 65 (1981): 518–23; Lynne Lawner, "The Riddle of the Dead Man (Raimbaut de Vaqueiras, 'Las frevols venson lo plus fort')," *Cultura Neolatina* 27 (1967): 30–49; and William Paden, "Utrum Copularentur: Of *Cors*," *L'Esprit Créateur* 19 (1979): 70–83.

51. Charles Jernigan, "The Song of Nail and Uncle: Arnaut Daniel's Sestina 'Lo ferm voler q'el cor m'intra,'" *Studies in Philology* 71 (1974): 149.

52. René Nelli, *Les Ecrivains anticonformistes du moyen âge occitan*. Vol. 1: *La Femme et l'amour* (Paris, 1977); Pierre Bec, *Burlesque et obscénité chez les troubadours: Pour une approche du contre-texte médiéval* (Paris, 1984).

53. Hans Robert Jauss, *Pour une esthétique de la réception*, trans. Claude

Maillard (Paris, 1978), p. 67. Jauss makes this remark with respect to the hermetic lyricism of Mallarmé and his circle, which enabled the "renaissance" or renewed appreciation of Baroque poetry.

CHAPTER 2

1. On this figure see the articles of Maria Dumitrescu, "Eble II de Ventadorn et Guillaume IX d'Aquitaine," *Cahiers de Civilisation Médiévale* 11 (1968): 379–412; and "*L'Escola n'Eblon* et ses répresentants," in *Mélanges . . . Rita Lejeune*, 2 vols. (Gembloux, 1969), vol. 1, pp. 107–18.

2. François Raynouard, *Lexique roman ou dictionnaire de la langue des troubadours*, 6 vols. (Paris, 1836–1844). Emil Levy, *Provenzalisches Supplement-Wörterbuch*, 8 vols. (Leipzig, 1894–1924), lists, additionally, a verb form, *se neblar*, having to do with plants ruined by fog. See also Kurt Baldinger, *Dictionnaire onomasiologique de l'ancien occitan*, part 1 (Tübingen, 1975), p. 39, under the entry *brouillard*; the earliest spelling as *neblo* appears in a context dated 1501. For a more extensive view of the evolution of Latin *nebula*, and various adjective forms, see Walther von Wartburg, *Französisches Etymologisches Wörterbuch* (Basel, 1955), vol. 7, pp. 69–72. In *Recherches linguistiques sur les chansonniers provençaux* (Geneva, 1987), François Zuffrey remarks that "the language of the troubadours is characterized by its polymorphism" (p. 313).

3. Louis Quicherat, *Thesaurus poeticus linguae latinae* (Hildesheim, 1967).

4. Adolf Kolsen, *Sämtliche Lieder des Trobadors Giraut de Bornelh*, 2 vols. (Halle, 1907), vol. 1, no. 48, p. 300. Citations are from this edition; Ruth Sharman's *The Cansos and Sirventes of the Troubadour, Giraut de Borneil* (Cambridge, England, forthcoming) was not yet available during the final stages of preparation of this book.

5. The songbook manuscripts are described by Alfred Pillet and Henry Carstens, *Bibliographie der Troubadours* (Halle, 1933), pp. x–xxiv. This list is brought up to date by Edith Brayer, "Chansonniers provençaux," *Bulletin d'Information de l'Institut de Recherche et d'Histoire des Textes* 2 (1953): 57–64, which details as well all the photographic holdings of the I. R. H. T. Succinct and useful is Martín de Riquer's description of the songbooks, vol. 1, pp. 11–19, in *Los trovadores*, 3 vols. (Barcelona, 1975). In *Recherches linguistiques*, pp. 4–6 (table) and 6–12 (rationale), François Zuffrey has now revised the conventional letter abbreviations of some of the minor Provençal songbooks, none of which are important to my discussion.

6. See Pillet and Carstens, *Bibliographie*, p. 59, for the list of manuscripts and folio numbers on which the lyric appears. For the modern edition, see Appel, no. 43, pp. 249–56.

7. Rupert Pickens, *The Songs of Jaufré Rudel* (Toronto, 1978). (Subsequent citations of Jaufre Rudel are from this edition.) Nevertheless, to save space (for a separate edition of each manuscript version of even such a small corpus of lyrics would be quite bulky), Pickens does collate very closely related versions in many instances, but never without giving full variants in notes. Another virtue of Pickens' edition he best describes himself: "An attempt has been made to elucidate all possibilities of multiple meaning and all ambiguities, when they have been perceived, by suggesting alternative translations and by the extensive use of notes: the translator, like the sensitive reader, cannot be allowed to make choices when multiple meanings emerge (neither, for that matter, can the edi-

tor!), but must take into account the fact that ambiguity is characteristic of the genre" (p. 43).

8. Paul Zumthor, *Essai de poétique médiévale* (Paris, 1972), pp. 70–75. For discussion of Zumthor's concept of "the text always in the process of becoming" applied to troubadour lyrics, see Pickens, pp. 34–39.

9. Pickens, "No sap cantar qui so non di," no. 6, p. 224. By contrast, Boccaccio's request for correction at the conclusion of his *Genealogy of the Gods* reveals his desire to produce an authoritative work, a written text that can be accepted as "sacred truth." Boccaccio asks his royal patron to make "necessary excisions, emendations, corrections of style"; but if the work is made public without such royal correction, he asks that all devout Catholics, and especially the renowned Petrarch, change any errors to "sacram veritatem" (XV). For an English translation, see Charles Osgood, *Boccaccio on Poetry; Being the Preface and Fourteenth and Fifteenth Books of Boccaccio's "Genealogia deorum gentilium"* (New York, 1956).

10. See the examples in Madeleine Tyssens, "Le Style oral et les ateliers de copistes," *Mélanges . . . Maurice Delbouille*, 2 vols. (Gembloux, 1964), vol. 2, pp. 673–75; and Dietmar Rieger, "Audition et lecture dans le domaine de la poésie troubadouresque: Quelques Réflexions sur la philologie provençale de demain," *Revue des Langues Romanes* 87 (1983): 76.

11. An important essay on this subject is Paul Saenger, "Silent Reading: Its Impact on Late Medieval Script and Society," *Viator* 13 (1982): 367–414. Saenger argues that word separation—an invention of the early Middle Ages in Latin—was what eventually enabled the reader to bypass syllabic pronunciation and thus to read silently:

> The introduction of word separation changed the way children were taught to read. Through the eighth century, they had learned to read [Latin] in the antique fashion from letters and syllables. In the ninth century, however, the young saint Samson was reported to have learned within a week to recognize *distinctiones* of letters as words. The recognition of words as visible units of letters which word separation made possible must undoubtedly have led to easier and swifter oral reading. True silent reading, that is, reading with the eyes alone, developed only with the evolution of a more rigorous intellectual life in the twelfth and early thirteenth centuries in the *studia* of Cistercian abbeys and at the cathedral schools of the eleventh and twelfth centuries from which universities would emerge.
> (p. 384)

Twelfth-century readers of vernacular texts would almost certainly still be reading in the old way, by pronouncing aloud the letters and syllables.

12. This example was given by Charles-Théodore Gossen, "Graphème et phonème: Le Problème central de l'étude des langues écrites du moyen âge," *Revue de Linguistique Romane* 32 (1968): 5. Sometimes differences in the spelling of the same word may also be due to spatial constraints such as the two-column format, which encourages abbreviation, as Zuffrey points out in *Recherches linguistiques*, pp. 15–17 and 319.

13. Saenger argues that in Roman times, "even in instances where a scribe worked individually to produce a single copy, he was forced by the undivided text of his exemplar to pronounce each line to himself and then to set it down from aural rather than visual recall" ("Silent Reading," p. 373). Something of this enters into the copying of medieval manuscripts before word division was regularized. The copying of the I and K songbooks, for instance, was probably

partly a matter of copying visual images of words—when these were recognizable—but also partly a matter of translating the letters into sounds and then back into images. Just because we have medieval visual representations of the copying of one text from another, as Saenger notes on p. 379, does not mean that copying had become a transcription of visual signs bypassing the voice. In his new book, *La Lettre et la voix* (Paris, 1987), Paul Zumthor emphasizes the "vocality" of the medieval written text. Writing was, he argues, a "temporary relay for the voice" (p. 135). What the scribe interiorized was not a visual image, but an acoustical image (p. 114), and this accounts for much graphological variation.

14. On the "acordansa" of consonant sounds in Provençal verse, see Joseph Anglade, ed., *Las Leys d'amors*, 4 vols. (Toulouse, 1919, 1920), vol. 2, pp. 42–46. Citations of the *Leys* are from this edition.

15. Saenger, "Silent Reading," pp. 370–71:

> The typical Roman book contained neither punctuation, distinction between upper- and lowercase letters, nor word separation. Latin writing, which consisted of undivided rows of capital letters or their cursive equivalents, was entirely phonetic and had no ideographic value. Since in ancient books verbal concepts were not represented by recognizable images, the Romans developed no clear conception of the word as a unit of meaning. Instead, Roman grammarians considered the letter and syllable to be basic to reading. The Roman reader, reading aloud to others or softly to himself, approached the text syllable by syllable in order to recover the words and sentences conveying the meaning of the text. Quintilian considered it a special facility of a scribe to be able to glance ahead as he read to see the end of a phrase before articulating it. For all Romans, the proper coordination of the eye and the tongue was an indispensable part of the activity of reading. A written text was essentially a transcription which, like modern musical notation, became an intelligible message only when it was performed orally to others or to oneself.

On the teaching of reading in antiquity by letters and syllables, see Henri-Irénée Marrou, *Histoire de l'éducation dans l'antiquité* (Paris, 1948), pp. 229–32.

16. Cesare de Lollis, "Il canzoniere provenzale A," in *Studi di Filologia Romanza* 3 (1891): 395–96.

17. Dejeanne, "L'iverns vai e·l temps s'aizina," no. 31, p. 146.

18. John A. Rea, "The Pilgrim Figure in Jaufre Rudel," *Neophilologus* 65 (1981): 518–23.

19. Pickens, no. 5, p. 168. Because "amor de loing" ends the second line of every other strophe in this version except the first ("d'auzels de loing"), I trust that "amon" here ought to be "amor."

20. Jacques Monfrin, "Notes sur le chansonnier provençal C," *Recueil . . . Clovis Brunel*, 2 vols. (Paris, 1955), vol. 2, p. 297. Zuffrey, *Recherches linguistiques*, p. 136, notes that the *æ* ligature occurs also in the M, D, and R songbooks.

21. For a photographic reproduction of this charter, see the plate accompanying Clovis Brunel's "Le Plus Ancien Acte original en langue provençale," *Annales du Midi* 34 (1922): 249–61. In the introduction to *Les Plus Anciennes Chartes en langue provençale: Supplement* (Paris, 1952), pp. v–vi, Brunel explains his editorial policy of using dashes to indicate modern word divisions: "The scribes of the period and regions concerned did not separate words according to their grammatical individuality as does modern orthography; they grouped them according to their phonetic interdependence. The groups thus constituted

give linguistic information easy to transmit without upsetting our habits. A hyphen henceforth marks the word divisions that present readers demand, but of which the authors of our manuscripts were unaware."

22. Saenger, "Silent Reading," p. 377.

23. On the use of these accent marks, which first appear in tenth-century Latin texts, see Clovis Brunel, "Remarques sur la paléographie des chartes provençales du XIIe siècle," *Bibliothèque de l'Ecole des Chartes* 87 (1926): 352–58. See also Åke Grafstrom, *Etude sur la graphie des plus anciennes chartes languedociennes avec un essai d'interprétation phonétique* (Uppsala, 1958), pp. 29–30; and M. B. Parkes, "Punctuation or Pause and Effect," in *Medieval Eloquence: Studies in the Theory and Practice of Medieval Rhetoric*, ed. James J. Murphy (Berkeley and Los Angeles, 1978), pp. 127–42.

24. See Leo Treitler, "The Early History of Music Writing in the West," *Journal of the American Musicological Society* 35 (1982): 237–79.

25. Rieger, "Audition et lecture," p. 78: "I maintain, then, that such a process of creation, which resorts obligatorily to the written form, has a *tendency* to make of this written form the principal basis of reception, and I affirm also that this tendency increases with the degree to which the poet feels the necessity of using the written form for composition."

26. Richard Rouse, "Roll and Codex: The Transmission of the Works of Reinmar von Zweter," *Paläographie* 32 (1981): 107–23, and a longer version with Franz Bäuml, "Roll and Codex: A New Manuscript Fragment of Reinmar von Zweter," *Beiträge zur Geschichte der deutschen Sprache und Literatur* 105 (1983): 192–231. For Gustav Gröber's thesis concerning the inscription of *Liederblätter*, see the first chapter of his "Die Liedersammlungen der Troubadours," *Romanische Studien* 2 (1877): 337–44. In *La letteratura medievale in lingua d'oc nella sua tradizione manoscritta* (Turin, 1961), D'Arco Silvio Avalle takes Gröber's thesis further, speculating on the stages of collection that lie behind the songbooks we own. See also Avalle's fine analysis, in his third appendix, of the mistaken assumptions of our nineteenth-century evolutionary model of medieval textual transmission.

27. Riquer, in *Los trovadores* (vol. 1, p. 15), argues that troubadour verse was first inscribed on wax tablets and then transferred to parchment, and he cites a *tornada* by Arnaut Tintinac (holder of the roll in the E songbook's miniature; see fig. 1) wherein Arnaut mentions writing: "Bos es lo vers, e chantador, / e volgra bon entendedor. / Per Dieu, bels clercx, tu lo·m escriu!" ("The verse is good and [so is] the singer / and it will seek good interpreters. / For God's sake, good cleric, write it down for me!") (ed. Jean Mouzat, *Le Troubadour Arnaut de Tintinhac* [Tulle, 1956], p. 17). Riquer also cites a similar envoy by Gauvaudan, "Vers es bos qui ben l'escriu" ("The verse is good if written well").

28. See Pasero, p. 110 n. 44, for examples of *trametra* used in this way. In this edition, the envoy strophe of "Farai un vers de dreyt nien" appears on p. 94; the C manuscript's envoy of "Farai un vers, pos mi sonelh" appears on p. 135.

29. Pickens, p. 119. On p. 35 n. 29, Pickens recollects, in order to reject as "too tenuous," Avalle's use of this strophe as "evidence that oral transmission (rather than just performance) was rare even in the twelfth century . . . (*La letteratura*, pp. 47ff.)." It seems to me that oral and written transmission need not be mutually exclusive; indeed, as we shall see, the coupling of the injunction to "sing or display" suggests a double transmission by reading or performing aloud and by the display of the written text.

30. Valeria Tortoreto, *Il trovatore Cercamon* (Modena, 1981), no. 3, p. 116. See also the new edition by George Wolf and Roy Rosenstein, *The Poetry of Cercamon and Jaufre Rudel* (New York, 1983).

31. Dejeanne, no. 33, p. 162; here, however, I have quoted the C manuscript version (Paris, B.N. fr. 856, fol. 177v), which has different rhyme words in the second and last lines: *fronzilh* and *estrilh*, instead of *foill* ("to leaf through") and *doill* (according to Dejeanne's interpretation, "hole").

32. Pickens, pp. 35–36.

33. Ernest Hoepffner, *Les Poésies de Bernart Marti* (Paris, 1929), no. 6, p. 19. Quotations of Bernart Marti are from this edition.

34. Stephen G. Nichols, Jr., *The Songs of Bernart de Ventadorn* (Chapel Hill, 1962), p. 131.

35. Pillet and Carstens, in their *Bibliographie*, pp. 56–57, give the folio numbers for the lyric in each different manuscript. I checked the variants by comparing all the photographs of this strophe in the collection of the Institut de Recherche et d'Histoire des Textes.

36. See, for example, Joan Ferrante, "'Ab joi mou lo vers e·l comens,'" in *The Interpretation of Medieval Lyric Poetry*, ed. W. T. H. Jackson (New York, 1980), p. 113. The many homonyms of the vernacular (Italian, but Provençal as well) are also the main source of its richness or obscurity of sense, which Dante contrasted with the clarity and openness of Latin in his *Convivio* (I.vii.8), *Tutte le opere di Dante. Vol. 8*, ed. Daniele Mattalìa (Milan, 1965). Citations of the *Convivio* are from this edition.

37. This strophe appears approximately as follows in the C manuscript (Paris, B.N. fr. 856, fol. 51v):

ia non partrai ama vida. tant
cum sia sals ni sas. que pus les
pigues issida. balaia lonc te͞ps
lo gras. e si tot no ses coitada.
ia per me non er blasmada. sol
mi do adenant semen.

My translation reflects the following grammatical analysis of the lines:

Ia no·n partrai a ma vida
tant cum sia sals ni sas
que pus l'espigu' es issida
balaia long temps lo gras
e si tot no s'es coitada
ia per me non er blasmada
sol mi do adenant semen.

38. Such an eroticizing reading is possible also with versions of the strophe that have "arma" in place of "espiga." In this case, one could understand "weapon" (rather than "soul" or "kernel").

39. Moshe Lazar, *Bernard de Ventadour, troubadour du XIIe siècle: Chansons d'amour, édition critique avec traduction, introduction, notes, et glossaire* (Paris, 1966).

40. Pointing to the "relatively high number of 'fractured' strophes" among the versions of Jaufre's seven lyrics, Pickens suggests that the basic formal structural unit of the troubadour lyric may not be the strophe (as Zumthor claims in *Essai de poétique médiévale*, p. 193). Instead, Pickens argues that the basic

compositional unit may be as small as "two lines not necessarily coupled by rhyme" (p. 29 n. 23).

41. With the exception of the *Leys d'amors*, J. H. Marshall has edited all of these texts: *The "Razos de Trobar" of Raimon Vidal and Associated Texts* (London, 1972), and *The Donatz Proensals of Uc Faidit* (London, 1969). The quotation from Uc Faiditz is from p. 255; page numbers cited in the text refer to Marshall's edition.

42. In his *Convivio*, Dante explains that "Latin is eternal and incorruptible, whereas the vernacular is unstable and corruptible" (I.v.7) and that "the vernacular follows usage, but Latin follows art" (I.v.14). Consequently, Latin is "clear" in displaying its meaning, whereas the vernacular is obscure and more richly evocative (I.vii.8). In other words, Latin had long been regulated; the vernacular had not.

43. For this vocabulary see Alphonse Blanc, "Vocabulaire Provençal-Latin," *Revue des Langues Romanes* 35 (1891): 29–87. The manuscript, Paris, B.N. lat. 7657, has been identified as a fifteenth-century Provençal one by Clovis Brunel, *Bibliographie des manuscrits littéraires en ancien provençal* (Paris, 1935), p. 64, no. 211, and p. 22, no. 67.

44. Louis de Landes, *Glossaire érotique de la langue française depuis son origine jusqu'à nos jours* (Brussels, 1861). See also Pierre Guiraud, *Dictionnaire érotique* (Paris, 1978). These draw examples from only a few Old French texts of an openly erotic nature.

45. The drawings of the *Vocabulaire* should also be reproduced in order to show how the scribe's play often consists in seeing things from different perspectives (as we do when we recognize a verbal pun). Beside the entry *parlar* (fol. 38r), for example, there is a curious abstract-looking design of ranks of backward *c* shapes with jagged insides. These probably represent toothy mouths open in talking (*parlar*).

46. For the derivation of *joi* from Latin *joculum*, see Charles Camproux, *Joy d'amor (Jeu et joie d'amour)* (Montpellier, 1965), pp. 122–25. Comparisons of different regional graphologies and pronunciations of Languedoc, as suggested by charters written between 1034 and 1200, may be found in Grafstrom, *Etude sur la graphie*. However, the relationship between graphology and phonology is an extremely vexed one in early vernacular documents. For an exposition of some of the difficulties, see Göran Hammarström, "Graphème, son, et phonème dans la description des vieux textes," *Studia Neophilologica* 31 (1959): 5–18.

47. Max Pfister, "La Langue de Guilhem IX, comte de Poitiers," *Cahiers de Civilisation Médiévale* 19 (1976): 111. See also Jacques Pignon, *L'Evolution phonétique des parlers du Poitou* (Paris, 1960).

48. Roger Dragonetti, *Le Gai Savoir dans la rhétorique courtoise* (Paris, 1982), pp. 21–22.

49. Monfrin, however, seems to see these double attributions in the C songbook as a sign of its compiler's critical acumen ("Notes," p. 294):

> In opening the book, one falls first on a table of the first lines of each piece in the order of transcription. . . . in thirty-odd cases, a second attribution is proposed concerning a given *incipit*. Up to now, no one has been able to give an exact account of this rough attempt at critical work. Let me only note one material detail: these secondary attributions are in red and they have been recorded by the rubricator (who, for that matter, does not seem, judging from his hand, to differ from the scribe) at the moment when he positioned the other rubrics: in effect, the flourishes of the pen that finish off the page pass around these words.

50. On the probable location of the C songbook's inscription, see Monfrin, "Notes," p. 310; Frank Chambers, "Matfre Ermengaud and Provençal MS C," *Romance Philology* 5 (1951–1952): 46; and Alfred Jeanroy, "Notes sur l'histoire d'un chansonnier provençal," *Mélanges . . . Emile Picot*, 2 vols. (Paris, 1913), vol. 1, esp. p. 526, where Jeanroy suggests, by graphological characteristics, that the manuscript was written in "Quercy or Haut-Languedoc, approximately between Cahors, Rodez, and Béziers." An even more thorough analysis of the linguistic characteristics of the C songbook is now available in Zuffrey's *Recherches linguistiques*, pp. 134–52. Zuffrey agrees with Monfrin in locating the C songbook in the region of Narbonne and detects, in addition, a Catalan influence in the final layer of scribal inscription.

CHAPTER 3

1. Virgilio Marone, *Epitomi ed Epistole*, ed. G. Polara, trans. Polara and Caruso (Naples, 1979). (Citations are from this edition.) For a consideration of Virgil's origins, with citations, see Mauriz Schuster, "Virgilius Maro, südgallischer Grammatiker," in *Paulys Realencyclopädie der classischen Altertumswissenschaft* (Munich, 1961), vol. 9, A–1, col. 187.

2. Michael W. Herren, *The Hisperica Famina. Vol. 1: The A-Text* (Toronto, 1974), p. 28. Citations are from this edition.

3. For these definitions see the dictionaries of François Raynouard, *Lexique roman ou dictionnaire de la langue des troubadours*, 6 vols. (Paris, 1836–1844); Emil Levy, *Provenzalisches Supplement-Wörterbuch*, 8 vols. (Leipzig, 1894–1924); and Frédéric Godefroy, *Dictionnaire de l'ancienne langue française*, 10 vols. (Paris, 1885; rpt. 1961). The word *goliard* may well be related to this same vernacular root: *gual* or *gal*.

4. *Epitomi*, "De catalogo grammaticorum," p. 164.

5. I am not the first to suggest such burlesque intentions. For a résumé of previous interpretations of Virgil's *Epitomies*, see Polara's introduction, p. xxi.

6. Jacques Fontaine, *Isidore de Seville et la culture classique dans l'Espagne wisigothique*, 2 vols. (Paris, 1959), vol. 1, p. 38:

> [In the preface to his *Differences*] Isidore explains how poetry and usage have altered the proper characteristics of terms and confounded the meaning of proximate words; it is necessary then to distinguish by means of the "difference" each of the confounded syllables in order to discover again its proper meaning, because "however similar they may be, yet they distinguish themselves from one another by their respective origins." This text enables us to see already the link between the "difference" and etymology. The latter is the very criterion of "difference" because it permits access to the origin of the word and, thereby, to its essential originality. This is why, in the *Origins*, etymology supercedes "difference" among the methods of Isidore's thought.

For the preface to Isidore's *Differences*, see J. P. Migne, *Patrologiae cursus completus . . . Series latina*, 221 vols. (Paris, 1844–1865), vol. 83, col. 9.

7. Cf. Marcabru's criticisms of troubadour *disciplina*, quoted in Chapter 1.

8. Herren, *A-Text*, p. 46. See also p. 48, where Herren notes that the root is supreme in Hisperic word formation, while the suffixes are merely ornamental variations (much as, for example, in Marcabru's rhyme words): "there is but a single principle of word formation acknowledged by the faminators, viz. that suffixes within the given categories of noun, adjective, and verb are semantically equal. . . . *Melchillentus*, *mellifluus*, and *mellitus* are virtual synonyms."

9. Descriptions of the Feast of Fools or Asses, of the Innocents, of the Circumcision, of the Boy Bishop, and the like may be found in E. K. Chambers, *The Mediaeval Stage*, 2 vols. (Oxford, 1903), vol. 1, pp. 274–371. For a collection of burlesque masses, see Paul Lehmann, *Die Parodie im Mittelalter*, 2d ed. (Stuttgart, 1963).

10. Edmond Faral, *Les Jongleurs en France au moyen-âge* (Paris, 1910), p. 43 n. 1: "We command all priests that they not allow truants or other errant scholars or goliards to sing verses set to the *Sanctus* and *Agnus Dei* either during mass or holy services."

11. The best single collection of goliard texts is contained in Lehmann's *Die Parodie*. Other collections of Latin verse and plays include *Carmina Burana*, ed. Alfons Hilka and Otto Schumann, 2 vols. (Heidelberg, 1930, 1941), esp. vol. 1, *Die moralisch-satirischen Dichtungen*; Thomas Wright, *The Latin Poems Commonly Attributed to Walter Mapes* (London, 1841); *Die Gedichte des Archipoeta*, ed. Heinrich Watenphul and Heinrich Krefeld (Heidelberg, 1958); *Die Oxforder Gedichte des Primas*, ed. Wilhelm Meyer (Göttingen, 1907; rpt. 1967); *Moralische-satirische Gedichte Walters von Chatillon*, ed. Karl Strecker (Heidelberg, 1929); *Three Latin Comedies (Geta, Babio, Pamphilus)*, ed. Keith Bate (Toronto, 1976); Gustave Cohen, *La "Comédie" latine en France au XII*[e] *siècle*, 2 vols. (Paris, 1931).

12. Cited by Faral, *Les Jongleurs*, p. 43 n. 1, along with other thirteenth-century ecclesiastical texts censuring the goliards. For a tenth-century injunction by Gautier of Sens, see p. 274: "We establish that ribald clerics, especially those commonly said to be of the family of Golias, should be shorn immediately, or even shaved, so that their clerical tonsure no longer remains."

13. For all of the surviving *vidas*, see Jean Boutière and A. H. Schutz, *Biographies des troubadours*, 2d ed. (Paris, 1973). Citations of *vidas* are from this edition. Peire Rogier's *vida*, just mentioned, is no. 40, p. 267; the Monk of Montaudon's, no. 46, p. 307; Giraut de Bornelh's, no. 8, p. 39; Peire Cardenal's, no. 50, p. 335; Arnaut de Maroill's, no. 7, p. 32. The translations of the *vidas* are my own, although there is also an English translation by Margarita Egan, *The "Vidas" of the Troubadours* (New York, 1984).

14. According to the chronicler Ademar of Chabannes, Guillaume the Great (the troubadour's grandfather) was "doctus litteris" from childhood. There may be a chastening reference to Guillaume's own studies in a letter of 1094 from Pope Urban II: "De te vero miramur, qui cum aliis bonis studiis, quantum ad militem polleas, in hoc a patris tui probitate degenerare perhiberis." Gerald Bond, *The Poetry of William VII, Count of Poitiers, IX Duke of Aquitaine* (New York, 1982), p. 101, translates this papal admonition: "But we are astounded that you who are outstanding in so many other good qualities, so far as a knight is concerned, depart from your father's worthiness in that you break the laws of churches and despoil those that he founded." "Bonis studiis" here may refer not only to Guillaume's "good qualities" or knightly endeavors, but also to his earlier intellectual education, intended to make him a better knight (but which evidently failed to indoctrinate Guillaume sufficiently in respect for the Church's power or property).

15. The *Regles de trobar* is edited by J. H. Marshall in *The "Razos de Trobar" of Raimon Vidal and Associated Texts* (London, 1972), p. 56: "eu En Iaufres de Fuxa . . . studiey e pessey a dar, segons lo meu saber, alcuna manera de doctrina en romanç; per que cells qui no·s entenen en gramatica, mas estiers han sobtil e clar engyn, pusquen mils conexer e apendre lo saber de trobar" ("I, Sir Jofre

de Foixa . . . have studied and attempted to give, according to my own knowledge, a kind of teaching in Romance [vernacular], so that those who do not understand [Latin] grammar, but otherwise have subtle and clever wits, can better know and learn the science of composition [poetic invention]").

16. Scholastic *agon* is the object of burlesque as early as the seventh century in Virgil's *Epitomies*, where he recounts the great debate among grammarians over the vocative of *ego*, a verbal battle that supposedly lasted fourteen days and nights.

17. For further discussion of these vignettes, see Chapter 5.

18. Ernest Hoepffner, *Les Poésies de Bernart Marti* (Paris, 1929), no. 4, pp. 11–12.

19. Alberto del Monte, *Peire d'Alvernha: Liriche* (Turin, 1955), no. 16, pp. 159–60, C ms. variants.

20. Adolf Kolsen, *Sämtliche Lieder des Trobadors Giraut de Bornelh*, 2 vols. (Halle, 1907), vol. 1, no. 14, pp. 68–70, C ms. variants. Citations in the text are from this edition.

21. Walter Pattison, *The Life of the Troubadour Raimbaut d'Orange* (Minneapolis, 1952), no. 5, p. 83, C ms. variants. Quotations are from this edition, wherein, unfortunately, Pattison does not list what he considers to be "minor variants of spelling" in different manuscripts' versions of the lyrics. This is, in fact, the unstated policy of many editors of Provençal lyrics, as I have discovered in trying to reconstruct the C songbook's versions from the printed variants in modern editions and then checking these against the manuscript.

22. Raimbaut d'Orange's views are not so different from Stéphane Mallarmé's, as expressed, for example, in his essay "Hérésies artistiques": "Let the masses read morality, but please don't give them our poetry to spoil" (*Poésies* [Paris, 1977], p. 144).

23. Boutière and Schutz, *Biographies*, no. 8, p. 39: "hom de bas afar."

24. Ibid., no. 6, p. 21, for the *vida* of Bernart de Ventadorn composed by Uc de Saint Circ, who names himself and his sources therein: "Et ieu, N'Ucs de Saint Circ, de lui so qu'ieu ai escrit si me contet lo vescoms N'Ebles de Ventadorn, que fo fils de la vescomtessa qu'En Bernartz amet. E fetz aquestas chansos que vos auziretz aissi de sotz escriptas" ("And I, Sir Uc de Saint Circ, what I have written about him was told me by the viscount, Sir Eble de Ventadorn, who was the son of the viscountess whom Sir Bernart loved. And he made these songs that you will hear written directly below"). Concerning Uc's authorship of this *vida*, see ibid., p. 25 n. 8.

25. Ibid., no. 33, p. 240.

CHAPTER 4

1. Every generalization has its exceptions. In the fourteenth-century Catalan Sg songbook's *vida* for Bernart de Ventadorn, there is an interpretation of the first strophe of Bernart's famous "Quan vei la lauzeta mover" that Pierre Bec believes to be a deliberate burlesque of Bernart's first strophe:

> E apelava-la Bernartz "Alauzeta", per amor d'un cavalier que l'amava, e ela apelèt lui "Rai". E un jorn venc lo cavaliers a la duguessa e entrèt en la cambra. La dòmna, que·l vi, leva adonc lo pan del mantèl e mes-li sobra'l còl e laissà-si cazer el liech. E Bernartz vi tot, car una donzèla de la dòmna li ac mostrat cubertament; e per aquesta razon fetz adonc la cançon que ditz: 'Quan vei l'alauzeta mover . . .'

And Bernart called her "Alouette" because of the love of a knight who loved her, and she called him "Ray." And one day the knight came to the duchess and entered the bedroom. The lady, who saw him, then lifted the skirt of her robe and put it for him over the neck and let herself fall on the bed. And Bernart saw everything, because one of the lady's maids showed it to him in hiding, and for this reason then he made the song that says, "When I see the Alouette move . . ."

This interpretation brings Bernart's first strophe down to the level of voyeurism. Instead of empathetic transport at the flight of a lark, the poet melts with sexual desire as, from a concealed position, he watches two lovers, who call each other by the *senhals* "Alauzeta" and "Rai," having intercourse on a bed in the lady's chamber:

Quan vei la lauzeta mover
De joi sas alas contra·l rai,
Que s'oblid' e's laissa cazer
Per la doucor qu'al cor li vai,
Ailas! Quals enveja me'n ve
De cui que veja jauzion!
Meravilhas ai, quar desse
Lo cors de dezirier no'm fon.

When I see the Lark move / its "wings" in joy against the Ray, / so that it forgets itself and lets itself fall / because of the sweetness that enters its heart [or, body], / alas! what envy overcomes me / of those whom I see enjoying themselves! / I marvel that right then / my heart [or, body] does not melt with desire.

Outrageous as this eroticizing explanation of the poet's reason for writing may seem to those of us who have been used to reading Bernart's first strophe as a metaphor for a more spiritual ecstasy, it illustrates very well the troubadours' sport of facetious exegesis, which was a burlesque, not of the lyric itself, but of *razo*—of serious (historicizing, moralizing, idealizing, or spiritualizing) interpretation. As we shall see later, the playful interpretation of Bernart de Ventadorn's verse often revolved around possible physical and phallic connotations of the word *cors* (or *cor*) in suggestive contexts such as this one, where *cors* is associated with "self-forgetting," "falling," "sweetness," "longing," "enjoyment," "desire," and "melting." How such a facetious, eroticizing explication came to be written down and later included with more serious ones in the Sg songbook is puzzling. This burlesque *razo* does not cut up or destroy the integrity of words; perhaps its historical explanation of the *senhals* and realistic, autobiographical staging of the lyric made it so appealing to later interpreters that, in this case, *sentenssa follatina* passed for *razo*. See Boutière and Schutz, p. 29, for this *vida*; or Pierre Bec, *Burlesque et obscénité chez les troubadours: Pour une approche du contre-texte médiéval* (Paris, 1984), p. 112.

2. See Clovis Brunel, *Bibliographie des manuscrits littéraires en ancien provençal* (Paris, 1935).

3. I am relying here on an informal judgment by François Avril of the Bibliothèque Nationale, Paris.

4. Margarita Egan, "Commentary, *Vita Poetae*, and *Vida*: Latin and Old Provençal 'Lives of Poets,'" *Romance Philology* 37 (1983): 37 n. 5.

5. See also A. H. Schutz, "Where Were the Provençal *Vidas* and *Razos* Written?" *Modern Philology* 35 (1938): 225–32.

6. Boutière and Schutz, no. 9, pp. 62–63.

7. Guiraut Riquier's *razo* on the "menor ters" is edited by Joseph Linskill,

Les Epîtres de Giraut Riquier (Liège, 1985), no. 13, pp. 273–330. Citations of Guiraut Riquier are from this edition, unless otherwise identified.

8. Raimon de Cornet's *razo* appears under the rubric "Le digz frayre R. Gloza," which identifies the lyric as a "gloss" (*gloza*) of an earlier poem by one "brother R." It has been edited by J. B. Noulet and Camille Chabaneau in *Deux Manuscrits provençaux du XIV*[e] *siècle* (Montpellier, 1888), pp. 56–61. (Citations of Raimon de Cornet are from this edition.) On p. 98 of the same edition see the *trufa* of Raimon de Cornet, wherein, after the style of a Guillaume IX, and in good *canso* form, he tells the story of how he was tricked and tonsured by one of his jealous mistresses and embarrassed to perform mass the following day in such a condition. Bec has anthologized and translated this lyric (*Burlesque*, pp. 114–17).

9. Matfre Ermengaud, *Le Breviari d'amor*, ed. Gabriel Azaïs, 2 vols. (Béziers, 1862, 1881; rpt. 1977), vol. 1, vv. 48–54. (Citations of Matfre are from this edition.) The "Perilhos tractat" alone is available in the edition of Peter T. Ricketts, *Le Breviari d'amor de Matfre Ermengaud (27252T–34577)*, vol. 5 (Leiden, 1976).

10. For comparison of the prose explication of Dante's *Vita nuova* to the Provençal *razos*, see Eduard Wechssler, *Das Kulturproblem des Minnesangs. Vol. 1: Minnesang und Christentum* (Halle, 1909), p. 404; Pio Rajna, "Per le 'Divisioni' della 'Vita nuova,'" *Strenna Dantesca* 2 (1902): 111–14; Paul Zumthor, "Autobiography in the Middle Ages?" trans. Sherry Simon, *Genre* 6 (1973): 43; and Jerome Mazzaro, *The Figure of Dante: An Essay on the "Vita Nuova"* (Princeton, 1981), pp. 65, 87–88.

11. Boutière and Schutz, p. viii. Along with its extensive historicizing *razos*, the P songbook (Florence, Laurentian, Plut. 41. cod. 42) contains the Provençal grammar of Raimon Vidal. Didactic considerations guided the compilation of this and other Italian songbooks. For example, the J songbook (Florence, B.N. Conv. Sopp. F, 4, 776) begins with a treatise on how men ought to learn to master their tongues, presents short pieces of wisdom literature and advice (copiously marked with *nota* signs in the margins), and places Peire Cardenal, probably for his sententiousness, at the head of its collection of Provençal verse.

12. Dante, *La Vita nuova*, ed. Kenneth McKenzie (Boston, 1922), XXV, pp. 70–74; English translation by Barbara Reynolds (London, 1969), p. 75. Subsequent quotations are from these editions.

13. Dante, *De vulgari eloquentia*, ed. Aristide Marigo, 3d ed. (Florence, 1957), II.xiii.12., pp. 272–73.

14. J.H. Marshall, *The "Razos de Trobar" of Raimon Vidal and Associated Texts* (London, 1972), p. 2.

15. Ibid., pp. 29–53, for Terramagnino of Pisa's *Doctrina d'acort*.

16. Ibid., pp. 51–52.

17. Adolphe Gatien-Arnoult, *Las Flors del gay saber*, 3 vols. (Toulouse, 1841–1843). Citations of the *Flors* are from this edition.

18. The *Flors* also has a section (vol. 2, p. 34) on equivocal names, beginning with proper names such as "Peyres, Guilhem, Arnaud, Bernad," some of the most common given names of the troubadours. For a modern analysis of what letters represented the same sounds in *langue d'oc* before the fourteenth century, see Åke Grafstrom, *Etude sur la graphie des plus anciennes chartes languedociennes avec un essai d'interprétation phonétique* (Uppsala, 1958), pp. 114–16 on *b* and *p*, for example.

19. See Michel Meylakh, "Troubadours et anagrammes (structures anagram-

matiques dans la chanson X d'Arnaut Daniel)," *Mélanges . . . Charles Camproux* (Montpellier, 1978), p. 153.

20. Many troubadours, including Marcabru and Raimbaut d'Orange, deformed the endings of words in rhyme position for the sake of difficult rhymes. Very rich rhymes are a form of paranomasia (Latin, *adnominatio*), which is defined in *Ad Herennium* (IV.xxi.29) as "the figure in which, by means of a modification of sound, or change of letters, a close resemblance to a given verb or noun is produced, so that similar words express dissimilar things" (trans. H. Caplan [London, 1954], p. 300). The ways *Ad Herennium* then lists of producing such puns and near-puns (thinning or contracting of the same letter, lengthening or shortening it, omitting, transposing, or changing letters, and the like) bear a close resemblance to the *Flors'* proscriptions against different kinds of "variable" words. The facetious troubadours seem to have interpreted quite literally the Latin grammarians' rules for producing *adnominatio* and to have taken these as a model and a license for modifying old words or coining entirely *new* ones, especially in rhyme position. In *Burlesque*, p. 102, Bec presents one exaggerated example of facetious troubadour play with the tails of words, a lyric in which every rhyme word is given an awkward and vulgar-sounding "-ul," "-ula," "-oira," or "-eira" ending.

21. That the troubadours thought of poetic composition in terms of the textile arts is suggested by the technical terms for composition that they used: *tresar* ("to braid"), *entrebescar* ("to weave"), *lasar* ("to lace"). Whereas, in the textile arts, patterns of colored threads are woven together to evoke visual figures, the troubadours wove together patterns of letters representing patterns of sounds evocative of abstract senses. The woven appearance of the initial letters in many medieval manuscripts bears witness to the medieval understanding of the inscribed text as texture. The initials are "texts" themselves, designs woven of natural and geometrical forms. The letters of the word *liber* (book) in an eleventh-century Bible from St. Martial of Limoges appear to be woven and interwoven. (See fig. 4.) Such images—and thinking of the written text as a woven fabric of letters—span the Middle Ages. Prefacing the verbal text of a sixth- or seventh-century manuscript of Augustine's commentary on the Gospels (Paris, B.N. lat. 12190), we find a sort of "carpet page" of woven designs showing different ways of linking and knotting colored strands, in effect, different kinds of *texere* (Latin meaning "weaving threads"). The picture illuminates or illustrates the writing process. The most striking illustrations of what it meant to read or write an early medieval text are the great initial pages of the *Book of Kells*, also known as "carpet" pages for their similarities to the intricate textile designs of Oriental rugs. To enter into the text of the Gospel books of *Kells*, or an eleventh-century Limousin Bible (see fig. 5), we must discover the very forms of the letters in their extraordinarily complex fabric.

22. Anglade, *Leys*, vol. 4, p. 122.

CHAPTER 5

1. Anglade, *Leys*, vol. 4, p. 49.

2. Gatien-Arnoult, *Flors*, vol. 1, pp. 256–62. "La Porquiera" is also included and translated into French in the anthology by Pierre Bec, *Burlesque et obscénité chez les troubadours: Pour une approche du contre-texte médiéval* (Paris, 1984), pp. 185–90.

3. Alfred Jeanroy, *Les Joies du gai savoir: Recueil de poésies couronnées par le*

Consistoire de la Gaie Science (1324–1484), trans. J. B. Noulet (Toulouse, 1914), p. xiv.

4. Ibid., p. xv.

5. For this Latin statute, see L. Deslisle, "Le Jeu des Cent Drutz," *Romania* 22 (1893): 274–75.

6. On the Roman *Floralia* games, Provençal *Calenda Maia*, and later medieval May festivities, see, for example, Marius Bonaria, *Romani mimi* (Rome, 1965); Alfred Jeanroy, *Les Origines de la poésie lyrique en France au moyen-âge* (Paris, 1889), pp. 88–89; E. K. Chambers, *The Mediaeval Stage*, 2 vols. (Oxford, 1903), vol. 1, pp. 160–79.

7. Adolphe Gatien-Arnoult, *Las Joyas del gay saber: Recueil de poésies en langue romane couronnées par le Consistoire de la Gaie-Science de Toulouse (1324–1498)* (Toulouse, 1849), pp. 3–6. Subsequent citations of prizewinning lyrics are from this edition.

8. Charles Jernigan, "The Song of Nail and Uncle: Arnaut Daniel's Sestina 'Lo ferm voler q'el cor m'intra,'" *Studies in Philology* 71 (1974): 127–51.

9. The possible ambiguity in this lyric of "crezens" and "crezensa," when understood as forms of *croire* or *croistre* ("to believe" or "to grow"), was pointed out to me by Sheila Delany.

10. On this folk belief, see René Nelli, *L'Erotique des troubadours* (Toulouse, 1963), pp. 86–87 n. 30.

11. Leo Steinberg, *The Sexuality of Christ in Renaissance Art* (New York, 1983). Michel Zink, in *La Prédication en langue romane avant 1300* (Paris, 1976), p. 290, notes wordplay with *virga* and *virgo* and their Romance equivalents in medieval sermons, where the "rod" associated with Mary is the tree of Jesse, or, less commonly, Moses' rod.

12. William P. Shepard, *The Oxford Provençal Songbook* (a diplomatic edition), Elliot Monographs 21 (Princeton, 1927), p. viii: "Of more interest are the signs *No* and *N* (= Nota) found at irregular intervals on each margin. Sometimes a series of verses is bracketed and thus marked. These passages or lines are generally of a proverbial or apocryphal character. They are all in the hand of the original scribe, and may serve to indicate the sayings that he regarded as significant or wise."

13. On the verso of the first folio of the K songbook (Paris, B.N. fr. 12473), Fulvio Orsini, who once owned the manuscript, wrote that it had been "tocco nelle margini di mano del Petrarca et del Bembo." See François Avril and Marie-Thérèse Gousset, *Manuscrits enluminés d'origine italienne*. Vol. 2: *XIII*[e] *Siècle* (Paris, 1984), p. 16, and Pierre de Nolhac, *La Bibliothèque de Fulvio Orsini* (Paris, 1887), p. 318.

14. D'Arco Silvio Avalle, *La letteratura medievale in lingua d'oc nella sua tradizione manoscritta* (Turin, 1961), pp. 179–81.

15. This statistic is from J. B. Beck, *Die Melodien der Troubadours* (Strasbourg, 1908), p. 8 n. 1.

16. Other Provençal songbooks that include musical notation are G (Milan, Ambrosian R 71 *supra*) and a Vatican collection of different genres (Rome, Chigiana C.V. 151). See J. B. Beck, *Die Melodien*, for descriptions of these. The fourteenth-century E songbook from Provence (Paris, B.N. fr. 1749) contains some marginal musical markings in the form of letters of the alphabet and names of Church songs and, on one occasion (p. 69), an "alleluia" written in the text at the end of a line. See pp. 51, 52, 53, and 175 in this manuscript, where

columns are rectified and additional space filled by means of red horizontal lines similar to those in some religious songbooks from St. Martial of Limoges.

17. The only study I know of the illuminations in the Provençal songbooks is quite inadequate: Joseph Anglade, "Les Miniatures des chansonniers provençaux," *Romania* 50 (1924): 593–604. The Italian songbooks in the Bibliothèque Nationale, Paris are now described by Avril and Gousset, *Manuscrits enluminés*. Avalle provides a list of the directions to the illuminator from the A songbook (*La letteratura*, pp. 179–81), but he does not point out how the actual images correspond to or differ from the directions. The typescript catalogue at the Pierpont Morgan Library in New York provides a descriptive list of the illuminated capitals of the N songbook in its collection (ms. 819). As well as black-and-white photographs of most of the songbooks, there are descriptive lists for the illuminations of many of the songbooks at the Institut de Recherche et d'Histoire des Textes in Paris. What is lacking in all cases is comparative analysis.

18. Mikhail Bakhtin, *Rabelais and His World*, trans. Hélène Iswolsky (Bloomington, 1984), p. 316.

19. Jean Lefèvre, *La Vieille*, ed. Hippolyte Cocheris (Paris, 1861), pp. 10–11.

20. According to Margarete Bieber, *The History of the Greek and Roman Theater* (Princeton, 1961), p. 248, "mimes did not wear masks, but actors with grotesque faces were used." The statuettes of Roman mimes illustrated on p. 249 of Bieber's book all have grotesque noses, as do the masks from Roman farce illustrated on p. 248. According to Heiko Jürgens, *Pompa diaboli: Die lateinischen Kirchenväter und das antike Theater* (Stuttgart, 1972), p. 220, unmasked players in the late antique theater painted their faces blue and red, and players of pantomime wore masks (p. 239). The jongleur masks or faces on the backs of the initials of the R songbook are painted a greater variety of colors.

21. On the court of Beaucaire and Guillem Mita, see Claude de Vic and Joseph Vaissète, *Histoire générale de Languedoc*, 15 vols. (Toulouse, 1872–1892), vol. 10, p. 284. See also the speculative note in Walter Pattison, *The Life of the Troubadour Raimbaut d'Orange* (Minneapolis, 1952), p. 140, about the derivation of the word *mita*: "The modern Provençal *mito*, *meto* has as one meaning *gros nez*, derived from the Latin *meta*, 'conical shaped,' from the shape of the *meta* or 'boundary post.'"

22. See, for example, Arnaut Daniel's use of the term *bec* in the first strophe of his "Pois Raimons e'N Trucs Malecs," anthologized by Bec in *Burlesque*, along with the other lyrics of the "affaire cornil," p. 147.

23. Religious songbooks contemporary with the earliest troubadours show a similar kind of *cap* play. One has but to leaf through the copious plates in Danielle Gaborit-Chopin's *La Décoration de manuscrits à Saint-Martial-de-Limoges et en Limousin du IXe au XIIe siècle* (Paris, 1969) to find many examples of heads forming or framed by initial letters beginning *capitula* (chapter or paragraph divisions of the text).

24. Jurgis Baltrušaitis, *Le Moyen-Age fantastique* (Paris, 1955), p. 20, fig. 9; p. 14, fig. 4; p. 16, fig. 6; p. 17, fig. 7.

25. In the earliest vernacular (Old French) use of the word *chimère* cited by Frédéric Godefroy, *Dictionnaire de l'ancienne langue française*, 10 vols. (Paris, 1883; rpt. 1961), vol. 2, p. 124, Gautier de Coinci links *chimère* with folly: "En est il bien fous et chimere / . . . Por fol le tiens et por chimere" ("He is quite foolish and chimerical / . . . I consider him to be a fool and a chimera"). The

occasional songbook chimera composed of a shaven-crowned human head on a changeling bestial body is interesting in this light, because the medieval natural fool was sometimes tonsured (making his head rather resemble a monk's) in the belief that this might cure him by allowing his excess melancholic humors to escape. For a fool with such a tonsure, although not chimerical in shape, see Claude Gaignebet and J. Dominique Lajoux, *Art profane et religion populaire au moyen âge* (Paris, 1985), p. 181, fig.2.

26. Bakhtin, *Rabelais*, p. 320, defines the classical body: "an entirely finished, completed, strictly limited body, which is shown from the outside as something individual. That which protrudes, bulges, sprouts, or branches off (when a body transgresses its limits and a new one begins) is eliminated, hidden, or moderated."

27. Bec, *Burlesque*, p. 17.

28. For the expression "cornar al cul," see the four lyrics anthologized by Bec, *Burlesque*, nos. 28–31, pp. 140–53. The names of two participants in the facetious debate are playful: Raimon de Durfort = Raimon the hard-strong; Turc Malec = sterile (*turg*) no-good lecher (*mal-lec*). The M songbook's illustration of "cornar al cul" is not unique in medieval manuscripts. In a fourteenth-century book of decretals, there is a *bas-de-page* illustration of a man applying a bellows to the anus of an ape who drums on two tabors fixed to the back of a dog. See Reinhold Hammerstein, *Diabolus in musica: Studien zur Ikonographie der Musik im Mittelalter* (Bern, 1974), fig. 75. Lilian M. Randall, *Images in the Margins of Gothic Manuscripts* (Berkeley and Los Angeles, 1966), p. 14, fig. 112, gives a *bas-de-page* from a book of Canticles of the Virgin that more closely resembles the M songbook's burlesque of Bernart de Ventadorn in that it too involves a trumpet or horn, but this time held with the bowl facing out from the hindquarters in a burlesque of "high" song (Canticles of the Virgin) with the "low" song of a fart.

29. See Hammerstein, *Diabolus*, pp. 25 and 31, on the connotations of fistula and tympanum (flute and drum) in medieval iconography. In "L'Erotisme dans la musique médiévale," in *L'Erotisme au moyen-âge*, ed. Bruno Roy (Montreal, 1977), pp. 83–107, Jean Gagné has treated the "instrumental" analogies for the sex organs and explicated some of the variations on the musical metaphor for lovemaking that involve wind or percussion instruments.

30. There are quite a few fighting *grylles* among the chimeras Baltrušaitis presents in *Le Moyen-Age fantastique*, as on p. 17, fig. 7, from the prayerful context of the *Hours of Therouanne*. Sometimes lone *grylles* are armed with sticks and clubs, as if to emphasize that their bodily parts are at odds; sometimes two *grylles* fight each other.

31. See J. N. Adams, *The Latin Sexual Vocabulary* (Baltimore, 1982), pp. 4–6, on ritual obscenity; and, on power symbols, Meyer Schapiro, "The Bowman and the Bird on the Ruthwell Cross and Other Works: The Interpretation of Secular Themes in Early Medieval Religious Art," *Art Bulletin* 45 (1963): 351–54.

32. This translation is from E. G. Holt, *Literary Sources of Art History* (Princeton, 1947), p. 19.

33. Randall, *Images in the Margins*, p. 14.

34. Ibid., fig. 29.

35. Even Guilhem Molinier, compiler of the *Leys d'amors*, signs his work playfully this way. He tells us his name is "Ernilimo qu'areyre va" ("Ernilimo that goes backwards," i.e., mo-li-ni-er, *Leys*, vol. 1, p. 32). In case this vernacular

riddle should be "too obscure," Guilhem gives us a second chance with a Latin one right afterward.

36. Sigmund Freud, *The Interpretation of Dreams*, trans. James Strachey (London, 1958), p. 755, for example, on punning associations in dreams: "The ideas which transfer their intensities to each other stand in the *loosest mutual relations*. They are linked by associations of a kind that is scorned by our normal thinking and relegated to the use of jokes. In particular, we find associations based on homonyms and verbal similarities treated as equal in value to the rest."

37. Jehan Bras-de-Fer, *Pamphile et Galatée*, ed. Joseph Morawski (Paris, 1917), p. 208, v. 2515.

38. See the illustrations in Charles Oursel, *Miniatures cisterciennes (1109–1134)* (Mâcon, 1960), esp. plates 27, 28, 29, 31, 33.

39. Ibid., plate 31.

40. Many examples of woven initials, all drawn from manuscripts in the collection of the Bibliothèque Nationale, Paris, may be found in Emile Van Moé, *La Lettre ornée* (Paris, 1949).

41. For examples of classical Latin wordplay involving *canere* ("to sing") and *canis* ("dog"), see the "canine cantos" section of Frederick Ahl's *Metaformations: Soundplay and Wordplay in Ovid and Other Classical Poets* (Ithaca, 1985), p. 31.

42. On this manuscript see Jacques Chailley, *L'Ecole musicale de Saint Martial de Limoges* (Paris, 1960), p. 93, and specifically for the tonary section, Michel Huglo, *Les Tonaires* (Paris, 1971), pp. 132–38.

43. On the dating and constitution of a Toulousain group of tonaries, see Huglo, who has suggested (*Les Tonaires*, p. 138 n. 3) that the illuminations of these tonaries may be determined by medieval musical theory, in that the dancer in Paris, B.N. lat. 1118, and also in London, B.L. Harley 4951, illustrates the fifth tone, which was called *subsaltans* or *lascivus*. The Harley tonary also presents a male jongleur who juggles six balls, none entering the text (Huglo, *Les Tonaires*, fig. 1).

44. Hammerstein, *Diabolus*, presents a series of twelfth- through fourteenth-century liturgical parodies in *bas-de-page* grotesques and sculpture (figs. 76–82 and 87). Within a divided frame in his fig. 64, from a twelfth-century English psalter, we see, on top, sacred music illustrated by King David playing a harp, to the accompaniment of other "high," soul-stirring instruments; in the lower register, the devil beats on a drum to the accompaniment of fiddle and horn, tumblers, and a group of men making gestures with their hands (mimes?), all representing jongleuresque music that stirs the senses. The jongleurs on fols. 107v and 111v in the eleventh-century Toulousain tonary of Paris, B.N. lat. 1118, were probably also meant to contrast with the more idealized Davidic string players seated in high chairs on fols. 104r and 110r of this manuscript.

CHAPTER 6

1. Reto Bezzola, *Les Origines et la formation de la littérature courtoise en occident (500–1200)*. Part 2, vol. 2: *Les Grandes Maisons féodales après la chute des Carolingiens et leur influence sur les lettres jusqu'au XII*[e] *siècle* (Paris, 1966), p. 262 n. 4. References to this volume will be abbreviated as *Les Grandes Maisons*.

2. Dietmar Rieger, "Guillaume IX d'Aquitaine et l'idéologie troubadoresque: Remarques sur l'emploi des noms propres chez le 'premier' troubador," *Romania* 101 (1980): 445–46.

3. Stephen G. Nichols, Jr., "*Canso→Conso*: Structures of Parodic Humor in Three Songs of Guilhem IX," *L'Esprit Créateur* 16 (1976): 16–29.

4. Charles Camproux, "'Faray un vers tot covinen,'" *Mélanges . . . Jean Frappier*, 2 vols. (Geneva, 1970), vol. 1, 164–67.

5. Rieger, "Guillaume IX," p. 448.

6. Pasero, no. 11, p. 278, for the C version: "Esgarda lai Falco d'Angieus / . . . Si Falco d'Angieus no·lh secor" ("I leave it in the guardianship of Fulk of Angers / . . . If Fulk of Angers does not come to his aid"). The majority of Italian manuscripts (DIK) and the Provençal R songbook read "Folcon" or "Folcos." The C scribe's spelling may be hypercorrect in this case to avoid the vulgar innuendo, substituting a more laudatory avian one.

7. Louis de Landes, in his *Glossaire érotique de la langue française depuis son origine jusqu'à nos jours* (Brussels, 1861), cites late medieval use of *boire* as a metaphoric expression for sexual intercourse (p. 42) and of *eau* as a metaphor for sperm. In the mid-twelfth century, Marcabru uses a form of the word *boire* to suggest intercourse in a context loaded with kitchen metaphors for sex:

> S'est estai en la cozina
> E cocha·l fuec el tuzo
> E beu lo fum de la tina [AKN "*con*tina"]
> De si donz na bonalfo.
> ("L'iverns vai e·l temps s'aizina,"
> no. 31, p. 148)

This one stays in the kitchen, / blows on the fire in the coals / and drinks the steam from the container / of his Lady, Lady Bonalfo [or, Bon-al-fo, "good-to-fuck"].

8. Pasero, no. 2, p. 46, minus his emendations.

9. Pasero, no. 3, p. 70. This lyric survives in a fragmentary state only in the E songbook. The rhyme and meter enable us to guess that the last line runs, as Bond suggests in his edition, "si·l dampn[atges no·i es ges]." For this reconstituted ending see Gerald Bond, *The Poetry of William VII, Count of Poitiers, IX Duke of Aquitaine* (New York, 1982), p. 12.

10. Lynne Lawner, "Notes towards an Interpretation of the *Vers de dreyt nien*," *Cultura Neolatina* 28 (1968): 156.

11. Pasero, no. 6, p. 166; however, I have corrected Pasero's C ms. variants from Paris, B.N. fr. 856, fol. 230v.

12. See Pasero, pp. 185–86, for a résumé of some modern interpretations of this crux.

13. *Thesaurus linguae latinae*, 10 vols. (Leipzig, 1900–), vol. 6, part 1, col. 41.

14. I cite the text and translation of this statement by Odericus Vitalis from Bond's appendix of historical documents relating to Guillaume IX, pp. 116–17 in *Poetry of William VII*.

15. Ibid., p. 120.

16. Ibid.

17. See Pasero, no. 5, pp. 133–135, for the C manuscript's version. The length of Guillaume's stay with the ladies is specified as "eight days and even more"

only in the N and V manuscript versions: "Ueit jorn ez ancar mais estei / az aquel torn" (or "sotorn," Pasero, p. 129).

18. In his notes on the C manuscript's version, Bond explains that he has emended to eliminate this syntactical ambiguity (*Poetry of William VII*, p. 84): "These lines are reversed in the MS. Syntax and context demonstrate the need to correct this aural or visual error (both lines begin with *e*-)." I would argue against the "need to correct" in this instance.

19. Rieger, "Guillaume IX," p. 447, links Guillaume's Ermessen with the she-wolf Hersant. For an interesting biographical interpretation associating the names Agnes and Ermessen with those of Guillaume's most pious female ancestors, Ermeson, wife of Guillaume VII of Aquitaine, and the Empress Agnes of Poitou, who retired to a convent in 1063, carried on a spiritual friendship with Peter Damian, and died when Guillaume IX was a young boy, see Rita Lejeune, "L'Extraordinaire Insolence du troubadour Guillaume IX d'Aquitaine," *Mélanges . . . Pierre Le Gentil* (Paris, 1973), pp. 485–503. It must be noted, however, that these seem to have been common female names among the nobility of the period. For example, an Agnes held the position of the first prioress of Orsan (a priory of Fontevrault), and Hersende of Montsoreau, who died in 1109, was the first prioress of Fontevrault itself.

20. Hans Spanke, *Untersuchungen über die Ursprünge des romanischen Minnesangs: Marcabrustudien*, Abhandlungen der Gesellschaft der Wissenschaften zu Göttingen, Philologische-historische Klasse, 3d ser., 24 (Göttingen, 1940), p. 37.

21. On melody as punctuation see Leo Treitler, "The Early History of Music Writing in the West," *Journal of the American Musicological Society* 35 (1982): 237–79; and "From Ritual through Language to Music," *Schweizer Jahrbuch für Musikwissenschaft* n.s. 2 (1982): 109–23: "melody was the medium for the oral recitation of the texts; it was an adjunct to language. The melodic realization of a text, if it is recorded in writing in a particular source, represents a particular way of reciting it. It records a 'reading' of the text in the sense of 'interpretation.' In this process melody plays a role something like that of punctuation, whose signs, as Cassiodorus put it, 'are, as it were, paths of meaning and lanterns to words, as instructive to readers as the best commentaries'" (p. 109).

22. This epithet for Guillaume was coined by Pio Rajna in an article on Guillaume's dualism, "Guglielmo, conte de Poitiers, trovatore bifronte," *Mélanges . . . Alfred Jeanroy* (Paris, 1928), pp. 349–60.

23. When excommunicated for repudiating his wife and refusing to break off his liaison with the Viscountess of Châtellerault, Guillaume, by William of Malmesbury's account, taunted the balding Bishop of Angoulême that the comb would run through the fugitive locks of the bishop's forehead before Guillaume would abandon the viscountess. For text and translation of this famous retort, see Bond, *Poetry of William VII*, pp. 128–29.

24. William of Malmesbury, *Gesta regum anglorum*, citation and translation from Bond, *Poetry of William VII*, pp. 128–29: "Legitima quoque uxore depulsa, vicecomitis cujusdam conjugem surripuit, quam adeo ardebat ut clypeo suo simulacrum mulierculae insereret; perinde dictitans se illam velle ferre in praelio, sicut illa portabat eum in triclinio" ("Also, when he had driven away his legal wife, he carried off the wife of a certain viscount, whom he lusted after so much that he vowed to engrave the image of the strumpet on his shield, saying again and again that he would support her in battle just as she did him in bed").

25. Bezzola, *Les Grandes Maisons*, p. 310:

> This astonishing song ends with two strophes that witness to the profound transformation undergone by the count under the influence of the religious mysticism surrounding him. . . . Before the mirage of "My Lady" that he had just created, the first troubadour remains himself filled with wonder. Does this superior being—dispenser of supreme joy, of health, of courtesy, of wisdom, of life itself, just as of illness, of crudeness, of folly, and of death—still have something to do with the real woman about whom the all-powerful count boasted, in his bawdy poems, of having made an easy conquest?

26. Bond, *Poetry of William VII*, p. xlix; Lawner, "Interpretation," p. 157; Leslie T. Topsfield, "The Burlesque Poetry of Guilhem IX," *Neuphilologische Mitteilungen* 69 (1968): 298. Nevertheless, Topsfield's order of treatment of Guillaume's lyrics in his *Troubadours and Love* (Cambridge, England, 1975), like Jeanroy's, Pasero's, and Bond's in their editions, tends to lend support to the old notion that Guillaume "progresses" from burlesques to more refined love lyrics. The progression, if there is one, may be, rather, to a more "refined" form of burlesque.

27. Peter Dronke, *Medieval Latin and the Rise of the European Love-Lyric*, 2 vols. (Oxford, 1965–1966). Concerning the mid-thirteenth-century treatise *Quinque incitamenta ad Deum amandum ardenter*, by the Cistercian Gérard de Liège, Dronke writes (vol. 1, pp. 61–62): "At times it is as if he were claiming that the 'real' meaning of profane love-songs was a divine one, at others as if he thought them a parody of the language of love. . . . This is to me the most striking thing that emerges from Gerard's juxtapositions: the more deeply religious the language, the closer to the language of *courtoisie*. The virtues acquired by the soul illumined by divine grace are exactly those which the lover acquires when his soul is irradiated by his lady's grace: they are truly a courtly lover's virtues."

28. Boutière and Schutz, no. 1, p. 7: "Lo coms de Peitieus si fo uns dels majors cortes del mon e dels majors trichadors de dompnas, e bons cavalliers d'armas e larcs de dompnejar; e saup ben trobar e cantar. Et anet lonc temps per lo mon per enganar las domnas." ("The Count of Poitou was one of the most courteous men in the world and one of the greatest beguilers of ladies, and a good knight at arms and generous in his gallantries, and he knew very well how to compose and sing lyrics. And he traveled through the world a long time seducing ladies.")

29. If we consider a songbook such as the thirteenth-century St. Martial collection of Paris, B.N. lat. 3719, as a "textbook" that might have been used in a monastic school—which formed young noblemen as well as future religious—we find that the peaceful skills it teaches include not only reading but playing chess (there are nearly three full pages in fine lettering, fols. 91v–92v, devoted to this subject); not only the singing of religious songs, many of which praise the Virgin, but also of profane ones on the seduction of girls. "Cortes" behavior might include all of this.

30. The judge is Geoffroi le Gros, in his *Life of Bernard of Tyre*, cited by Bezzola, *Les Grandes Maisons*, p. 268 n. 3: "Guillelmus, dux Aquitanorum . . . totius pudicitas ac sanctitatis inimicus."

31. Bond, *Poetry of William VII*, pp. 120–21, for text and translation.

32. Bezzola, *Les Grandes Maisons*, pp. 284–88. On the voluntary submission of the brothers of the order of Fontevrault to the sisters, see Jacques Dalarun,

L'Impossible Sainteté (Paris, 1985), p. 260, and p. 37 for Robert d'Arbrissel's deathbed request that the brothers continue to observe their vow of obedience to the sisters and that the sisters, in turn, consult with the brothers in making decisions.

33. In his edition of Guillaume's verse, Pasero relegates to an appendix "Farai chansoneta nueva" (no. 8) which survives only in the C songbook, where it is attributed to "coms de peytius." Bond labels it "poem of doubtful attribution." The main basis for this modern interpretive decision is the novelty of its feminine rhymes and the term *chansoneta* in the opening line, rather than *vers*, the label Guillaume gives his other lyrics. (Cf. A. Monteverdi, "La 'chansoneta nueva' attribuita a Guglielmo d'Aquitania," *Syculorum Gymnasium* n.s. 8 [1955]: 6–15; and Bond, *Poetry of William VII*, p. lxxvii). Any argument based on rhyme or metrics seems rather flimsy, in light of Guillaume's creativity and the previous use of many feminine rhymes in religious songs. As Pasero notes (p. 302 n. 1), *chansoneta*—as compared to *canso*—is a rare word in any case, although used once later by Bernart de Ventadorn and by Peire Vidal. Why might Guillaume not have invented it—or borrowed or modified it from a popular word form—rather than Bernart or Peire? The C manuscript compilers did not seem to be daunted by such technical arguments against attribution to Guillaume, especially when there was an important thematic reason for assigning it to him: its parody of monastic piety and devotion to the Virgin.

In two early strophes, the speaker plays the monk. He uses images of religious submission and obedience to praise his lady. Because she is whiter than ivory (whiter, perhaps, than ivory carvings of the Virgin or the saints), he professes to "adore" only her: "Que plus ez blanca qu'evori, / per qu'ieu autra non azori" (Pasero, no. 8, p. 299). He will give himself up to his lady (like a novice entering the monastery) so that she may write him down in her charter: "Qu'ans mi rent a lieis e·m liure, / qu'en sa carta·m pot escriure." Each of the strophes containing such religious-sounding professions of submission ends with an incongruously sensual statement of the speaker's physical desire, his "hunger" for her love, his dying for a kiss. Finally he bridles against asceticism in love:

Qual pro i auretz, dompna conja,
si vostr'amor mi deslonja?
Par que·us vulhatz metre monja!
(p. 300)

What will it profit you, sweet lady, / if you distance your love from me? / It seems that you want to become a nun!

In the next strophe the speaker explicitly affirms the joy "of this world" against monastic asceticism, deliberately reversing the biblical maxim "What will it profit you if you gain the whole world . . .":

Qual pro i auretz s'ieu m'enclostre
e no·m retenetz per vostre?
totz lo joi del mon es nostre,
dompna, s'amdui nos amam.

What will it profit you if I cloister myself / and you don't hold me for your own? / All the joy of the world is ours, / lady, if both of us love.

This sounds like Guillaume to me. If he did not write "Farai chansoneta nueva," the lyric nevertheless expresses anti-ascetic sentiments similar to his and does so in a facetious manner not unlike Guillaume's in other lyrics that are more surely his, such as "En Alvernhe, part Lemozi."

34. Dronke, *Medieval Latin*, vol. 1, p. 235.

35. Dronke edits and translates this lyric from Paris, B.N. lat. 3719, fol. 23. It is copied again on fols. 37v–38r in an alternating series of religious and profane songs on love and birth. For example, immediately following the secular song "De ramis cadunt folia" (fol. 49r), with its winter topos opening and the poet's profession of his burning desire for a girl (see Dronke, *Medieval Latin*, vol. 1, pp. 288–90, for text and translation), there appears a song announcing the nativity of Christ and Mary's reparation, through His birth, of the defects of man and nature brought about by sin (fol. 49v): "Nata est hodie / virgo pura / data est leticie / humana creatura" ("Today is born / a pure maid; / joy is given / to human creatures"). Similar kinds of alternation occur several times. Songs about the seduction of girls in springtime, which end in grief to the girls and complaints about pregnancy, as on fol. 37r, are juxtaposed in a striking fashion, through opening word choice, to songs on Christ's nativity, as on fol. 38v, "Uterus hodie virginis floruit" ("Today the womb of a virgin flowers").

36. Cf. Canticles 5:1: "Veniat dilectus meus in hortum suum" ("My beloved is come into his garden").

37. Cf. Canticles 5:2–4, where the beloved, not having a key, must knock at the door and call "Aperi mihi" and try to force the opening with his hands: "Dilectus meus misit manum suam per foramen" ("My beloved put his hand through the opening").

38. Dronke, *Medieval Latin*, vol. 1, p. 274.

39. Hans Spanke, "Zur Formenkunst des ältesten Troubadours," *Studi Medievali* n.s. 7 (1934): 72–84, and *Marcabrustudien*; Guido Errante, *Marcabru e le fonti sacre dell'antica lirica romanza* (Florence, 1948).

40. Peire Rogier's *vida* (Boutière and Schutz, no. 40, p. 267) states that he was "canorgues de Clarmon" (canon of Clermont-Ferrand), and Peire d'Auvernhe, in "Cantarai d'aqestz trobadors," reproaches him for singing secular love songs, instead of singing his psalter in religious processions:

car chanta d'amor a prezen;
e valgra li mais un sautiers
en la glieis'o us candeliers
tener ab gran candel'arden.
(Del Monte, no. 12, p. 120)

Because he sings about love now, / and it would be better for him to carry a psalter / in the church, with a candlestick / and a big burning candle.

Peire Cardenal's *vida* (Boutière and Schutz, no. 50, p. 335) also mentions his education as a canon: "E cant era petitz, sos paires lo mes per quanorgue en la quanorguia major del Puei; et apres letras, e saup ben lezer e chantar" ("When he was little, his father placed him as a canon in the great canonry of Le Puy, and he learned [Latin] letters and knew how to read and sing well"). Peire d'Auvernhe was also from the bishopric of Clermont-Ferrand, according to his *vida* (ibid., no. 39, p. 263). Both Clermont and Le Puy were early centers of Mariology, with statues of the Virgin and cathedrals named for her. That Peire d'Auvernhe was once a colleague of Peire Rogier's at Clermont-Ferrand we know from Bernart Marti's response to Peire's criticism of himself (Hoepffner, no. 5, p. 16):

E quan canorgues si mes
Pey d'Alvernh' en canongia,
A Dieu per que·s prometia
Entiers que pueys si fraysses?
Quar si feys fols joglares,
Per que l'entier pretz cambia.

And when Peire d'Auvergne assumed the position / of canon in a canonry, / why did he promise himself entirely / to God since afterward he broke [his promise]? / Because if he plays the foolish jongleur, / it appears that his perfect reputation has changed.

41. See the Monk of Montaudon's *vida* (Boutière and Schutz, no. 46, p. 307).

42. See William Paden, Jr., "*De monachis rithmos facientibus*: Helinant de Froidmont, Bertran de Born, and the Cistercian General Chapter of 1199," *Speculum* 55 (1980): 669–85. According to their *vidas* and other documents, two early troubadours, Bernart de Ventadorn and Bertran de Born, became Cistercians in the Limousin monastery of Dalon.

43. See Istvan Hajnal, *L'Enseignement de l'écriture aux universités médiévales*, 2d ed., revised by László Mezey (Budapest, 1959), p. 69: "When the child, under the direction of the canon, had finished study of the psalms, with what that involved of reading and fragmentary knowledge of Latin, he had the right to the title of cleric." On this subject see also Henri-Irénée Marrou, *Histoire de l'éducation dans l'antiquité* (Paris, 1948), pp. 445–46.

44. Leon Gautier in his *Histoire de la poésie liturgique au moyen âge: Les Tropes* (Paris, 1886), p. 182, noted that the greatest number of religious tropes celebrate the Nativity and Incarnation. They were composed for the festivities of the Christmas season, when youthful choirs—the monastery's or cathedral's *scola*—performed in honor of Christ's infancy. Gautier has also suggested (p. 73) that, along with the masters, the more advanced students set themselves to the composition of new tropes as a kind of grammatical and rhetorical exercise, whence the great abundance and variety of trope collections. Variation was prescribed: the intention behind such compositions was to sing an ever-new song to the Lord.

45. Bezzola, *Les Origines* . . . . Part 2, vol. 1: *L'Essor de la société féodale et les lettres* (Paris, 1966), p. 29. References to this volume will be abbreviated as *L'Essor*.

CHAPTER 7

1. Henri-Irénée Marrou, *Les Troubadours*, 2d ed. (Paris, 1971), pp. 175–76:

We have sometimes exaggerated, antedated, the influence on our poetry of Marian piety as a result of not knowing the stages of the development of the latter very well. Some have maintained that under the veil of worldly love, the earliest troubadors really addressed the Virgin, or even that the cult of Mary was at the source of courtly love, properly speaking. We must remember that in the West, Marian theology had long remained stationary; it was only after 1100 that it took new flight, but the piety and mysticism of the twelfth century are still above all Christological and Trinitarian, and it is on this sound and solid foundation that Mariology will be able to develop.

Courtly love and Marian piety represent two parallel movements; if there was influence, it was, instead, in the opposite direction. It is the love poetry that is to

> furnish more emotional means of expression to piety, the more affectionate piety of the thirteenth century and of the end of the Middle Ages.

Views similar to Marrou's are expressed by Etienne Gilson in an appendix entitled "St. Bernard and Courtly Love," pp. 170–97 in *The Mystical Theology of Saint Bernard*, trans. A. H. C. Downes ([French ed. 1934] London, 1955). Both Gilson and Marrou are also at pains to prove (with the implication that there could be no serious imitation) that the "objects" of courtly and religious love were different—one profane, the other sacred; one carnal, the other spiritual. They both entertain the question, in passing, without pursuit, of whether courtly love might be a deliberately perverse parody of religious love: "We may still ask ourselves whether the courtly conception of love, although oriented in the opposite direction to the Cistercian, was not a kind of reversed copy of it, at least in some respects" (Gilson, "St. Bernard," p. 178).

The weight of Gilson's judgment was enormous; he effectively (although unfairly) discredited Eduard Wechssler's comparative chapters in *Das Kulturproblem des Minnesangs*. Vol. 1: *Minnesang und Christentum* (Halle, 1909). Nevertheless, a few scholars have not been wholly intimidated: Guido Errante, *Marcabru e le fonti sacre dell'antica lirica romanza* (Florence, 1948); Nicolas J. Perella, *The Kiss, Sacred and Profane* (Berkeley and Los Angeles, 1969); Raymond Gay-Crosier, *Religious Elements in the Secular Lyrics of the Troubadours* (Chapel Hill, 1971). These have accepted only half of Gilson's and Marrou's judgment—that the cult of Mary in the West developed, at the earliest, along with the troubadour cult of the *domna*—and then they have gone on to explore what they saw as a seriously parodic relationship between contemporary or later (especially Bernardine) expressions of religious love and the language of the troubadours. However, their work is flawed by their choice of twelfth-century and later religious texts for comparison. Even a cursory examination of the religious verse from the third through the fifteenth century collected by Henry Spitzmuller in his *Poésie latine chrétienne du moyen âge* (Bruges, 1971) shows that songs of supplication to Mary as patron and intercessor, not to mention more general praise for her part in man's redemption, were common in the West from at least the tenth century. See also Hubertus Ahsmann, *La Culte de la Sainte Vierge et la littérature française profane du moyen âge* (Utrecht, 1929).

2. Peter Dronke, *Medieval Latin and the Rise of the European Love-Lyric*, 2 vols. (Oxford, 1965–1966), vol. 1, pp. 91–92 and p. 92 n. 1:

> in one of the oldest and greatest hymns to her [Mary] she is not only a figure of Sapientia, but explicitly a figure with the functions of the *nous poiêtikos*, envisaged with all its mystical connotations, and intimately associated with the language of love. This is the *Hymnos Akathistos*, the canonical hymn to the Virgin of the entire Byzantine Church in the Middle Ages, written in Greek in the first quarter of the sixth century, and known in the West in a Latin translation at least from the ninth century . . . : "Hail, you state of love surpassing all love, . . . you who bring the contraries together, . . . you who contain the divine Sapientia and are a token of God's providence."

3. See C. A. Maurin, *Les Saluts d'amour*. Vol. 1: *Les Troubadours de Notre-Dame*, part 1, *Des premiers siècles au quatorzième* (Montpellier, 1932), p. 42.

4. For the Greek text see J. P. Migne, *Patrologiae cursus completus . . . Series Graeca*, 161 vols. (Paris, 1857–66), vol. 98, col. 317. The poem is translated into French, from which I have translated it into English, in *Louanges mariales du*

premier millénaire des églises d'orient et d'occident, ed. C. Berselli et al. (Paris, 1981), p. 72.

5. Maurin, *Les Saluts*, p. 161; cf. Canticles 4:10–11.

6. See, for example, the figures in W. W. S. Cook and José Gudiol Ricart, *Ars Hispaniae*. Vol. 6: *Pintura e Imaginería Románicas* (Madrid, 1950); or Georges Duby, *Adolescence de la chrétienté occidentale (980–1140)* (Geneva, 1984), p. 100.

7. Such interpretations of the Canticles are, of course, not the only reasons for changing church design. Abbot Suger of St. Denis, for example, relied on texts of the pseudo-Dionysius in trying to "illuminate" his church. Sometimes artistic innovations were carried out in order to reify new textual interpretations; sometimes the direction of influence must have been just the opposite, with new interpretations of old texts invented to substantiate the desired artistic innovations.

8. Both the English translation and the edition of this song from Cambridge, Trinity B. I. 16, fol. 2r, are from Dronke, *Medieval Latin*, vol. 2, pp. 516–17, who groups it under the heading of "sapiential verse" but regards it as a lyric of profane love imitating the language of the Canticles:

Luce fruor gaudio, noctibus suspirio;
Mesta que sum tenebris luce fio celebris.

En per montes saliens et colles transiliens;
Venit quem optaveram, michi loqui cupiens.

Per fenestras et cancellos me videre voluit;
Ad contactum manus sue venter meus tremuit.

Vox dilecti sonuit, favo michi dulcior,
Cuius sole facies est claro preclarior:

"Columba mea nitida, amica mea splendida,
Surge! veni! propera! postponendo vetera.

. . . .

Sponsa mea, veni, veni, surge, veni, propera!

. . . .

Tibi dabo munera— Mecum tanges ethera!"

See Canticles 2:9–13, 5:4.

9. The closing lines of the Canticles (8:10) may also have suggested the towers flanking the facade of some Romanesque and Gothic church portals. The bride/Ecclesia speaks: "Ego murus et ubera mea sicut turris ex quo facta sum coram eo quasi pacem reperiens" ("I am a wall and my breasts are like towers, from which I am made in his presence, as if finding peace").

10. See Cook and Ricart, *Pintura*, and Emile Mâle, *Notre-Dame de Chartres* (Paris, 1983), p. 26: "the superhuman Virgin of Chartres, majestic like a theological idea, is the first that had been seen in France on the tympanum of a church."

11. Cited by Mâle, *Notre-Dame de Chartres*, p. 26, from the cartulary of Notre-Dame de Chartres.

12. The glorification of Mary/Ecclesia is evident even earlier in certain monastic milieus, as, for instance, in the imagery of Notker of St. Gaul's ninth-century verses for the dedication of a church (Spitzmuller, *Poésie latine chrétienne*, p. 314): "Psallat Ecclesia, mater illibata/et virgo sine ruga" ("Sing,

Church, mother unpolluted / and virgin without imperfection"). The Church is a Virgin Mother; "within her, impregnated by the Holy Spirit, grace gives birth to a new progeny."

13. Philippe Verdier, *Le Couronnement de la Vierge: Les Origines et les premiers développements d'un thème iconographique* (Paris, 1980), p. 69. This manuscript from the monastery of Jumièges is now in the library of Rouen (Y 109, fol. 4r).

14. Spitzmuller, *Poésie latine chrétienne*, pp. 454–58, attributes the poem hesitantly to St. Anselm.

15. Léon Gautier, "La Poésie religieuse dans les cloîtres des IX–XIe siècles," *Revue du Monde Catholique* 91 (1887): 484.

16. Ibid.

17. Such linguistic exaggeration is easy to tilt into burlesque. Without knowing the original context and manner of performance of such verses, it is often hard to judge whether the exaggeration is intended to magnify or to mock. For example, Dronke quotes and translates (*Medieval Latin*, vol. 2, pp. 513–15) an eleventh-century lyric that he judges, probably correctly, to be a burlesque of the extravagances of encyclopaedic learning:

> Mater materne   rationis, adesto superne!
> Matrem devote   filius audio te.
>   Ecce, lyram recito:
>
> Quantum gauderet   si se semel ire deceret
> Imantapoda gens,   poplitibus peragens
>   Cursus retrograda—
>
> Alysinus quantum   miratur flumine cantum,
> Aut antropophagus   quam cupit ore vagus
>   Cognato pasci—

> Mother of mother wit, be present on high! / I, your son, hear you devoutly, mother. / See, I recite my canticle:
>
> As greatly as the bandy-legged tribe would rejoice if for once it were able to walk, / the Himantopodoi marching / backwards on their knees—
>
> As much as the Alisian marvels at the song of the river, / as much as the wandering anthropophage longs / to chew his blood-relative—

In this lyric, which goes on in this vein for several more strophes, "mater materne rationis" (mother of mother wit or reason) may refer to Mary as bearer of the Word, *sedes sapientia*, figure for the Church as gateway to learning, an *alma mater* who nourishes the worshipper, as he finally proclaims, with the "honey-dripping goblets / of [her] doctrine ("dogmatis, alma, tui / Pocula melliflua"). Might this be serious praise of Mary/Ecclesia, whom all creatures adore, including the fantastical humanoid creatures described by the encyclopaedists? Is this a serious putting-to-religious-use of even the most extravagant classical learning? With Dronke, I suspect a comic intention in this lyric—but no one has questioned the seriousness with which the same encyclopaedic learning is reified in the stone sculptures of fantastical humanoid creatures surrounding and adoring Christ over the portal of Vezélay (in virtually the same position as the sculpted figures of the liberal arts at Chartres).

18. Dronke, *Medieval Latin*, vol. 1, pp. 268–69.

19. Karl Young, *The Drama of the Medieval Church*, 2 vols. (Oxford, 1933).

20. F. S. Schmitt, *Anselmi . . . opera omnia*, 6 vols. (Edinburgh, 1940–1961), vol. 3, pp. 13–25. Citations of Anselm are from this edition.

21. Dronke, *Medieval Latin*, vol. 1, p. 265.

22. See, for example, the anonymous tenth-century sequence beginning "Missus sacer a supernis ad Mariam angelus," pp. 1276–78 in Spitzmuller's anthology, *Poésie latine chrétienne*. This song seems to require a narrator and two figurants, Gabriel and Mary, who might either form a mute tableau while the narrator sang their words, or, less probably, sing their own lines.

23. Spitzmuller, *Poésie latine chrétienne*, pp. 350, 410.

24. Dronke, *Medieval Latin*, vol. 1, p. 185.

25. Ibid., pp. 264–65.

26. Spitzmuller, *Poésie latine chrétienne*, p. 410.

27. Ibid., p. 1276.

28. On Peter Damian's letter, see Dronke, *Medieval Latin*, vol. 1, p. 199 n. 2. Of interest, too, is the tradition, even if mistaken, that attributes Mariological verses such as "In laudem sanctae Mariae" to the sixth-century Bishop Fortunatus (from Byzantine Ravenna). Like Reto Bezzola, medieval interpreters may have understood these as veiled love-songs to Fortunatus's female religious patrons, Queen Radegonde and Abbess Agnes, who in the sixth century founded and headed a convent outside Poitiers dedicated to the Virgin. (See Bezzola, *Les Origines. . . .* Part 1: *La Tradition impériale de la fin de l'antiquité au XIe siècle* [Paris, 1968], pp. 65–74.)

To show how, "sacred or profane, the language of love can at times remain virtually a constant," Dronke offers an example of a fourteenth-century interpretation committed to writing in a marginal gloss (*Medieval Latin*, vol. 2, pp. 518–19). Such slight pointing might also be done with the voice or gesture. Beside the statement "I am not with you now in the body, yet in my senses with you ardently," the glossator writes "scilicet in celo" to clarify that the beloved is in heaven, where the speaker yearns to join her. The same gloss spiritualizes the "place for love" that the speaker longs for "right now." More radically, the glossator rubs out one half-line and adds a religious epithet that clearly identifies the beloved as Mary: "post Christum patris Sophia" ("you who after Christ are the Wisdom of the father"). This change and the addition of the title "Ad dei genitricem Mariam" are not shocking in the context of the heavily Mariological language of the lover's praise of his lady, which begins "Instar solis, ave! totius luminus atque . . ." If, indeed, the poet was writing in praise of a living lady, which is not entirely certain, he was appropriating the language of Mariology. Thus, the fourteenth-century glossator had little to do to redirect the object of the lover-speaker's words upward once more, "in celo." "Who is the object of the lover's desire?" is a kind of riddle, an interpretive game played with the texts of both medieval Latin and vernacular love lyrics.

29. Dronke, *Medieval Latin*, vol. 1, p. 314.

30. Ibid., p. 271.

31. Reedited from Paris, B.N. lat. 1118, fol. 247v. See also, from this songbook, the somewhat emended edition of Guido Maria Dreves and Clemens Blume, *Analecta hymnica medii aevi*, 55 vols. (Leipzig, 1886–1922), vol. 11, no. 91, pp. 57–58.

32. This is not the only "nothing" that the makers of Paris, B.N. lat. 1139, turn into the sign of something. On fol. 110r, for example, a smaller hole is circled in red to form the capital *O* of the word *Oris* and to imitate, perhaps,

a mouth open in singing praises. The previously discussed large hole in the middle of folio 51 is also outlined in red on the recto, where it may signal *con* play, especially because of its shape and red outline, positioned above a song beginning "Congaudeat ecclesia."

33. For early examples, including one from St. Martial, of festive dancing in churches, gleaned mostly from ascetic opposition to it, see L. Gougaud, "La Danse dans les églises," *Revue d'histoire ecclésiastique* 15 (1914): 5–22, 229–45.

34. Hans Spanke, "Zur Formenkunst des ältesten Troubadours," *Studi Medievali* n.s. 7 (1934): 75–76. Spanke does not discuss the appearance of "Promat chorus hodie" on the manuscript page. He does note (p. 77) that the metrical models of some of Guillaume's and other early troubadours' songs are festive conductuses and songs that would have been sung by youthful choirs, songs such as "In laudes Innocentium," the model for Guillaume's "vers de dreyt nien." Léon Gautier, in his *Histoire de la poésie liturgique au moyen âge: Les Tropes* (Paris, 1886), p. 182, suggests that it was especially choirs of children who celebrated the infancy of Christ with the tropes and songs of the Christmas season: "They were the kings then, and these songs were sung by the choirboys alone: 'Gratulentur parvuli,—Nato rege parvulo' [Paris, B.N. lat. 1139, fol. 40v]; and another, 'In laudes innocentium—Psallat chorus infantium' [fol. 40r]; and yet another, 'Sint infantes—Festivantes—Et sonorus—Psallat chorus' [Paris, B.N. lat. 3719, fol. 43v]."

CHAPTER 8

1. See Heiko Jürgens, *Pompa diaboli: Die lateinischen Kirchenväter und das antike Theater* (Stuttgart, 1972), p. 234.

2. For example, Chaucer's Alison in the "Miller's Tale" is not fooled for a minute about Absalon's intentions as he stands under her window wooing her in the yearning language of the Canticles: "What do ye, hony-comb, sweete Alisoun, / My faire bryd, my sweete cynamome?" . . . "Go fro the window, Jakke fool," she sayde; / "As help me God, it wol nat be 'com pa me'" (F. N. Robinson, *The Works of Geoffrey Chaucer*, 2d ed. [Cambridge, Mass., 1957], p. 53, vv. 3698–99, 3708–9).

3. On youth groups organized as "abbeys" and their activities in the late Middle Ages and the Renaissance, see Natalie Zemon Davis, "The Reasons of Misrule," *Society and Culture in Early Modern France* (Stanford, 1975), pp. 104–23.

4. Bezzola, *Les Grandes Maisons*, p. 288.

5. Examples of the saints' revenge could be drawn from many sources. Saints were believed to be able to provoke the same diseases they cured. For more ingenious saintly punishments befitting human misdemeanors, see the twelfth-century accounts of Gerald of Wales in his *Journey through Wales*, trans. Lewis Thorpe (London, 1978). See also Jean Delumeau, *La Peur en Occident* (Paris, 1978), pp. 61–62; Patrick J. Geary, "La Coercition des saints dans la pratique religieuse médiévale," in *La Culture populaire au moyen âge*, ed. Pierre Boglioni (Montreal, 1979), p. 156; and Pierre-André Sigal, *L'Homme et le miracle dans la France médiévale (XIe–XIIe siècle)* (Paris, 1985), esp. pp. 276–82.

On the patron-client relationship in the worship of the saints, see Peter Brown, *The Cult of the Saints: Its Rise and Function in Latin Christianity* (Chicago, 1981), pp. 55–68.

6. Peter Dronke, *Medieval Latin and the Rise of the European Love-Lyric*, 2 vols. (Oxford, 1965–1966), vol. 1, p. 48.

7. In "L'Erotisme dans la musique médiévale," *L'Erotisme au moyen-âge*, ed. Bruno Roy (Montreal, 1977), Jean Gagné has discussed the playing of wind instruments as metaphors for lovemaking. I have encountered no other instances of "faissoner con" used in this way, but the Provençal expression "cornar al cul" (instead of *con*) is the musical metaphor for a perverse sexual encounter, used in a burlesque debate on the proper behavior of a lover. The topic of the three-sided debate among Arnaut Daniel and characters with the equivocal names of Raimon de Durfort and Turc Malec is whether or not a knight named Cornil (nil-heart/horn) should try to fulfill the conditions of "cornar al cul" ("to horn the behind") set for obtaining her love by the Lady Aia (whose name is erotically evocative, rather like the previously discussed *a* and *o* refrain of a Latin burlesque of the Canticles). For this burlesque debate see the edition and translation of Pierre Bec, *Burlesque et obscénité chez les troubadours: Pour une approche du contre-texte médiéval* (Paris, 1984), nos. 28–31, pp. 140–53.

8. Reto Bezzola is the leading upholder of the sudden-conversion theory of Guillaume's poetic development. Bezzola asks:

> How does it happen that, at the end of the eleventh or at the beginning of the twelfth century, a great poet of the southwest, Guillaume IX . . . , author of strictly sensual songs, begins all of a sudden to sing a nearly mystical love for a lady whom he sometimes exalts as a superior being, unique, i.e., unreal? How does it happen that the first troubadour of whom we know, after having rimed his gallant adventures in a saucy fashion, even downright obscene, aimed at an audience of jovial companions in debauchery, suddenly changes style and presents to a woman his most humble tribute, if not the most refined? . . . And how does he know, all of a sudden, this "joy" of love—so spiritualized after having evoked others so completely material?
>
> (*Les Grandes Maisons*, pp. 249–50)

On the other hand, in "Guillaume IX and Courtoisie," *Romanische Forschungen* 73 (1961), especially pp. 336–38, Peter Dronke gives us convincingly sensual readings, but without calling attention to erotic wordplay, of the same passages Bezzola and other idealists have treated as keystones of Guillaume's new courtly-ascetic notion of love.

9. Gerald Bond, *The Poetry of William VII, Count of Poitiers, IX Duke of Aquitaine* (New York, 1982), p. 116.

10. Ibid., p. 120, for Latin text.

11. Albert Blaise, *Dictionnaire Latin-Français des auteurs chrétiens* (Paris, 1954), p. 723.

12. Gisela Scherner-Van Ortmerssen, in *Die Text-Melodiestruktur in den Liedern des Bernart de Ventadorn* (Münster, 1973), has studied how melody meshes with sense in the works of one troubadour, always assuming a serious intention on the part of the composer. See also Hendrik Van der Werf, *The Chansons of the Troubadours and Trouvères: A Study of the Melodies and Their Relation to the Poems* (Utrecht, 1972).

13. Brunetto Latini, in his mid-thirteenth-century *Li Livres dou tresor*, II.xxxvii.1, emphasizes this self-mockery along with mockery of others in his definition of the "gengleour" (jongleur) as "celui ki gengle entre les gens a ris et a gieu, et moke soi et sa feme et ses fiz et tous autres" ("he who jangles on in company, laughing and playing, and mocks himself and his wife and his

children and everyone else"). For this citation see the edition of *Li Livres dou tresor* by Francis Carmody (1948; rpt. Geneva, 1975), p. 204. The best general works on medieval jongleurs are by Ramon Menéndez Pidal, *Poesía juglaresca* (Madrid, 1957), and Edmond Faral, *Les Jongleurs en France au moyen-âge* (Paris, 1910).

14. Quintilian begins his section on "pronunciation" in the *Institutiones*, XI.iii, by equating it with "action" (*actio*) both of the voice and of bodily gesture. He cites the authority of Cicero, who defined *actio* as a sort of language, the body's eloquence. See *Quintilien: Institution oratoire*, ed. Jean Cousin, 7 vols. (Paris, 1975–1980), vol. 6, pp. 222–23. Citations of books and sections of the *Institutiones* are from Cousin's edition.

15. W. M. Lindsay, *Isidori . . . Etymologiarum sive originum*, 2 vols. (Oxford, 1911), vol. 1, X.95.

16. For chronologically ordered collections of ecclesiastical fulminations against mimes and jongleurs, see especially Jürgens, *Pompa diaboli*; Marius Bonaria, *Romani mimi* (Rome, 1965); Faral, *Les Jongleurs*, Appendix 3; E. K. Chambers, *The Mediaeval Stage*, 2 vols. (Oxford, 1903), vol. 1, p. 35; and Menéndez Pidal, *Poesía juglaresca*, where he quotes censure as early as the sixth and seventh centuries in Spain for "burlesque songs that were accompanied by the clap of the cymbals" (p. 342).

17. From Roman times, mimes seem to have distinguished themselves by bright combinations of colors. See Jürgens, *Pompa diaboli*, p. 231.

18. On this character, "king" of *histriones*, see C. de Vic and J. Vaissète, *Histoire générale de Languedoc*, 15 vols. (Toulouse, 1872–1892), vol. 10, p. 284.

19. Boutière and Schutz, no. 80, p. 500 (Cadenet); no. 76, p. 493 (Gillems Magretz); no. 63, p. 425 (Aimeric).

20. Ibid., no. 9, p. 59.

21. For an explication of Arnaut's tour de force, see Charles Jernigan, "The Song of Nail and Uncle: Arnaut Daniel's Sestina 'Lo ferm voler q'el cor m'intra,'" *Studies in Philology* 71 (1974): 149.

22. Rita Lejeune, "L'Extraordinaire Insolence du troubadour Guillaume IX d'Aquitaine," *Mélanges Pierre Le Gentil* (Paris, 1973), pp. 485–503.

23. This better kind of vernacular jonglerie, epitomized by St. Francis, who called himself God's jongleur, celebrated spiritual rather than mundane matters. The Church also seems to have encouraged non-subversive vernacular recitations by jongleurs of *chansons de gestes* (of "lineages"/"deeds"/"gestures"), especially of secular heroes who fought the pagans, and saints' lives. By the end of the thirteenth century, in his *Penitential*, the Englishman Thomas Cabham distinguished several kinds of vernacular entertainers. He called the "good" ones *joculatores* (jongleurs who sang the histories of saints and Christian heroes without unseemly mimetic action). The "bad" ones also had musical instruments and sang, but frequented public gatherings of a sinful sort and performed lyrics that excited desire ("diversas cantilenas ut moveant homines ad lascivam"). Quotations are from Faral, *Les Jongleurs*, p. 67. Likewise, in the late thirteenth century, the "last" troubadour, the didactic Guiraut Riquier, tried to distinguish between good jongleurs and bad ones by giving them different names ("bufon" for the bad and "ioglar" for the good). See his verse treatise beginning "Sitot s'es grans afans," ed. C. A. F. Mahn, *Die Werke der Troubadours in provenzalischer Sprache*, 4 vols. (Berlin, 1853), vol. 4, pp. 182–91.

24. Menéndez Pidal, *Poesía juglaresca*, p. 39. This book includes many reproductions of manuscript illuminations of jongleurs performing lyrics. For

sculptural representations of jongleurs of all types, mostly on Romanesque capitals, see Jan Svanberg, *Gycklarmotiv i romansk konst* (Stockholm, 1970).

25. Charles Oursel, *Miniatures cisterciennes (1109–1134)* (Mâcon, 1960), plate 25.

26. There are a few illustrations in the Italian songbooks of troubadours as jongleurs playing musical instruments, mainly when such ability is mentioned in the adjacent *vida*. For example, in the A songbook, we know from the scribe's note to the illuminator, ".I. jogalar cu[n] una viola," that the standing figure playing the fiddle on fol. 50v (see fig. 36) is Elias Cairel, "playing badly" in illustration of his *vida*'s remark: "E fetz se joglars . . . e mal violava" (Boutière and Schutz, no. 35, p. 252). In the I songbook (fol. 123r), there is an unusual image of Aimeric de Sarlat, whose *vida* merely says that he was a jongleur, with a whistle or very short pipe in his mouth and a tiny tabor hanging around his neck, in his hand a stick to beat it. Images of jongleurs playing "high" stringed instruments such as fiddles (Elias Cairel in the A songbook or Albertetz on fol. 133v of the I songbook) more commonly depict jongleuresque musical accompaniment than do images of jongleurs playing "low" wind or percussion instruments. This may be due more to the Italian compilers' notions of propriety than to actual performance practices.

27. Boutière and Schutz, no. 8, p. 39.

28. Ibid., no. 50, p. 335.

29. *Poetria nova*, ed. Edmond Faral in *Les Arts poétiques du XIIe et du XIIIe siècles* (Paris, 1958), p. 259, under the rubric "L'action."

30. Cousin, *Quintilien*, vol. 6, III.iii.87. For the entire discussion of hand gestures, see III.iii.85–131.

31. Juan Ruiz debunks the rhetoricians' idealistic notion that the language of gesture is universally understood in the exemplum from his *Libro de buen amor* with which I began Chapter 1: the learned Greek doctor and the Roman hoodlum completely misinterpret each other's hand signals.

32. Quintilian, for example, abhorred the "singing" of arguments by lawyers and students, that is, their attempt to persuade by pleasing their auditors with artificially melodic patterns of speech. He ridiculed the practice by suggesting that if "singing" was to be permitted at trials, they might as well go all the way and accompany the song with strings, woodwinds, and cymbals, "which suit the monstrous practice best" (Cousin, *Quintilien*, vol. 6, XI.iii.57–59).

33. On late antique mimetic art see Bonaria, *Romani mimi*; Margarete Bieber, *The History of the Greek and Roman Theater* (Princeton, 1961); W. Beare, *The Roman Stage* (London, 1950); and Hermann Reich, *Der Mimus, ein litterar-entwickelungsgeschichtlicher Versuch* (Berlin, 1903).

34. Alain de Lille, *De arte praedicatoria* (J. P. Migne, *Patrologiae . . . latina*, 221 vols. [Paris, 1844–65], vol. 210, col. 112), also cited by Edgar de Bruyne, *Etudes d'esthétique médiévale*, 3 vols. (Bruges, 1946), vol. 2, p. 282.

35. Faral, *Les Arts poétiques*, p. 166.

36. Ibid., p. 153. De Bruyne, *Etudes*, vol. 2, p. 16, judged that Matthew equated elegy with mime because he had a very muddled understanding of what antique drama and mime were all about.

37. D. R. Sutherland, "L'Elément théâtrale dans *la canso* chez les troubadours de l'époque classique," *Revue de langue et littérature d'oc*, nos. 12–13 (1962–1963): 95–101.

38. Roy Rosenstein, "Locus Amoenus: Love, Play, and Poetry in Troubadour Lyric," Ph.D. diss., Columbia University, 1980, p. 46.

39. Sutherland, "L'Elément théâtrale," p. 97.

40. It is perhaps worth remembering that not only did the actors of Atellan farce wear grotesque masks, but part of the costume of male characters was a large red phallus. See Bieber, *Greek and Roman Theater*, pp. 248–49 and figures 827b, 828; and Beare, *The Roman Stage*, p. 153 n. 17, for classical descriptions of the shaven heads of mimes, the phallus, and other aspects of their costume.

41. On the grounds of suffering for love, Bernart de Ventadorn explicitly compares himself, in "Tant ai mo cor ple de joya," to Tristan:

plus trac pena d'amor
de Tristan l'amador,
que·n sofri manhta dolor
per Izeut la blonda.
(no. 44, p. 262)

I bear more pain for love / than Tristan, the lover / who endured many sorrows / for Iseut the blond.

In other passages it is not clear, although editorial capitalization tries to make it so, that the word "tristans" is a *senhal* for Bernart's lady. It is as likely to be a gerundive describing Bernart's own lover persona, a kind of signature in the last lines of several lyrics, as in "Can vei la flor, l'erba vert e la folha" (no. 42, p. 244): "Amics Tristans, car eu no·us pos vezer, / a Deu vos do, cal que part que m'esteya" ("Friend, sorrowing [or, Friend Tristan,] because I cannot see you, / I commend you to God, wherever I may find myself"); or in "Lo rossinhols s'esbaudeza" (no. 29, p. 177): "Tristan, si no·us es veyaire, / mais vos am que no solh faire" ("Tristan [or, Sorrowing], even if it is not apparent to you, / I love you more than ever"); or in the final lines of Bernart's famous "Can vei la lauzeta mover," where the sorrowing lover vows to give up love and song (no. 43, p. 254):

Tristans, ges no·n auretz de me,
qu'eu m'en vau, chaitius, no sai on.
de chantar me gic e·m recre,
e de joi e d'amor m'escon.

Tristan [or, Sorrowing], you will have nothing more from me, / for I am leaving, miserable, I don't know where; / I abandon and refrain from song / and hide from joy and love.

There are similar ambiguities in the usage of "T/tristan" in the passages Frank Chambers lists from other troubadours in *Proper Names in the Lyrics of the Troubadours* (Chapel Hill, 1971), pp. 258–59.

42. Bec, *Burlesque*, p. 111; Boutière and Schutz, p. 29.

43. Bec, *Burlesque*, pp. 173–75.

44. Del Monte, no. 12, p. 121:

E·l tertz, Bernartz de Ventedorn,
q'es menre de Borneill un dorn;
en son paire ac bon sirven
per trair'ab arc nanal d'alborn,
e sa mair'escaldav·l forn
et amassava l'issermen.

And the third, Bernart de Ventadorn, / who is one hand smaller than [Giraut de] Bornelh, / had for his father a servant good / at shooting a bow at a laburnum ring, / and his mother heated up the oven / and gathered together the vine shoots.

45. James Wilhelm, in a brief analysis in *Seven Troubadours: The Creators of Modern Verse* (University Park, 1970), p. 116, has been one of the few modern readers to recognize the humor implicit in Bernart's verse: "One notes that Bernart, not his lady, gradually emerges as the idealized figure: He is the noble sufferer, clinging to his ideals, willing to undergo the tortures of his unwilling Milordess. Only when one realizes that the poem is constructed around sex do the attitudes and postures become genuinely funny." On later instances of punning about love's "pains" (Latin *poena*) in Andreas Capellanus, see Betsy Bowden, "The Art of Courtly Copulation," *Mediaevalia et Humanistica* n.s. 9 (1979): 67–85.

46. Bernart de Ventadorn's contemporary, Peire Rogier, seems to have used many of the same techniques as Bernart for encouraging his audience to make fun of his lover persona. In "Per far esbaudir mos vezis," Peire sets out to compose a new love song, he says, in order to amuse his neighbors. In this lyric, the lover continually vaunts his refinement, but the name of the jongleur to whom Peire entrusts the lyric is a crude one, Bastart. Peire seems to have intended a ludicrous clash—to burlesque effect—between these two personas. The vulgar performance style of a Bastart would bring out conventional near-puns, such as, in the second strophe, *ric/rege* ("powerful"/"stiff," from Latin *rigidus*) or, in the fifth strophe, the lover's desire to "die" loving. Equivocation of this kind could provoke the mockery and laughter of Peire's lady, Never-in-the-wrong (Tort-n'avetz), and of his audience of "neighbors":

De midons ai lo guap e·l ris,
e suy fols s'ieu plus li deman,
ans dey aver gran ioy d'aitan;
a dieu m'autrey;
no n' ai donc pro quan sol la vey?
Del vezer suy ieu bautz e letz;
plus no m'eschai,
que ben o say,
mas d'aitan n'ai ieu ioy e pretz
e m'en fauc ricautz a sazos
a guiza de paubr' ergulhos.

(Paris, B.N. fr. 856, fol. 194r; also edited by Derek Nicholson, *The Poems of the Troubadour Peire Rogier* [Manchester, 1976], pp. 60–61)

I have the mockery and laughter of my lady, / and I am a fool if I ask more of her, / but, rather, I ought to rejoice in so much. / I give myself to God. / Does it not profit me just to see her? / From looking I am gay and light-hearted; / I don't deserve more, / well I know this; / but from so much I get joy and prestige / and I make myself arrogant, when the time is right, / after the fashion of a proud pauper.

One wonders if this was not an old joke: the only way a proud poor man might become arrogant or "ricautz" (which sounds much like *rege autz*, "stiff high") was by having an erection. Bernart de Ventadorn seems to have used the same near-pun in "Chantars no pot gaire valer," in a strophe full of sensual description of his lady's appearance and its effect on him, which he sums up in the last line: she has made him "powerful":

Mout ai be mes mo bon esper,
cant cela·m mostra bels semblans
qu'eu plus dezir e volh vezer,
francha, doussa, fin' e leiaus,
en cui lo reis seria saus.
bel' e conhd', ab cors covinen,
m'a faih ric ome de nien.
(no. 15, p. 87)

I have placed my good hope very well / when she whom I most desire and want to see / shows me a pleasant expression, / sincere, sweet, pure, and loyal, / [she] by whom the king would be saved; / beautiful and gracious, with a well-formed body, / she has made me a powerful man from nothing.

47. On the interpretation of *aizimens*, see Roger Dragonetti, *Aizi* et *aizimen* chez les plus anciens troubadours," in *Mélanges . . . Maurice Delbouille*, 2 vols. (Gembloux, 1964), vol. 2, pp. 127–53.

48. Pasero, no. 7, p. 197.

49. On forgeries and distrust of writing see M. T. Clanchy, *From Memory to Written Record: England, 1066–1307* (Cambridge, Mass., 1979), esp. pp. 248–57. Presumably English monks were not much different from their Continental brothers: "Monks' propensity to forgery does not imply that they are unreliable in all their statements, but only in those which particularly concern the honour of their patron saint or the status of their house. Where there was doubt, they were determined to establish the truth for posterity. By truth about the past they meant what really should have happened" (p. 120). In the investiture controversy between St. Anselm and Henry I of England, for example, the king's men refused to admit the authenticity of the papal letters, denigrating them as mere "skins of wethers blackened with ink and weighted with a little lump of lead" (p. 209).

50. Pasero, no. 10, p. 252.

51. Rita Lejeune, "La Part des sentiments personnels dans l'oeuvre du troubadour Guillaume IX d'Aquitaine," *Orbis mediaevalis: Mélanges . . . Reto Bezzola* (Bern, 1978), pp. 251–52.

52. Clanchy, *Memory to Written Record*, p. 203: "Before conveyances were made with documents, the witnesses 'heard' the donor utter the words of the grant and 'saw' him make the transfer by a symbolic object, such as a knife or a turf from the land. William the Conqueror went one better and jokingly threatened to make one donee 'feel' the conveyance by dashing the symbolic knife through the recipient abbot's hand saying, 'That's the way land ought to be given.'"

CONCLUSION

1. On the "verbalization of trial" with specific reference to the Provençal *canso* and other medieval debate forms, see R. Howard Bloch, *Medieval French Literature and Law* (Berkeley and Los Angeles, 1977), pp. 167–89.

2. Valería Tortoreto, *Il trovatore Cercamon* (Modena, 1981), no. 8, p. 200, beginning "Car vey fenir a tot dia."

3. Dejeanne, no. 30, pp. 137–41, the *pastourelle* beginning "L'autrier jost'

una sebissa," and nos. 25 and 26, pp. 121–29 and 131–35, the lyrics beginning "Estornelh cuelh ta volada" and "Ges l'estornels non s'ublida," wherein the lover's messenger is a talking starling.

4. For the *senhal* "na Cropa fort," see Dejeanne, no. 34, p. 167, where Marcabru complains that ladies reward vulgar rascals for their "services," and promises to prove this "Per ma domna na Cropa fort / Mas ja no la vuelh decelar" ("by Milady Strong Crupper, / but I don't want to reveal her identity"). In the C songbook's version of these lines, Dejeanne reads the *f* of "fort" as an *s*. A more interesting variation is the R manuscript's spelling of the last word in the strophe as "desellar," which may point to a "saddling" pun: "but I don't want to unsaddle her."

5. Alfred Jeanroy, *Les Poésies de Cercamon* (Paris, 1922), no. 3, p. 9.

6. Michel Zink, *La Prédication en langue romane avant 1300* (Paris, 1976), p. 37.

7. According to surviving manuscripts from monastic libraries, the Canticles was the most frequently commented text in the twelfth century. See Jean Leclercq, *L'Amour des lettres et le désir de dieu* (Paris, 1957), pp. 84–86.

8. Dejeanne, no. 41, pp. 202–3:

> Tans n'i vei dels contraclaviers,
> Greu sai remanra conz entiers.

> I see so many counterkeys / that here a cunt will with difficulty remain whole.

9. Erich Köhler, *Trobadorlyrik und höfischer Roman* (Berlin, 1962), p. 8:

> Courtly love bestowed an "honor" that the petty nobles no longer derived from feudal [land] tenure. The renunciation of fulfillment in love is a response directly corresponding to the renunciation, forced by historical actuality, of material possession. In the possession- and rank-indifferent, dematerialized value system of courtly love poetry, the interests of all levels of nobles tended toward the harmony of a single class consciousness.

10. See Köhler, *Trobadorlyrik*, the chapter entitled "Reichtum und Freigebigkeit in der Trobadordichtung," especially pp. 59–65, for discussion of the theme of the *rics* in troubadour verse.

11. Clifford Geertz, *The Interpretation of Cultures: Selected Essays* (New York, 1973), p. 433.

Index

Medieval authors are listed under their first, or given, names.

Compositor: Wilsted & Taylor
Text: 10/13 Galliard
Display: Galliard
Printer: Braun-Brumfield, Inc.
Binder: Braun-Brumfield, Inc.